All About American Holidays

Also by Maymie R. Krythe

All About Christmas

ALL ABOUT

AMERICAN HOLIDAYS

by Maymie R. Krythe

Harper & Brothers, Publishers, New York

To Margaret Ellen Kirschbaum

Contents

Foreword

Since the United States of America has long been the "melting pot" of the world, various peoples have brought with them native celebrations. Many of these customs have been accepted and observed here. Therefore it is interesting to trace their origins and evolution, and to note how they have influenced our present-day holiday observances.

From primitive times man has observed various feast days: some connected with religious worship (hence the word, "holiday," from "holy day") or with changes of seasons and historical events. Several modern celebrations are concerned with interesting our citizens in certain worthwhile movements.

In Compton's Pictured Encyclopedia we read: "Of all the states, Oklahoma has the most holidays, 20. Its special days include Will Rogers Day, Senior Citizens Day and Jefferson Day. The District of Columbia has the least—only 8 days."

The six days most widely celebrated in the United States are New Year's Day, Washington's Birthday, Independence Day, Labor Day, Thanksgiving, and Christmas. Next in popularity are Lincoln's Birthday, Memorial Day, Columbus Day, Election Day, and Veterans' Day.

New Year's Day—January 1

IMPORTANCE OF NEW YEAR'S DAY

New Year's Day is the most important January holiday, and the only one the entire world observes, regardless of race or religious belief. No doubt the greeting, "Happy New Year!" in various languages has been most often heard around the globe.

New Year's Day is a legal holiday in all our states, the District of Columbia, Canal Zone, Guam, Puerto Rico, and the Virgin Islands. (There are no "national holidays" in the United States; for each individual state has jurisdiction over the dates it observes. The President and Congress can designate holidays "only for the District of Columbia and Federal employees, throughout the nation.")

In early times in such places as Cambodia, New Guinea, Peru, Burma, Babylon, Greece, there was "a period of suspended animation," observed "with fasting and austerity," before the dawn of a new year. The Hebrews and the Natchez Indians in America also noted such a time.

Since the advent of a new year is symbolic of the fact that "Life is in the end victorious and that Death is swallowed up forever" (Theodore Gaster), the day has long been looked forward to, and greeted with joy. Early men rejoiced because nature was taking on new life; they stopped work, and joined with families and friends in a season of good fellowship. Quarrels were settled; friendships, renewed; rich and poor greeted each other; and many persons observed religious rites on New Year's Day.

This holiday is the oldest one; and both primitive and civilized peoples have noted its arrival with some kind of festivity. Through the centuries, numerous traditions and customs have become associated with New Year's Day; therefore, when we moderns celebrate the day, we engage in some practices that are reminiscent of antiquity.

1

VARIOUS DATES OF NEW YEAR'S DAY

Even before methods of measuring time were established, primitive man welcomed the new year. Since they reckoned time in their own ways, the date of this holiday varied in different parts of the world.

Some began their time cycle in accordance with certain natural phenomena, such as the winter solstice; the waxing and waning of the moon; sowing and reaping of crops; or the return of flowers and other plants to earth.

Egyptians started a new year when the Nile overflowed its banks; this occurred during our summer; the Greeks, with the first new moon after June 21; the Babylonians, Persians, and Russians, from the spring equinox, when nature showed new life in the form of fresh growth. Some American Indians connected the idea of a new year with the ripening of acorns and the salmon run. This made their time cycle begin in August.

The Festival of Ancyclia opened the Roman year. This included religious processions, general rejoicing, and feasting. At first the Roman year began in March and had only ten months. Numa Pompilius (716 to 672 B.C.) added January and February.

This system lasted until about 45 B.C. when Julius Caesar decided to reform the calendar, because of the differences between solar and religious years. He ordered an Egyptian astronomer, Sosigenes of Alexandria, to devise a new one. This Julian calendar provided for leap years, and set January 1 as the date for New Year's Day.

During the Middle Ages, various countries began the new year on different dates; and this made timekeeping difficult. For example, Italy and France started theirs in March; Spain and Germany on Christmas; while Belgium and Holland used Easter. Several other European countries regarded the vernal equinox as the proper date.

As years passed, errors appeared in the Julian calendar; for natural time dropped behind, and the vernal equinox rushed ahead. In 1582 Pope Gregory decreed that October 5 of that year would become October 15; also that the first year of each century must be divisible by 400 (instead of by 4) to make it a leap year. And January 1 was established as New Year's Day.

At once the Roman Catholic lands accepted this Gregorian calendar. However, the Protestants kept to the Old Style, or Julian calendar, until 1752. (Scotland had accepted the New Style in 1600.)

March 25 was used as the first of the year. Both England and the American colonies waited until September 3, 1752, to accept January 1 for this holiday. George Washington was born February 12 (Old Style), but it was not until about the beginning of the nineteenth century that his birthday was observed on February 22.

However, the Orthodox Eastern churches continued to use the Julian calendar, making their New Year fall on January 13. The Chinese have a "movable feast" for theirs, which occurs between January 21 and February 19. The ancient Jewish year began on March 25; but now it is on the first day of Tishri, and may fall between September 6 and October 5.

EARLY NEW YEAR CELEBRATIONS

It is said that Babylonians observed New Year's Day as early as 2600 B.C. This holiday occurred in March, and was considered their most important feast day. The festival, called Esagila, continued for eleven days, at the great temple of Marduk.

In one of the ceremonies, the King was humiliated; his crown and royal regalia were taken away by priests; he was obliged to kneel before Marduk and confess his sins, or declare his innocence. If he wept on this occasion, it was considered a good omen for the year; if not, ill luck would follow. During the course of the festivities, there were contests, and dramas were presented; one of these showed the death and resurrection of Marduk. In addition there was a sacred procession, followed by the "Fixing of Destiny," the "magical determination and course of the New Year."

Early in the Christian Era, Christ's adherents observed New Year's Day with religious rites, to show the contrast between the pagan revelry and their own devout celebration. In India, on this holiday, Hindus offered sacrifices to the god of wisdom, then spent the rest of the day in general rejoicing.

In Scotland the first day of a new year was their favorite holiday. Even the soberest Scots—it is said—relented on this date and enjoyed themselves. Everyone who could possibly do so went to his home for a family reunion.

"First-footing" was a Scottish custom, very popular with all. After the midnight church service, attendants went calling from twelve to one o'clock. It is said there were more persons on the streets at that time than were seen at noon.

With a loud shout of "Welcome!" the host opened his door to his guests. To assure good luck to their friends in the ensuing months, callers were expected to bring small gifts. The first guest was the most important. It was considered unlucky, for a woman, a criminal, a person with a squint, or a deformity, or for a red-haired individual to come into the house first on that night. There was a belief that the household would be fortunate if a dark-haired man entered first, after midnight. "First-footing" was also connected with love-making; the young men hurried to their sweethearts' homes to be first to cross the threshold.

On this night older boys in Scotland often dressed in fantastic costumes and wore masks. Then they knocked at doors of well-to-do villagers. After being invited in, the group performed a folk play that dealt with the adventures of a national hero, Galshan, and resembled the story of St. George and the Dragon.

For many years Scottish people of all types used to meet on the streets to enjoy New Year's fun together. But as time passed, numerous pickpockets mingled with the gay crowds. They plied their trade so diligently that members of the higher classes of society, stopped joining in the noisy and unprofitable outdoor festivities.

In ancient England, on the first day of the new year (then March 10) druids went out to cut sprigs of mistletoe from sacred trees. They gave these bits of greenery to their people to assure them of blessings in the following days.

On New Year's Day there was general merriment and much feasting in "Merrie England." Staying up to see the old year out and the new one come in was a long-established custom. New Year's Eve was termed "Singing E'en" because at that time, the final Christmas carols were sung.

At midnight it was customary for a householder to open all doors and allow the spirit of the old year to leave, and to invite the new one to enter and warm itself. In Derbyshire, a hostess put her wedding ring in the posset pot (a drink made of hot milk, curdled with wine, and spiced). Then each unmarried guest tried to pick up the ring with his ladleful of the hot drink. The one who succeeded was sure to marry in the new year.

In some British villages, young boys called "Howlers," went out on New Year's Day and beat fruit trees, while begging them to produce abundant fruit. Also at this time, farmers "wassailed" their apple trees by sprinkling them with cider and singing a song; this was supposed to encourage good crops.

In England the Puritans did not take any note of New Year's Day; and since January was named for a pagan deity, they called it "First Month." The Pilgrims, who settled at Plymouth, followed the same belief that the observance of this holiday savored of improper and unchristian reverence for the heathen god, Janus.

Germans welcomed a new year with merrymaking and street celebrations. They followed an old pagan tradition of dressing in animal skins, parading around town, or of riding on hobby horses. The idea of representing a new year as a baby is said to have started in this same country during the fourteenth century. However, some claim that the Greeks used to carry a baby around in a basket as a symbol of this holiday.

NEW YEAR'S NOISEMAKING

Mingled with the raucous din of welcoming in a new year is the old cry, "Happy New Year!" Noisemaking on this date is one of the earliest and longest continued customs known to mankind. This idea is said to have come from Babylon and India, where hilarity and much noise accompanied their New Year observance.

Our modern celebrations, such as that in Times Square in New York City, are featured by pealing of bells, wailing sirens, tooting of whistles, blowing of car horns, and by shooting off firecrackers, rockets, or firearms. All this din is a relic of the past and comes from primitive times when men had reasons for indulging in such loud noises.

There was an ancient belief that the old year should be driven out before the arrival of the new one. And in the Scottish highlands, the passing year was represented by a dummy, called the "Auld Wife," which was set on fire. In Bohemia a similar rite was carried out by German children. At one Austrian town, a straw effigy, known as "The Death," was drowned in a nearby river. This was to protect the community from diseases, including the plague. The same custom prevailed on the Island of Guernsey. After parading a straw figure through their community, the people buried it in an out-of-the-way spot. This was termed "burying the fag-end of the year."

There was also much noisemaking associated with getting rid of evil spirits at the beginning of a new year. For "man was more afraid of Nature than of his fellowmen." Therefore, various noises were concocted to frighten away undesirable beings thought to be roaming the earth at this season. This pastime was claimed to be "a device to beat the Devil at his own game." However, this was important business for our ancestors; and even today some primitive tribes seriously consider similar ceremonies.

In Siam, guns were fired on the last day of the old year to frighten off demons. The approach of the new period was also hailed in this fashion in Japan. Dancers went from home to home; inside they rattled bamboo sticks, making a loud clatter to expel unwanted spirits. Chinese used firecrackers to scare away evil beings; lamps, too, burned all night for this purpose. After the Chinese made New Year calls at midnight, they went out to the graves of their ancestors to set off firecrackers.

In some European countries, too, people believed they should rid themselves of undesirable elements; and they expelled witches during the twelve days between Christmas and Epiphany. In some parts of Russia, it was customary to beat the corners of the house with sticks to drive Satan out. On New Year's Eve in Bohemia, young boys gathered in a circle in the square to fire a gun into the air three times. This was intended to shoot down any black-clad spirits that might be riding about in the sky on their broomsticks.

All through March, in Calabria, Italy, church bells were rung to scare away witches, while in the Tyrol houses were cleaned and faggots burned "to smoke out such beings." And in Switzerland and Germany boys and girls got up early on New Year's Day to march around, beating drums and making a commotion to banish harmful beings.

Here in the United States (especially in some southern sections) an old custom still exists—shooting off guns to greet a new year. It was brought in by early settlers over a hundred and fifty years ago.

Cherryville, North Carolina, still clings to this custom. Recently, forty or more citizens marched to the city hall. Each was armed with an ancient musket. At one minute after midnight, eighty-five-year-old Sidney Beam greeted the mayor with a shout, "Good morning to you, sir!" Then his companions sent "a shattering volley into the air." Next they marched around the streets and out into the country, shooting off their old weapons. These southern revelers saluted the new year on into the afternoon.

For centuries the pealing of bells has been an important part of the coming of New Year's Day, a pleasant and welcome sound. Charles Lamb once remarked that the most striking bell sound is "the peal that rings out the old year."

In the British Isles church bells were rung muffled, until twelve midnight, to show grief at the passing of the old year; then the bells were unmuffled so they would sound out clearly to announce the arrival of a new one, with its hopeful promise.

> In olden times, the advent of New Year was signalized by the ringing of church bells, and by dancing, singing, music, horn-blowing, and many other such proceedings on the streets.
> —Wright, in British Calendar Customs

Today around the globe church bells peal out as people gather on the streets at midnight to rejoice together. And modern man, in a lighter mood than his ancestors, greets New Year's Day, with the perennial noisemaking.

NEW YEAR'S OMENS AND PORTENTS

Through the ages, varied superstitions have been connected with New Year's Day. For instance, there was a widespread belief that the first day of the year was symbolic of, or could portend, what the following ones would bring with them.

Therefore, people put on clean clothes, did some work to bring them good fortune, settled accounts by paying their debts, and returned things borrowed from friends. It was considered harmful to allow a candle or light to be taken from a home at this date. Before the first of January came, some people filled their cupboards so the shelves would not be empty during the ensuing weeks.

There was a tradition in Germany that each person should wear his best clothes and live on this day as he wished to the rest of the year. The idea, too, was to avoid unpleasant things, such as visits to the dentist.

In some lands, on New Year's Day there was much scanning of the skies to discover what they foretold about the weather for the coming months. The Old Shepherds' Calendar for 1709 stated:

If New Year's Day in the morning open with dusky red clouds, it denotes strife and debates among great ones, and many robberies to happen that year.

Long ago on the Isle of Man, women sprinkled ashes on the kitchen floors on New Year's Eve. Next morning they looked carefully to see whether there were any footsteps among them. If they saw prints leading toward the door, it was a sign there would be a death in the home. If the steps were reversed, it portended an addition to the family.

Chimney sweeps in Austria went around on this date, singing New Year's songs. When these boys were not looking, people tried to steal some of their broom straws, which they tied together and preserved as a token of ensuing good fortune. Also, to foretell events in following months it was customary to drop melted lead in water; then from the shapes the metal assumed, individuals tried to figure out future happenings.

In Scotland if one met a beggar, sexton, gravedigger, or a person with empty arms on New Year's Day that presaged ill fortune. However, if one encountered a rich man, or someone with his arms loaded, this was a sign of good luck. And in Lancashire to share a lighted match with another was sure to bring harm. In some localities, chimneys were cleaned out to assure prosperity. It was a belief of the Spaniards that if a person had a gold coin in his pocket on the first day of the year, he would never lack for cash in the coming months.

There's an old superstition that some still follow today; and not only at New Year's. It is the attempt to prophesy the future by "dipping" into the Bible at random. A person places his finger on a certain spot, reads the passage, and then tries to make it foretell his future.

NEW YEAR'S DAY FOODS

Since New Year's Day is the time for reunions of families and friends, feasting naturally is a chief pastime. And throughout the world this holiday is associated with certain foods believed to bring good luck to the diners. Often, too, there is an exchange of dishes between friends. Some modern eating customs on this date can be traced to ancient eras. Serving sweets, for example, goes back to the time when sugar cane was discovered. A favorite Roman food was honey; apples dipped in honey were also a feature of Hebrew New Year observances, which take place sometime between September 6 and October 5.

Since some American Indians associated New Year's Day with acorns and salmon, they made a ceremony of eating these foods at this time. In our southwestern states, Texas, for instance, there was a belief that good fortune would come to those who ate black-eyed peas on January 1. This goes back to England from which settlers brought the idea to Virginia. Black-eyed peas were considered a delicacy from the time of our first President. And the turkey has long been the main dish on many tables in the United States when friends gather to honor a new year.

In some lands of northern Europe, "meal cakes," made from the first grains harvested, are served. The French eat pancakes tossed on the griddle to bring good fortune. Their most important New Year's Day event is the evening dinner, usually at the home of the head of the family.

On this holiday Swedes serve a meal that is much like the Christmas feast. It begins with many appetizers, followed by lutfisk, served with cream sauce, boiled potatoes, ham, and their special rice pudding. In Switzerland housewives pride themselves on a distinctive bread, containing milk, butter, eggs, raisins, as well as other ingredients.

For years it was the habit of an Austrian family to serve a big noontime dinner. The Hungarians, at their New Year's feast, served a roasted pig, with a four-leaf clover or an apple in its mouth, as the chief article of food. Greek women make "Basil cakes" (the Feast of St. Basil falls on January 1), while dressed in their best attire. Even wealthy ladies, when baking such cakes, don their finest jewelry.

Bannocks, with holes in them, like our doughnuts, are made especially for this occasion in County Antrim, in Ireland. The Scots prepared "hot pot," spiced, sweetened ale, sometimes with spirits added; and when the clock struck twelve midnight, the family drank together. Then they carried the pot outside and shared the contents with neighbors.

On the first day of a new year in some old European monasteries, a bowl of wine, called the "Loving Cup," was brought to a refectory table. After the superior had drunk a toast to his brother monks, he passed the cup to them.

As this day was one of much rejoicing, feasting, and drinking in "Merrie England," the traditional wassail bowl was sure to be in evidence. The word, "wassail," comes from the old Gaelic words for good health. The great bowl was passed around, and each wished his companions "Was Hael!" After drinking this in their homes, they took the bowl out with a good supply of cakes, and offered such refreshments to their friends.

Often in the British Isles, a young person rushed to the well to be the first to drink from it at the advent of a new year; for this was a sign of future good times. People of Coventry were known for their "god-cakes," small triangular mince pies, given as presents, while in Northumberland neighbors often gathered to drink wine, served with rich cakes.

Hollanders drank hot spiced wine, and with it ate apple fritters and their traditional doughnuts. Fish is eaten in Germany to increase one's riches, also white cabbage, symbolic of silver money, and carrots, of gold. Swabian women make rings of bread, emblematic of the year's cycle. When whipped cream is served in Switzerland on this holiday, it is proper to drop a bit on the floor, and let it remain, as a symbol of "fatness and richness."

In some parts of the globe, people believe that a full salt shaker foretells a good year. India serves only new foods at this date, as they think the cooking of new rice assures prosperity. Rice cakes are used as New Year offerings in Ceylon. At some places, there are taboos on certain edibles on this date. For example, the Chinese refrain from rice, and Germans from dumplings.

Bulgarian women bake cakes with center holes. At midnight, on New Year's Eve, boys knock at the doors, then sing songs. The youths receive cakes, which they slip on long sticks. Sweets are served in Albania, to be sure of a year of sweetness. There is also a cake with a coin in it; and the finder will be lucky. At midnight, when an Armenian family gathers for the blessing of the grandmother, or oldest member of the family, all enjoy a feast of fruit, candies, and cakes together.

NEW YEAR'S DAY GIFTS

The giving of presents on New Year's Day is an old habit. Some say it started first to propitiate the gods, then the rulers, later the lawmakers. Finally, it was practiced for selfish reasons only, in many cases. Some sources claim this started in southern Asia, before the time of Christ, while others attribute the idea to the Romans. The practice was mentioned by such writers as Tacitus and Suetonius. Julius Caesar once declared he had dreamed that Roman senators were presenting him gifts on the first day of the new year.

Romans sent friends good luck tokens, sometimes exchanging small copper coins with the head of Janus on one side, and a boat on the other; for he was the protector of ships and trade. Little Roman presents, such as gilded nuts, were known as "strenae." Gradually presents became more costly, and the Roman rulers exorbitant in their demands for expensive gifts.

For instance, the notorious Caligula used to stand in the hall of his palace on New Year's Day, to collect offerings from his subjects. This became such a "racket" in Italy, that, in 458, Pope Leo the Great abolished the custom, declaring it "a relic of heathen superstition."

Ancient Egyptians had a special New Year's gift, an earthenware flask (with a neck shaped like a lily), called a "pilgrim's bottle." On it was an inscription—a wish that the receiver would have only good fortune in the new year.

The New Year's greeting card is really a form of gift; this custom is credited to the Chinese, who have sent such cards for over a thousand years.

Perhaps the Saxons learned from the Romans the idea of giving presents at this holiday. Gradually in England it became customary for subjects to send costly gifts to their monarchs. Often the royal wardrobes were kept almost completely supplied by these annual presents. Queen Elizabeth accumulated—so the story goes—hundreds of pairs of jeweled gloves. This practice continued in Great Britain until the era of Cromwell and the Commonwealth.

The English kings used "silent persuasion" frequently to fill their empty coffers. In 1249, for instance, Henry III forced wealthy London merchants to pay him high tribute; and in 1584 the Archbishop of Canterbury had to present Elizabeth I forty pounds. In addition, persons sometimes were compelled to give presents to lords, or town officials. The Earl of Leicester is said to have received the most costly gifts of any noble. But, fortunately, by 1647 the ruling was made that it was no longer necessary to give "heathenish and superstitious New Year's gifts" to the Lord Mayor and aldermen of London.

The last day of the old year, in Scotland, was called "hogmanay." This was the most popular of the "daft days," as the Christmas holidays were named. Poor children went around on December 31 to sing before various homes, and called out, "Hogmanay." Housewives usually responded with presents of fruit, nuts, candy, or small coins. The youngsters also begged for bread and cheese. All gifts were stored in the capacious folds of the draped sheets the children wore as costumes.

In England it was customary for the head of the house to give presents to his servants and to those who worked for him at Christmas, but gifts for relatives and friends were usually reserved for New Year's Day. When the English emigrated to the New World, they continued to follow the practice of exchanging presents on January 1 instead of at Christmas.

Belgian children saved their money to buy gaily decorated paper, on which to write greetings to their parents. Of course they practiced writing these at school, until they could make perfect copies. Then, on New Year's morning, each child read his message aloud to the family.

Gifts and greeting cards are exchanged in France on the first day of the year. Children often make small tokens for their parents, and present them, with good wishes for the new year. Shop owners usually send something to their patrons; and at this date servants and clerks sometimes get an extra month's pay.

In some parts of India lemons are used for gifts, while in Persia (Iran) eggs, symbolizing the beginning of life, are exchanged. Many Dutch children hurry from their beds to be the first to shout "Happy New Year!" to their parents. On this day, bachelor uncles, or grandfathers, give money to their small relatives, when all enjoy a gala dinner together.

German boys and girls carry presents to their teachers, apples being given in some cases. In this country, too, people send New

Year's Day greetings; but on this date presents are usually given only to servants, postmen, or janitors.

NEW YEAR CELEBRATIONS IN THE UNITED STATES

Calling on friends on New Year's Day is said to have been started centuries ago by the Chinese. And in the United States, especially in cities, such as New York, this custom began early. Dutch settlers are credited with beginning this pleasant practice. The men called on the women; so the ladies saw men friends at least once a year. It is said that George Washington was surprised by this custom when he went to New York, as the first elected Chief Executive. Gradually, the calling idea spread from the East coast to other states, and for many decades was a popular way of opening a new year.

Our first President started the precedent (which continued to this century) of holding open house for the general public on January 1. He and his wife, Martha Washington, continued such social affairs during the seven years the national capital was in Philadelphia. Although John and Abigail Adams moved into the White House in Washington, D.C., before it was completed, they managed to hold a reception there on New Year's Day in 1800.

Thomas Jefferson followed their example. In 1804, for example, he held open house, from twelve noon until 2 P.M. During this period, a large number of guests arrived, including government officials, diplomats, military officers, and even some Cherokee Indian chiefs, along with "most of the respectable people of Washington and Georgetown." On this notable occasion, the Marine band played, and "abundant refreshments" were served.

Other Chief Executives continued the custom for many years; also the wives of Cabinet members and various Washington social leaders received friends and constituents on New Year's Day.

In eastern cities like New York and Philadelphia, it was quite "the proper thing" to give and attend such annual functions. During the latter part of the last century, anyone who wanted to be considered in the upper social brackets took part in these social affairs.

It was customary for men to call on ladies on New Year's afternoon; for younger people to visit older friends, while women paid calls on each other the following day.

During the Gay Nineties, hostesses often announced in the newspapers the hours they would receive guests on this holiday.

People arrived in their best finery—men in silk hats, with chamois skin gloves, and ladies in "stiff bombazine with sealskin tippets."

Callers placed their cards on trays in the reception hall, greeted the host and hostess, then went to the dining room, where tables held such substantial foods as roast beef, turkey, ham, relishes, along with all kinds of fancy pastries. Of course, punch and the traditional eggnog were dispensed in large quantities.

After their guests had departed, the host and hostess often made a round of calls on their friends. As a result, the affair became a real calling marathon. Persons rushed around in their "stylish turnouts," drawn by teams of matched horses, to see how many calls they could make. At times, undesirables managed to crash the parties; also guests who had imbibed too much at different homes sometimes caused hostesses embarrassment.

While Easterners were carrying on this New Year tradition, it is interesting to note what Westerners, in Southern California, for example, were doing to observe the amenities of this holiday.

Even in the 1850's, after the state had entered the Union and Los Angeles was just a small pueblo, her people always celebrated the coming of a new year. Some Angelenos attended midnight Mass at the old church, still standing at the plaza. Others showed their joy by shooting off guns and pistols.

On January 1 friends got together for roast turkey and "all the fixings." The *Los Angeles Star*, in January 1855 reported as follows:

> Christmas and New Year's festivities are passing away with the usual accompaniments, namely bull fights, firing of crackers, fiestas, and fandangoes. In the city, cascarones commanded a premium, and many were complimented with them as a finishing touch to their headdresses.[1]

By 1877, many Angelenos were attending church services on the morning of New Year's Day; and later, prominent citizens entertained at their homes. "The ladies wore their prettiest smiles, and dispersed the customary refreshments in the most graceful and hospitable manner." It was said that a certain hostess entertained more than "thirty gentlemen in her parlor" at one time. That eve-

[1] "Cascarones" are blown-out egg shells, filled with bits of colored papers, confetti, etc.

ning the elite of the city gathered at Union Hall for a brilliant formal ball.

In those days people all over the United States were big eaters. If you had been invited to a New Year's Eve ball in the 1870's and 1880's, after several hours of dancing, you and your partner would have joined the other guests in the dining room "to partake of" a meal that would fortify all sufficiently to continue the gay festivities until dawn. Here is a sample menu:

SUPPER

Cold Collations

Roast Chicken   Boiled Ham   Tongue   Steak and Kidney Pie

Veal and Ham Pie   Cold Joints

Meringos	Derbys
Lemon Drops	Queen's Drops
Lady Fingers	Fruit Cake
Genoa Cake	Coventrys
Banbury's Cheese Cakes	Jellies
Compotes	Ice Cream
Raisins and Nuts	Apples and Pears

Mixed Candies

Tea   Coffee

Claret   White Wine

Eldorado   Sherry

Madeira   Port

Angelica

Gradually the custom of extensive calling on New Year's Day died out in most places. Nowadays, many socially minded persons prefer to celebrate the coming of the holiday by spending New Year's Eve in hotels and cafés. After a gala dinner, a floor show, and dancing, the noisemaking keeps up until midnight; then it reaches a crescendo, followed usually by a brief pause when the new year is welcomed in with "Should Auld Acquaintance Be Forgot," the song that has become associated with this annual event:

> For auld lang syne, my dear,
> For auld lang syne,
> We'll take a cup of kindness, yet,
> For auld lang syne.

Afterwards, the festivities are resumed and may last the rest of the night.

Because of the different time zones in the United States, the West can hear or see by means of radio or television, the earlier celebrations in the East, such as that in Times Square where pandemonium reigns when the old year is over.

While many Americans celebrate New Year's Eve in this hilarious fashion, others consider its arrival more seriously. Therefore, they "take stock" of themselves, review their mistakes and failures of the past months, and, following the advice of Sarah C. Woolsey, "Yesterday's errors let yesterday cover," resolve to do better.

Making New Year's resolutions has long been an American custom on this holiday. Even though some scoff at the idea, and few succeed in keeping all of their resolutions, we are encouraged in the attempt by the poet, Alfred Tennyson, who wrote:

> I hold it truth with him who sings
> To one clear harp on divers tones
> That men may rise on stepping stones
> Of their dead selves to higher things.

When numerous Americans are attending gay social events on New Year's Eve, others prefer to take part in Watch Night services at some church. These meetings are said to have originated with early Methodists. They held the first such gathering in this country at Philadelphia in 1770. Members left their homes, met for a season of prayer and praise, and after midnight bells had rung in a new year, these worshipers went thoughtfully to their homes.

Nowadays, in some churches, members and friends meet early for an informal program, and then enjoy an hour or so of good fellowship, with refreshments. Sometimes these exercises are followed by Holy Communion. The congregation is inspired by the religious aspect of the season, which "emphasizes the fundamental purpose of the new year—to bury the past and start anew."

Or the Watch Night service may begin at 11 P.M. in a candle-

lighted sanctuary. There is special music; the minister gives a meditation on the significance of the hour; and all join in familiar hymns.
There is a solemnity about the time and place; as midnight bells peal
in the new year, they recall the words of Emily H. Miller: "The
old goes out, but the glad young year comes newly in tomorrow."

At the Watch Night service in New York's noted Riverside
Church, there is an "hour of great significance"; then the carillon in
the tower announces the arrival of a new year. This is a great contrast to the noisy observance in Times Square, but both are typical
of the way the United States heralds the coming year. No matter
how one celebrates, he no doubt will wish with William Cullen
Bryant: "The good old year is with the past, oh be the new as kind!"

New Year's Day coincides with the Circumcision which is observed in the liturgical churches to commemorate the circumcision
of Christ eight days after His birth, in accordance with Jewish practice. Members of these churches, the Anglican or Episcopal, the
Roman Catholic, and the Greek Orthodox are expected to attend
services either on New Year's Eve or New Year's Day.

On this holiday many Americans enjoy staying at home for family
dinners or entertaining friends. Naturally the football enthusiasts
who are unable to attend the Rose Bowl game watch it on the screen
and later enjoy informal suppers.

Today our modern American celebration of New Year's Day is
highlighted by two famous events: in the East, at Philadelphia, the
colorful Mummers' Parade is held, while the celebrated Pasadena
Rose Tournament is staged in the West. Both have gained national
acclaim; and annually millions of local people and tourists throng to
see them.

The Mummers' Parade goes back to the time when the Swedish
emigrants came over and settled along the Delaware River. At
yuletide they kept up their celebration until New Year's Day.
Dressed in grotesque outfits, they roamed around the towns and
countryside in gay bands, creating fun for neighbors and townspeople. English settlers brought with them their traditional mummers' holiday plays. As the years went by, groups of Swedish masqueraders and English mummers paraded together on New Year's
Day, shooting their firearms and making as much noise as possible.

Just before the famous Centennial of 1876 in Philadelphia, some of the citizens had organized the Silver Crown New Year's Association. This was the first large society to take part in the Mummers' Parade, which was still a rather unorganized affair. In 1901 the city government recognized the mummers and allowed them to stage a parade in which forty-two clubs joined. By 1930 this had become an important event, with prize money amounting to thirty thousand dollars.

In 1955 more than eight hundred thousand people witnessed the Mummers' Parade, a ten-hour long spectacle, presided over by King Momus. That year pink was the predominant color, but there were other costumes in varied pastel shades. These handsome outfits are fashioned from gleaming satin with fine embroidery work on them, and some are ornamented with spangles and sequins.

There was, as usual, much noise: shrieking sirens, firecrackers, and car horns, while clowns and other comics lampooned national and international celebrities. String bands, decorated with colorful plumes, marched to traditional banjo rhythms. The top prize of two thousand dollars was won by the Polish-American band, whose members did the can-can.

In 1957 the mummers staged their fifty-seventh annual parade. A crowd of several hundred thousand lined the four-mile route along Broad Street to the judges' stand at the City Hall. Philadelphia provided fifty-two thousand dollars in prize money that year for three classes of entrants: comic, fancy, and string. The comics were dressed to represent famous politicians, popular television personalities, and other notables. Preparations for this event had begun a year before; and in this parade twelve thousand Mummers strutted along and gave New Year's Day a rousing official welcome.

One newspaper stated that the participants had spent about half a million dollars on their costumes. There were one hundred bands, and such old-time favorites as "Oh Dem Golden Slippers" and "Four-Leaf Clover" were often heard along the line of march. An unusual feature of this Mummers' Parade in the "City of Brotherly Love," is that no women are allowed in it. However, many men impersonate women in this colorful event.

Out on the Pacific coast, on this same holiday the Pasadena Tournament of Roses Parade is seen by millions of Californians, and by visitors from all over the world. It is always hailed as one of the best annual American festivals in the entire country.

Charles F. Holder, founder of the Valley Hunt Club, is really responsible for the first such parade, held in the city of Pasadena on January 1, 1886. On that day, members of the Hunt Club decorated their carriages and buggies with real flowers. After they had paraded around the town, they gathered that afternoon to watch varied athletic contests.

For several years the Valley Hunt Club financed the parade; then the city of Pasadena took over the responsibility. Finally the Tournament of Roses Association was formed as the permanent sponsor of this unique celebration.

This event has gone through several stages of development. At first it was just a parade of decorated vehicles, then floats were added and prizes given. In 1902 a football game was played in the afternoon. For several years chariot races were put on.

Each year since 1905 there has been a beautiful queen to rule over the event, and a celebrity has led the long procession as grand marshal. The Rose Parade has become a larger and more expensive affair with the passing years. Only *fresh* flowers can be used on a float; and one of these beautiful creations often costs several thousand dollars. A different theme is chosen yearly and all floats carry out the central idea. Numerous bands are interspersed between the exquisite floats, so the mood of gayety and celebration is sustained.

Another special feature of the parade is the sight of hundreds of spirited, prancing horses (including handsome golden palominos), their silver trappings glittering in the bright sunlight, as they are put through their paces by skilled riders.

Such headlines as the following described the 1959 parade:

1,500,000 HAIL DAZZLING ROSE PARADE
63 BRILLIANT FLOATS THRILL VAST THRONG

That year the top prize—the sweepstakes—was won by the city of Glendale, California:

The sweepstakes prize went to the city of Glendale, for its magnificent "Adventures in Fantasy."

It was a worthy champion—10,000 vanda orchids, 6,000 roses and innumerable narcissus and chrysanthemum blooms, fashioned into a sedan chair from which a queen of fantasy ruled a fairyland.

A canopy of strung orchids stretched above the chair and tiers

of pink, lavender, and white chrysanthemums led upward to a
platform where three princesses reposed on blossoms.

—Long Beach Press-Telegram,
January 2, 1959

It is estimated that over a million and a half people watch both
the parade and the Rose Bowl football game between eastern and
western teams, which was instituted in 1916 and has become a permanent afternoon feature on New Year's Day.

Feast of Epiphany—January 6

On January 6 the Feast of Epiphany occurs. It is also called "Old Christmas," "Twelfth-tide," or the "Feast of the Three Kings." In Spain this date has been celebrated as Christmas, and in Italy as "Befana Day." The preceding evening—Twelfth Night—January 5, was the end of the "Twelve Days of Christmas," and marked the close of yuletide festivities.

The word Epiphany means a bodily manifestation or "appearance, commonly used of the appearance of a deity in visible form." Western branches of the Christian church observed January 6 as the occasion to commemorate the "manifestation to the Gentiles" (the visit of the Three Kings to the manger in Bethlehem). At their Epiphany services, they also read Scriptures relating to Christ's baptism, and to His first miracle at Cana. This was termed the "Three-fold manifestation." Authorities say that the Greeks used this feast day to observe Christ's manifestation—at His baptism—of His messiahship. Also after the fourth century, Western branches emphasized God's manifestation of Himself in Christ to the entire world.

The first reference to Epiphany is said to have been made in Egypt, during the latter part of the second century, when Clement of Alexandria stated that on January 6 (or 10) some Gnostic Christians celebrated the Feast of Epiphany in remembrance of John's baptism of Christ and the descent of the spirit of God upon Him.

One writer states that the date of Epiphany "does not rest on any certain tradition of time, either of Christ's nativity or baptism . . . but was obviously chosen in conscious rivalry to popular pagan festivals of the day." At least—among Eastern churches (until the close of the fourth century) the feast occurred on January 6; and this custom continued for more than a century.

Earlier (350 A.D.) December 25 had been set as the time to observe the birth of Christ; and this was an important part of church liturgy.

"It is not possible to fix the date when the change from January 6 to December was made," according to one source. During the fourth century Western churches adopted the Feast of Epiphany in addition to that of Christmas on December 25. It is claimed that the first really *separate* feast was held in 813. Pope Julius I is given credit for teaching people to distinguish between the Nativity and Epiphany.

During the Middle Ages, at Epiphany, Western churches often staged miracle plays in their sanctuaries to teach attendants the significance of the visit of the Magi, or Three Kings. One drama, *The Feast of the Star*, was played by three priests, representing the Wise Men.

When these productions gradually took on secular tones, with the introduction of jests and revelry, the plays were no longer permitted in the churches.

However, the tradition of drama productions at Epiphany (or Twelfth Night) continued; for this occasion afforded a gay conclusion to the Christmas holidays. At the English court, at universities, and Inns of Court, such performances were put on with splendid settings. Shakespeare's *Twelfth Night* was written for production on this holiday. Ben Jonson's masque, *Hymen*, was staged at the court on January 6, 1606; and another play was given at Whitehall in 1613.

For centuries France featured Twelfth Night with its "Cake of Kings," which contained a bean. The lucky finder reigned as monarch during that day. In 1563, Mary Queen of Scots celebrated the holiday with such a game at her palace of Holyrood. But instead of a king, a queen ruled over the gay festivities.

The observance of Twelfth Night in "Merrie England" (presided over by the Lord of Misrule and a jester) became quite boisterous during the reign of Elizabeth I (1558–1603) and lost all religious significance. At court, gambling was one of the chief pastimes on Twelfth Night; and often hundreds of pounds were wagered and lost by the ruler and his courtiers.

In *British Calendar Customs* Wright tells of a ceremony that prevailed for several centuries in connection with this holiday:

> It had long been a custom of the kings of England to attend personally, or by proxy, the arrival of Epiphany service in St. James, the Chapel Royal and offer gold, frankincense, and myrrh in commemoration of the offering of the Magi.

After the change of the calendar in Great Britain, in 1752 the Twelfth Night celebrations lost in popularity in higher social circles. But the merriment continued in the rural districts, and included masques, wassailing the wheat fields, sprinkling apple trees with cider, and lighting bonfires. Some of these ceremonies still survive in remote sections of the country.

Today, in general, Epiphany is observed with solemnity as a major church festival to commemorate Christ's manifestation as "the Son of God and Saviour of Mankind." In the churches which formally observe the date, the hymns and Scripture have as their theme, "A manifestation of the Light to all the world."

Here in the United States there are two outstanding church celebrations which stem from the Greek Orthodox Church. At Epiphany, its ceremonies always included the "Blessing of the Waters." After a procession to the riverbank, the priest threw a crucifix into the waters. There was much rivalry among the young men to recover it; for the priest gave a special blessing to the successful diver.

Now, for many years this colorful ceremony has been observed at Tarpon Springs, Florida, home of numerous Greek sponge fishermen. And at Long Beach, California, in January 1952, Greek church authorities started a similar observance on the shores of the Pacific Ocean. Each year thousands of spectators throng to both communities to witness this old and interesting Epiphany celebration.

Aside from denominational observances, in recent years the United States has carried out a special Twelfth Night ceremony of its own that has become increasingly popular. On January 5, Christmas trees, wreaths, holly, and pine branches are taken to city parks; there they are set on fire with appropriate ritual, the flames of the great bonfires lighting up the winter sky. This is in accordance with an old superstition that all holiday greenery must be taken down and burned on this date.

In some localities the merrymaking includes cutting a Twelfth Night cake, so the lucky finder of the bean can rule as monarch over the ceremonies. All join around the fire in singing the final Christmas carols; so this community event concludes the holiday season and celebrates Twelfth Night in happy modern fashion.

Inauguration Day—January 20

(EVERY FOUR YEARS)

In 1933, by the 20th Amendment to our Constitution, Congress set January 20 (instead of March 4) as the time for the inauguration of the President and Vice-President of the United States. Franklin Delano Roosevelt was the first Chief Executive to take office on this new day (at his second inauguration in 1937). Now January 20—Inauguration Day—is a legal holiday in Washington, D.C., only.

The ceremony takes place on a platform built over the steps at the east front of the Capitol; and the oath of office is administered by the Chief Justice of the Supreme Court. This important event attracts thousands of visitors; and no one who has seen it with its distinctive parade and visiting celebrities can ever forget the colorful scenes.

It is an impressive moment when the President Elect declares:

> I do solemnly swear that I will faithfully execute the office of President of the United States, and will, to the best of my ability, preserve, protect and defend the Constitution of the United States.

After kissing the Bible, he delivers his inaugural address. And as the crowds cheer, the new Chief Executive is escorted to the reviewing stand to watch men from all branches of the service, accompanied by numerous bands, march down Pennsylvania Avenue. That evening the traditional inaugural ball is staged.

When Washington became our first President, his term was to begin on March 4, 1789. However, the inauguration did not take place until April 30, at the old City Hall in New York City. Washington drove there in a coach drawn by six white horses. After the general had taken the oath, Chancellor Livingston turned to the spectators and cried, "Long live George Washington, President of the United States."

Apparently the event was a strain upon him, for one writer declared that "this great man was more agitated and embarrassed than

24

ever he was by a leveled cannon or pointed musket . . ." When he was re-elected, Philadelphia was the national capital; so George Washington took the oath of office that time at Independence Hall.

Thomas Jefferson was the first President to be sworn in at Washington, D.C. He was escorted to the Capitol by the militia and many citizens, and the ceremonies took place in the Senate Chamber.

James Madison was the first Chief Executive to take the oath in the House of Representatives, the first to have his wife, Dolly, by his side, first to address the crowd from the eastern portico of the White House, and he also attended the first inaugural ball ever given.

In 1817, James Monroe moved the ceremonies outside. As the British had burned the Capitol during the War of 1812, a temporary building had been erected for the occasion. But since some people did not think the structure safe, the exercises were held out-of-doors.

After President Andrew Jackson's inauguration, he rode on horseback down Pennsylvania Avenue to the White House. There tables had been spread in the East Room; this was soon thronged with "backwoods" friends of the new official; and their actions scandalized upper-class Washington society. The excitement was too much for "Old Hickory" (saddened by the death of his beloved wife); therefore several friends took him out of the White House, to an inn, where he got some much-needed rest.

William Henry Harrison gave the longest address on record—one hour and forty minutes—at his inauguration in 1841. However, on that day he rode in his carriage without coat or hat, took cold, and in one month was dead of pneumonia, having served the shortest term of any President.

Inauguration Day was a sad one for Franklin Pierce and his wife; for their eleven-year-old son had been killed in a railway wreck just a short time before.

As Abraham Lincoln rode to his installation, he was closely guarded by soldiers, and sharpshooters were stationed on the roof of the Capitol. He was the first to be sworn in at this building, as now completed.

As years passed, and the parades and ceremonies became more elaborate, many visitors arrived to see the impressive rites. One of the best attended was the inauguration of General Grant, following the Civil War.

A committee of Senators was in charge of arrangements for the event until the time of William McKinley, who suggested that a joint group from both Houses take care of this project. Since the days of Ulysses S. Grant, each President has chosen a selection from the Bible appropriate to the trend of the times.

Because of bad weather, William Howard Taft took the oath of office in the Senate Chamber. Afterwards the jovial 323 pound President Taft remarked, "I knew it would be a cold day when I was made President of the United States."

Franklin D. Roosevelt made inaugural history by taking the oath four times. When he was sworn in the last time, in 1945, he gave the shortest address (559 words) except for that of George Washington, at his second inaugural, which had only 133 words in it.

Here are several inaugural "firsts": Zachary Taylor was first to travel by train to his inauguration; John Quincy Adams, to wear long trousers instead of knee breeches; William H. Harrison, to dance at his own inaugural ball; Calvin Coolidge, to have his speech go out over the radio; and Herbert Hoover to have his address broadcast around the globe.

Only seven Chief Executives have been in their forties, when taking the oath of office: Presidents Polk, Pierce, Grant, Garfield, Cleveland, Theodore Roosevelt, and Kennedy.

No doubt the 1961 inaugural ball will long be remembered; one reporter declared it "the biggest and splashiest" since Franklin D. Roosevelt took office in 1933. The three-day affair included many major events: receptions, a national symphony concert, a gala "star-studded" Hollywood show, the official swearing-in ceremonies, the long parade, and several inaugural balls. Even though the weather was inclement and there was plenty of snow, thousands of shivering Americans lined the streets.

The Parade Committee announced that no other parade had ever had so many horses in it as this one—275 plus 22 mules and 1 burro. The theme of the procession was "World Peace through New Frontiers." There were 40 marching military units (15,800 men), including cadets of all services with their bands. Each state had a section, with its governor, one float, a band "of not more than 100 members," and a marching unit of 200 or less.

Of course the high point of the day was the solemn swearing-in ceremony at noon. Members of four religious faiths, Jewish, Protestant, Roman Catholic, and Greek Orthodox prayed for the success

of the new administration. There were musical selections by the
Marine band; and Marian Anderson sang "The Star-Spangled
Banner."

The Speaker of the House, Sam Rayburn, swore in the new Vice-
President, Lyndon B. Johnson, while Chief Justice Earl Warren
administered the oath of office to John F. Kennedy. In his inspiring
fourteen-minute address, the new President made an appeal for
world peace; he declared that the United Nations is "our last hope
in an age where the instruments of war have far outpaced the instruments of peace."

And in words that no doubt will go down in our history, President Kennedy appealed to his fellow Americans: "Ask not what
your country will do for you—ask what you can do for your
country."

Chinese New Year

A distinctive New Year's celebration occurs yearly in the Chinese sections of our large cities. This is especially elaborate in San Francisco, which has the largest of American Chinatowns. Within a small area, this district has a normal population of 42,000. The Orientals do not observe the coming of a new year on January 1. Their festival of several days is held on varying dates between January 21 and February 19.

Before the colorful holidays, Chinese throng Grant Street and do their buying for the festival. Pavements in front of stores are heaped high with crates of Chinese vegetables, and boxes of imported delicacies. People buy large quantities of flowers at this time for they want to beautify their homes for the new year. Children receive good luck money wrapped in red paper so they can buy sweetmeats and novelties during the Dragon Parade.

On their New Year's Eve at the closing meal of the old year, the Chinese eat no meat but drink several toasts. Next day is devoted to the family; members of the group either stay at home together or go to their temple.

The following day is given over to visiting, exchanging presents, and feasting. Those of us who enjoy Oriental dishes really envy the Chinese during these festive days; they feast on such delicious foods as deep-fried prawns, capon (sprinkled with sesame seeds and covered with a red, sweet–sour glaze), tasty spareribs, a salad of shredded lettuce, chicken, deep-fried strips of "Schow See Gai," Chinese peas, water chestnuts, and other delectable items.

The 1959 observance in San Francisco's Chinatown was especially colorful. It was their New Year, Number 4,657—"The Year of the Boar"—symbolic of good spirits and alertness.

The celebrants began the festival by choosing a "Miss Chinatown"; the activities included band concerts, dancing, a fashion show, and processions, featuring the long dragon. On a single evening more than 150,000 visitors crowded into Chinatown to view the unusual sights. Everyone is gay during this period and when Oriental friends meet, they salute each other with these words: "Gong Hay Fot Choy," which means, "Wishing you a prosperous New Year!"

The 1960 celebration lasted from February 4 until February 7, opening "The Year of the Rat," the 4,658th one of the Chinese lunar calendar.

The spectacular parade on February 5 contained a 150-foot dragon, imported from Hong Kong. It was propelled by "scores of human legs" as it belched forth "brimstone." Also there were groups of Chinese carrying lanterns, a dancing lion, military and other marching units, various floats, and a drum and bugle corps. Street entertainment during the days of festivity was put on by Chinese performers, and all through the celebration, shops on Grant Avenue had special displays of imported articles. As usual, this annual celebration was enjoyed both by the participants and their neighbors.

Candlemas—February 2

The Feast of the Purification of the Virgin, on February 2, gets its popular name, "Candlemas," from the ceremonies observed on this date. These include the blessing of candles by the clergy and their distribution to worshipers, who then carry the lighted tapers in a procession around the church.

This festival stems from the ancient custom that each Jewish mother was required to present her child at the temple forty days after its birth, and appear for her purification. This was in accordance with the law as set forth in Lev. 12:6—

> And when the days of her purifying are fulfilled, for a son, or for a daughter, she shall bring a lamb of the first year for a burnt offering, and a young pigeon, or a turtledove, for a sin offering. . . .

Then after the mother had brought her sacrifice to the altar, the priest made atonement for her and she was considered "clean."

Thus Candlemas commemorates the visit of the Holy Family to the temple, as related in Luke 2:22. At that time it was revealed to the devout Simeon that this Child was the long-awaited Son of God. When he took the Babe in his arms, Simeon praised God, and declared that He was "The Light to lighten the Gentiles, and the glory of thy people, Israel." On this same occasion, an elderly prophetess, named Anna, recognized Jesus as the Saviour of the world.

From early times, Christians observed this holy day. When, in 350 A.D., December 25 was set as the date to celebrate Christ's birth, Candlemas fell on February 2. One source states that this feast day was established by Emperor Justinian I, in 542 A.D. It is said that Constantine and other rulers often gave churches valuable lands and other possessions; and for maintaining lighted churches, rulers presented them with abundant supplies of candles and tapers.

At the old Roman Feast of Purification, celebrated the same

month as Candlemas, Romans paraded around with lighted candles in their hands. This stemmed from the old story that after Pluto, the god of the Underworld, had carried off Proserpina, her mother, carrying a lighted candle, roamed around, searching for her.

As in other cases it apparently was difficult to persuade early converts to do away with their old pagan festivals. So some say that Candlemas was grafted upon the earlier Roman celebration. As someone has said,

"This was deemed sufficient ground by the Roman Church, whereon to adopt the torch-bearing of the pagans in honor of their own deities, as a ceremony, in honor of the presentation of Christ in the Temple."

Therefore—so it is claimed—since the Fathers were unable to stop the heathen custom completely, they ordained that candles be carried to honor the Virgin Mary. Also, as light had become associated with this day, by Simeon's declaration of Christ as the Light, the custom of blessing candles on this date arose—hence the name—"Candlemas."

In early times, people preserved the remains of candles blessed on this holiday; for they believed these fragments could ward off evil spirits and dangers from their homes. After the Reformation in England, such candle ceremonies were not done away with entirely. In 1539 Henry VIII decreed that candles should be carried in memory of Christ, the "Spiritual Light of the World."

For many years the British considered Candlemas the end of the holiday season. They believed it was unlucky for Christmas greens to remain up after February 2. ("The Christmas greens are removed before Candlemas, if Septuagesima occurs first.") In reference to this custom, the noted poet, Robert Herrick, declared: "Down with the rosemary and bays . . ."

On Candlemas in Scotland children took gifts of money to their teacher. The boy and girl giving the largest amounts were selected as king and queen for this holiday; they were carried around in royal thrones formed by the clasped hands of their classmates. The teacher used some of the funds for refreshments, and kept the rest for himself. After "a jolly time together" the children were allowed to leave school.

Another Scottish custom on Candlemas was the playing of football. Often married men were matched against the bachelors, or a team from one part of a town played against a group from another section.

The festival of Candlemas is still observed by the Roman Catholic, Greek Catholic, and Anglican churches. It has been a custom for the Pope to officiate on this date in the Chapel of the Quirinal in Rome. After blessing the candles and sprinkling them with incense, he distributes them to those kneeling before him: cardinals, bishops, canons, priors, abbots, priests, and sacristans.

After the candles are lighted, the Pope is carried in his chariot in a procession around the church, while the choir chants an anthem. For "this solemn procession represents the entry of Christ, who is the Light of the World, into the Temple at Jerusalem." Later the hangings are taken down from the throne; the Pope and cardinals doff their gold and crimson robes, put on the ordinary ones, and then the regular Mass is sung.

The Church of England and the Episcopal Church in the United States have in their Book of Common Prayer a collect and gospel for "the day of the presentation of Christ in the Temple, commonly called the 'Purification of St. Mary, the Virgin'" and "the presentation of the Babe to the Lord, and the prophecies of Anna and Simeon."

Groundhog Day—February 2

Perhaps most Americans do not think of February 2 as Candlemas, but as Groundhog Day. Several interesting weather superstitions are connected with this date. And some European lands held the belief that the six-weeks' period following Candlemas Day would have weather just the opposite from that on February 2.

Medieval folk thought that various hibernating animals came to the surface of the ground on Candlemas morning to observe the state of the weather. If the hedgehog (badger, in Germany) saw the sun, he became frightened by his own shadow and crawled back into his hole to sleep for six more weeks. This came to mean to farmers that more cold weather would follow, and that the result would be poorer crops that year.

However, if the skies were dull and cloudy, the animal stayed above ground; for this presaged that cold weather would soon give way to balmy spring days. Naturally the farmers preferred unpleasant weather on Candlemas (or Groundhog Day). The English and Scots referred to the prevailing weather beliefs in such rhymes as these:

> If Candlemas be fair and bright,
> Winter will have another flight;
> But if it is dark with clouds and rain,
> Winter is gone and will not come again.
>
> The hind would as lief see
> His wife on the bier
> As that Candlemas Day
> Should be pleasant and clear.

This superstition about the hedgehog was brought to America by early settlers from Germany, where many farmers planted their crops in accordance with this belief. Since the newcomers did not find the true animal here, they transferred the idea to the groundhog (marmot, or woodchuck).

Pennsylvania is the home of the "groundhog fables"; and several groups of fun makers in this state have organized clubs to observe groundhog movements on February 2, and to engage in the fine art of weather forecasting. There is much rivalry between the different organizations; and they challenge each other's predictions and activities.

In northeastern Pennsylvania is the Punxutawney Ground-Hog Club, which boasts that it has been in business since 1898; and it "looks down" on later groups. They declare their town is the home of "traditional weather forecasting groundhogs." Each year since 1898, on the second day of February, members have trudged up to Gobbler's Knob in the Allegheny foothills to observe and record the behavior of the groundhog. In 1952 this group mourned the death of Dr. Frank Lorenzo, who had been the head of their internationally known club for thirty years.

The scornful rival of the Punxutawney Club is found in Lancaster County; it is the Slumbering Groundhog Lodge of Quarryville, Pennsylvania, and was started in 1908. The older group sneers at this one and calls the members upstarts. In return the Quarryville people dub the Punxutawney organization "The upstart gang of Gobbler's Knob" and declare it is just a "paper" group, to promote the sale of cookbooks on how to cook and serve groundhog meat!

The members of the Quarryville Lodge have a creed concerning their faith in the groundhog, which contains these statements:

> We believe in the wisdom of the groundhog,
> We declare his intelligence to be of a
> higher order than that of any other animal . . .
> We rejoice that he can, and does, foretell
> with absolute accuracy the weather conditions
> for the six weeks following each second day
> of February . . .

Because of this faith in the animal, the members solemnly pledge to defend him with all their powers.

Each year the Quarryville Lodge elects an outstanding person as an honorary member in their unique club. In addition, they "go all out" in their fancy dress when they observe groundhogs along Octoraro Creek; for they don top hats, swallowtail coats, white togas, or long fur coats.

In 1959 the new chairman of the board of Hibernating Governors, Robert W. Herr, announced that eight squads of observers had been on duty before daybreak; that at least six animals had been noted; also that the groundhog saw his shadow that day at exactly seven minutes after sunrise. Mr. Herr stated that there had been 90 per cent accuracy in the animals' prognostications during the fifty-one years of the group's observations.

In Quarryville on the second of February the whole day is given over to fun. In 1959 there was an elaborate, televised ceremony to show the elevation of Charles F. Hess (an active participant for fifty years) to the position of "Emeritus Provost Hibernating Governor and Illustrious Patriarch." Mr. Hess rode in a sulky, drawn by a donkey.

That evening the "brethren" assembled at 6 P.M. and marched "in their unique cadence" behind the Groundhog Band to the Spanish Tavern, there "to sup and discuss the profundity of the day's message, as delivered by the sage groundhog." At this annual meeting, they conduct business, take in new members, and sing their club song, to the tune of "John Brown's Body." Here is the first stanza with the chorus:

> Let the scientific fakirs gnash their teeth and stamp with rage—
> Let astrologers with crystals wipe such nonsense from the page—
> We hail the King of Prophets, who's the world's outstanding Sage—
>
> TODAY THE GROUNDHOG COMES!
>
> Glory! Glory! to the Groundhog,
> Glory! Glory! to the Groundhog,
> Glory! Glory! to the Groundhog,
> TODAY THE PROPHET COMES!

Another Pennsylvania club is named the Greater Philadelphia Groundhoggers, while one in Allentown is designated as the "Grundsow Lodge Nummer Ains on da Lechaw" (Number One on the Lehigh). Freely translated this means "they can do anything better than anyone else."

Since the groundhog clubs of Pennsylvania have become known not only nationally but internationally, one midwestern state—Wisconsin—not to be outdone, started its own group. This Sun Prairie Groundhog Club began in 1948 purely as a "fun" organization; of course, every February 2 each member solemnly swears with a straight face that he has seen the groundhog emerge from his hole.

Anyone born on this date can be a full member; those born that month, associates, while others rate merely as woodchucks. Outside of the town of Sun Prairie is a sign, saying WELCOME TO THE GROUNDHOG HEADQUARTERS OF THE WORLD.

Naturally this irritated members in Pennsylvania; so each year there is a spirited exchange of insulting messages. The Punxutawney group declared the Prairie Sun groundhog a mere prairie dog; then came the retort: "There is so much coal dust in the Pennsylvania air, you can't tell a shadow from a smudge."

This feud even got into the Congressional Record. On February 4, 1952, Mr. Davis of Wisconsin addressed the House on the subject of Groundhog Day, declaring that the Honorable Mr. Gavin of Pennsylvania had "presumptuously claimed the title of groundhog capital of the world," when it really belonged to Sun Prairie. In his reply, Mr. Gavin stated that this Wisconsin town was just a wide place in the road; also that their groundhog was "a coddled, faint-hearted pig" in comparison with the "rough, tough Punxutawney groundhog."

On the second of February, members of the Sun Prairie Club, wearing top hats and white or striped clothes, go out at sunrise to observe the doings of the groundhog. Often they have some special feature on this day, such as the wedding of two woodchucks. Also when their groundhog died, they gave the animal a funeral that rated headlines in the local paper. At their Parish Hall, they have a floor show, stunts, with prizes for young and old, and serve "groundhog sandwiches," a special pork sausage concoction.

Each year the club puts out an original "cover," which is highly prized by collectors. These go all over the United States and abroad and have brought the community much publicity. And they actually *do* have groundhogs in the vicinity on which to base their claims.

Some time ago the National Geographic Society declared this whole groundhog idea ridiculous, and said the day ought to be abolished. And one weatherman asserted not long ago:

> Using temperature and precipitation figures for the past 60 years, we found that Mr. Groundhog would have done very much better by remaining in his burrow and not bothering us civilized folks. Groundhog was right only 28% of the time.

In spite of such assertions, groundhog adherents swear with poker faces that the animals *have* been more accurate than the United States Weather Bureau.

Even though few take this holiday seriously, these clubs will no doubt continue to challenge each other and to support their favorite animal and its ability to forecast the weather on February 2. And since this day affords us good laughs, it would be too bad if this unique bit of Americana were abolished.

Lincoln's Birthday—February 12

Each year, on the twelfth of February, Abraham Lincoln's birthday is observed in numerous places. It is a legal holiday in most states but not in these: Alabama, the District of Columbia, Florida, Georgia, Idaho, Louisiana, Maine, Massachusetts, Mississippi, New Hampshire, North Carolina, Oklahoma, Rhode Island, South Carolina, Texas, Virginia, and Wyoming.

It was on February 12, 1866 that the first formal celebration of Lincoln's birthday occurred. On that date, President Johnson met with his Cabinet, the Justices of the Supreme Court, Senators, Representatives, diplomats, navy and army officers, and others to honor the late President. The Marine band played, there was a prayer, followed by eulogies by such speakers as the president of the Senate, and the famous historian George Bancroft who spoke on the Great Emancipator.

On that same date in 1866, a group of private citizens met in Jersey City to observe Lincoln's anniversary. This gathering became the Lincoln Association; and each year, at their dinners, famous speakers addressed them. In 1887, at the noted restaurant, Delmonico's in New York, Chauncey M. Depew, the celebrated after-dinner speaker, addressed three hundred members of the newly formed Republican Club.

It was in 1891 that Hannibal Hamlin of Maine suggested that Lincoln's birth date be made a national anniversary. A year later, Illinois set the day apart as a legal holiday; and soon other states followed her example.

When the year 1909 was approaching—the one-hundredth anniversary of Lincoln's birth—although there had been many observances up to this time, plans were made for a special and really fitting celebration. A memorial association purchased the Lincoln farm in Hodgenville, Kentucky, with the cabin where Abraham was born.

On February 12, 1909, President Theodore Roosevelt delivered the address at the laying of the cornerstone of the marble structure that shelters the noted log cabin. On this same date, there were meetings in New York, with the main one at Cooper Union, where Lincoln had made an important address; in Springfield, Illinois, distinguished guests included William Jennings Bryan, and the English and French ambassadors. The Daughters of the American Revolution held a reception on that particular day at the Lincoln home. Also memorial tablets were affixed to the church which the Civil War President had attended, and at the place where he had had his law office. On the courthouse lawn citizens planted a tree in Lincoln's honor.

Booker T. Washington, the distinguished Negro educator, spoke before the Republican Club at the centennial observance. In Chicago store windows were filled with Lincoln pictures, mementoes, and Civil War items. Several meetings were held in Chicago; and at the chief affair, Woodrow Wilson, then president of Princeton University, made the main address.

At Boston (1909) Senator Henry Cabot Lodge was the speaker; Julia Ward Howe read a poem; and several cornetists played her "Battle Hymn of the Republic" from the belfry of the Park Avenue Congregational Church.

That year there were observances of this one-hundredth anniversary of Lincoln's birth all over the country. In the South, for the first time, schools took note of the holiday. There were also celebrations abroad, in London, Berlin, and Paris; at the last-named city, the well-known writer, Henry Van Dyke, gave the address.

Because of the renewed interest shown in 1909 in the memory of our distinguished Civil War President, Congress passed a bill proposing the erection of a Lincoln memorial in our national capital.

This impressive monument, one of the most visited spots in Washington, D.C., was designed by Henry Bacon of New York; and the famous sculptor, Daniel Chester French, was chosen to make the statue. On February 12, 1915, the cornerstone was laid, and the memorial was dedicated in May 1922. After the poet, Edwin Markham, had read a poem about Lincoln, several addresses were given; then William Howard Taft, chairman of the commission, presented the building to President Warren Harding.

Nowadays, Lincoln's birthday usually is not formally observed by cities; however, many schools hold special assemblies with programs that inform students of his life and character. Other groups also commemorate the holiday. For instance, on February 12 the Illinois State Society of Long Beach, California, holds a picnic at Bixby Park, followed by a program paying tribute to "The Rail Splitter."

One of the finest ways in which Lincoln's birthday is now remembered is by setting apart the Sunday just preceding it as "Race Relations Sunday." This is a cooperative project, carried on by Protestants, Roman Catholics, and Jews. The last group observe the day on their Sabbath, the preceding Saturday.

This worthwhile event is sponsored by the National Council of Christian Churches (Protestant and Orthodox), the Central Conference of American Rabbis, and several Roman Catholic organizations. All join with the National Association for the Advancement of Colored People "in proclaiming the unity of all mankind under a common Father."

Each community carries out this inter-faith idea as it wishes; and sometimes there are exchanges of pulpits between pastors of white and Negro congregations. Such matters as respect for other races and friendly attitudes toward all are stressed in sermons and speeches. This is truly a fitting tribute, and one of the best ways we can pay our respects to the memory of our great President, Abraham Lincoln, when the anniversary of his birth occurs.

St. Valentine's Day—February 14

Just before St. Valentine's Day, store windows feature valentines. Adults as well as children are attracted by the displays of artistic cards and gifts. Even though this holiday has lost some of its romance, many still like to observe it by sending affectionate messages or by giving gay parties.

There are conflicting ideas about the origin of St. Valentine's Day. Some sources say it goes back—perhaps to the third century—when there were hordes of hungry wolves outside Rome. The god, Lupercus, was said to watch over the shepherds and their flocks. Therefore, in February Romans celebrated a feast, called the Lupercalia, in his honor. Even after the danger from these fierce animals was over, people still observed this festival.

When Christianity became prevalent, the priests wanted their converts to give up former heathen practices. Therefore, the officials Christianized the ancient pagan celebration and called the Feast of Lupercalia St. Valentine's Day. Sometimes a priest placed names of different saints in a box or urn; the young people drew these names out; then during the following year each youth was supposed to emulate the life of the saint whose name he had drawn.

According to the Acta Sanctorum, there were actually eight men with the name, Valentine, seven of whose feast days were on February 14. Also on this date occurred "the veneration of the head of the eighth."

These men are said to have lived in different parts of the world, including Spain, Africa, Belgium, and France. However, the three most important ones were a priest, beheaded at Rome in 269, a bishop of Umbria (both of the third century), and the third, Valentine, who was put to death in Africa. Tradition has preserved several accounts of these saints; but some authorities believe many of the stories have no historical value.

One source states that a Valentine served as a priest at a beautiful temple during the reign of the cruel Emperor Claudius. Romans revered this priest; and young and old, rich and poor, thronged to his services. When the Emperor tried to recruit soldiers for his wars, he met much opposition. For the men did not want to leave their wives, families, or sweethearts. Then the angry monarch declared that no more marriages would be performed, and that all engagements were canceled.

This was not fair to young lovers—so Valentine thought—therefore, he secretly joined several couples. Claudius declared that no one, not even a priest, could defy him; so he threw Valentine into prison where he died. Then his friends got his body and buried it in a churchyard in Rome.

Another version is that St. Valentine was seized for helping some Christians; while in prison he cured a jailer's daughter of blindness. This made Claudius angrier than ever; he had Valentine beaten with clubs and then beheaded. His death is said to have occurred on February 14, 269 A.D. In 496 Pope Gelasius set aside this date to honor him. Another legend says that Valentine fell in love with the jailer's daughter and wrote her letters, signed "From your Valentine."

So gradually as time passed this new Christian holiday became a time for exchanging love messages, and St. Valentine emerged as the patron saint of lovers. There was also an old European belief that on February 14 of each year the birds began to choose their mates. In his "Parliament of Foules," Chaucer wrote: "For this was Seynt Valentine's Day when every foul cometh ther to choose his mate."

The old custom of drawing names on St. Valentine's Eve continued in England and some parts of the Continent. When a youth drew a girl's name, he wore it on his sleeve, and attended and protected her during the following year. Thus she became his valentine, and they exchanged love tokens. Later on, only the men gave presents. Often the gifts were without names, and signed "with St. Valentine's Love."

Shakespeare and other writers mentioned this holiday. The poet, Drayton, wrote verses entitled "To His Valentine," in which he expressed the idea of the birds' mating on this day:

> Each little bird this tide
> Doth choose her beloved peer,
> Which constantly abide
> In wedlock all the year.

There was also a belief that the first person of the opposite sex whom one met on the morning of this holiday would be the individual's valentine. Gay, the poet, wrote of this:

> Last Valentine, the day when birds of kind
> Their paramours with mutual chirpings find,
> I early rose, just at the break of day,
> Before the sun had chased the stars away,
> A-field I went, amid the morning dew,
> To milk my kine (for so should housewives do)
> Thee first I spied—and the first swain we see,
> In spite of fortune shall our true love be.

One of the earliest creators of valentines, called "poetical or amorous addresses," was a young Frenchman, Charles, Duke of Orleans. He was taken prisoner at the Battle of Agincourt in 1415 and for several years was confined in the Tower of London. From this prison he sent many poems, or "valentines," to his wife in France.

During the period of the popular diarist, Samuel Pepys, both married and unmarried men could be selected by the fair sex as valentines. In 1667 Pepys reported that "little Will Mercer" was his wife's valentine; that Will had presented her with his name, written in gold letters on blue paper. Pepys himself drew "Mrs. Pierce's little girl" as his partner.

Usually valentine gifts were simple; often men presented their sweethearts with bouquets of flowers. Later, lacy valentines and heart-shaped candies were popular. However, sometimes costly presents were given on this holiday; for instance, Miss Stuart received a jewel worth eight hundred pounds as a valentine gift from the Duke of Richmond. Another nobleman gave his lady a gem valued at three hundred pounds. On February 14, 1668, Pepys wrote in his diary that his wife had had a special ring made for him.

The date also came to be marked by social gatherings; the evening before St. Valentine's Day was often chosen as a time to give an elaborate ball; and those fortunate enough to be on the guest list decked themselves out in their best and flocked to attend.

In England, the holiday has been observed for centuries; and various customs grew up around it. Little children used to go about singing of St. Valentine and collecting small gifts. Also it was customary to place valentines on friends' doorsteps.

One old valentine (made during the fifteenth century) showed a drawing of a knight and a lady, with Cupid in the act of sending an arrow to pierce the knight's heart. By the seventeenth century some persons were making and sending original valentines. They either created their own messages or copied them from booklets containing appropriate poems. Oliver Cromwell frowned upon valentines as "immoral"; but the custom of giving them returned during the reign of Charles II, when such gifts as perfumed gloves and jeweled garters were popular.

The first commercial valentines appeared about 1800. Originally they were rather simple, but by the 1830's and 1840's experts had mastered the art of creating delicate and really artistic messages; some of these sold for high prices. Such missives were made of fine papers and decorated with satin, ribbon, or lace. They had pictures of turtledoves, lovers' knots in gold or silver, bows and arrows, cupids, and bleeding hearts—all emblems connected with love and lovers. Mechanical valentines were introduced during the 1840's.

Messages on these early valentines included such expressions as "Love," "I fondly, truly love thee," "Love protects," "My orb of day departs with thee," or a stanza like this:

> I love thee! Oh! I love thee!
> Dearer art thou than life.
> I love thee! Oh! I love thee!
> Say, wilt thou be my wife?

One valentine sold in 1840 carried this injunction:

> 'Tis Valentine's Day, to the church let's away;
> No longer I'll wait, let us marry.
> You promised, dear maid, that you would be mine,
> If I, till today, would tarry.

The Victorian period was the golden age of valentines in the British Isles; then gradually the custom died out. But it is said that American soldiers stationed there during World War II revived the idea.

Credit for creating the first worthwhile valentines in this country goes to Miss Esther Howland, a student at Mount Holyoke College a century or more ago. Her father, a stationer in Worcester, Massachusetts, used to import valentines from England, as did other American merchants.

However, Esther decided to create her own messages; as a result, she was one of our first career women. About 1830 she started to import lace, fine papers, and other supplies for her business. This grew so rapidly that she had to employ several assistants. Her brothers marketed her justly popular "Worcester" valentines, and sales amounted to about a hundred thousand dollars annually.

These messages remained at the height of their popularity in the United States until the Civil War era. Valentine's Day is said to have ranked next to Christmas in holiday importance. Many early valentines, hand-painted and expertly trimmed with lace work, are now collectors' items. Even though some have faded, we are still charmed by their delicate colors, unique designs, and tender sentiments.

In later decades valentines became less artistic and frequently they were overornamented—especially through the Gay Nineties—with garish decorations of spun glass, mother-of-pearl, imitation jewels, or silk fringe. So the finer handmade greetings gave way to unattractive, cheap-looking ones.

Another type that lessened the popularity of valentines was the "vinegar valentine," or so-called "comic." Printed on cheap paper, in crude colors, they were first concocted by a New York printer, John McLaughlin. Such messages ridiculed certain types of persons: old maids, teachers, and others. This unkind custom made many people unhappy; for the valentines were certainly not in tune with the real spirit of St. Valentine.

Fortunately, from the beginning of this century there has been quite a change in the missives sent on February 14. The heavy sentimentality of earlier days has given way to the "light touch." Naturally, too, living in the Space Age has affected our valentines.

At times a husband will "go all out" on this holiday to impress his wife. Some time ago the comedian, Garry Moore, hired four planes to do some sky writing. This included a heart three miles wide, pierced by an arrow, six miles long. Inside the heart were the names, "Garry and Nell."

Nowadays, adults usually purchase valentines to accompany a more elaborate gift, such as candy, flowers, or perfume. School children enjoy buying or making valentines for their friends and teachers; they like to baffle the receivers by printing the old "From guess who," on the messages. Even in quite modern schools youngsters want a gaily decorated box with a slot in the top where they can "mail" their valentines. Usually each classroom has one and the distribution at the end of the school day is eagerly awaited.

Naturally St. Valentine's Day, like some other holidays, has become commercialized. The designing and manufacturing of valentines is one of the most important parts of the greeting card business. (It is estimated that, in 1959 for example, at least 150 million such messages went through the United States mails.) Some artists give their entire time to planning these cards; and the charming verses are, of course, the work of real professionals.

And there's a certain city in Colorado, named Loveland, whose post office does a land office business around this speical holiday. It all began in 1947 when some individuals sent their valentines to this town, where they are stamped with an appropriate crimson seal, and then remailed with the postmark, "Loveland," on them.

Even though today most of us don't care for the overly sentimental valentines of bygone days, we are glad that the spirit of good St. Valentine is still prevalent. For our simpler present-day greetings do convey the same good feelings that the older ones did. And no doubt the saint—whoever he was—is glad to know he started a custom that brings happiness to many persons.

Washington's Birthday—
February 22

George Washington's birthday, February 22, is now a legal holiday in all states, the District of Columbia, the Canal Zone, Guam, Puerto Rico, and the Virgin Islands.

In colonial times it was customary to observe the British king's birthday each year; then, following the American Revolution, observance of our first President's anniversary took its place. The idea of celebrating George Washington's birth date was of rather slow growth, but it became a time of general thanksgiving and rejoicing for our forefathers. (At first the occasion was noted on February 11, according to the Old Style Calendar, and many years passed before February 22 was the accepted time.)

In the winter of 1778, when Washington had his headquarters at Valley Forge, the band of the Fourth Continental Artillery marched to his quarters, and serenaded him on his birthday. Three years afterwards, in 1781, when the French allies under Count Rochambeau were at Newport, Rhode Island, the officers honored our commander-in-chief by a dinner.

The count wrote General Washington of this affair. From his headquarters at New Windsor, New York, the latter in his reply said: "The flattering distinction paid to the anniversary of my birthday is an honor, for which I dare not attempt to express my gratitude. . . ."

There seem to be conflicting claims as to who actually had the idea of giving the first real celebration. *The Virginia Gazette* (or *American Advertizer*) of Richmond, Virginia, stated that on February 11, 1782 the birthday "of our illustrious Commander-in-Chief" was observed "with demonstrations of joy."

A year later several gentlemen met at Talbot Courthouse in

Maryland, where they recited odes, and drank toast after toast. "All, before they went reeling and singing home, agreed to assemble in the future and make merry over the birthday of Washington."

That same year there were salutes in New York Harbor; a company of men met at a New York hotel and several after-dinner speeches praising Washington were given and the usual thirteen toasts drunk. Cambridge, Massachusetts, also celebrated this holiday.

During the early part of Washington's term of office, New York was the national capital. The President and his wife lived not far from Trinity Church on lower Broadway; Congress held its sessions in the old City Hall at the corner of Wall and Nassau streets. In 1790, during Washington's first year in the Presidency, Congress adjourned on his birthday and extended him congratulations.

The Tammany Society, formed in 1789, held a real celebration in 1790 with the customary thirteen toasts. These included tributes to their founders, the Fourth of July, their chief sachem, the Constitution, etc. Here is an excerpt from a news report of the affair:

> At a meeting of the Tammany Society, at their wigwam in this city on Monday last, after finishing the ordinary business of the evening, it was unanimously resolved: That the 22nd day of February be, from this day and ever after, commemorated by this society as the birthday of George Washington. The society then proceeded to the commemoration of the auspicious day, which gave birth to the distinguished chief, and the following toasts were drunk in porter, the produce of the United States, accompanied with universal acclamations of applause . . .

By 1791, when George Washington reached the age of fifty-nine, the national capital had been moved to Philadelphia. There, on February 22, a parade of military men took place; and the Chief Executive received congratulations and good wishes.

The Baltimore Advertizer described an anniversary ball at Wise's Tavern in 1791 in this fashion:

> The meeting was numerous and brilliant. Joy beamed in every countenance. Sparkling eyes, dimpled cheeks dressed in smiles prompted by the occasion, with all the various graces of female beauty, contributed to heighten the pleasure of the scene. At an interesting moment, a portrait of the President, a striking likeness, was suddenly exhibited. The illustrious original had often been seen in the same room in the mild character of a friend, a pleased and pleasing guest. The song

of "God Bless Great Washington, Long Live Great Washington" succeeded. In this prayer, many voices and hearts united. May it not be breathed in vain.

The President and Martha Washington were honored by a banquet in Philadelphia in 1792. For the patriotic citizens of this community enjoyed paying homage to their Chief Executive. The anniversary in 1793 was noted by a parade of militia, and officers called at the Washington home to express their congratulations.

On that day, officers of the First Pennsylvania Brigade held a meeting at Mr. Hill's tavern with such guests as the governor, Speaker of the House, and others. After the thirteen toasts, "the afternoon and evening were spent agreeably in social pleasures, and convivial mirth. . . ."

There is no doubt that the University of Pennsylvania has held regular exercises in honor of Washington's birthday longer than any other such institution. In 1794 the faculty members marched to the President's house in Philadelphia to pay their respects.

In 1797 when the general reached his sixty-fifth year, he was honored at a ball in New York, attended by about five hundred persons. That same year several smaller cities also staged banquets and balls, thus showing their patriotism and ways of entertainment. During the decade of the 1790's, there was some opposition to the observance of this holiday, for certain individuals declared it was too partisan. John Adams approved the celebrations; but later Thomas Jefferson ignored the occasion, as did others of his political party.

Not long after George Washington's death (late in 1799) Congress passed a resolution that February 22, 1800 should be observed as a day of mourning. The New York State Society, for example, marched to the New Dutch Church, and in other localities notice was taken of the day. In Philadelphia, all business was suspended; government officials and other citizens attended church services; and in a parade from the State House a horse "caparisoned in full dress" was led.

In 1832, the one-hundredth anniversary of Washington's birth, some places that had not celebrated before did so. The first important observance occurred in Boston; also that year in New York, bells pealed, cannon sounded, and citizens gathered in the churches.

That evening buildings were lighted and a grand ball took place at which the general's sword, pistols, etc. were on display.

Four years afterwards Philadelphians did not celebrate as joyously as before because the city was covered by a heavy snow. But in spite of this many persons gathered on the streets, and at one place a whole ox was roasted and eaten by celebrants.

During ensuing decades Washington's birthday continued to be noted in varied ways all over the country. Often on these occasions such celebrities as Presidents Taft, Theodore Roosevelt, and Chief Justice Hughes gave eulogies.

However, the most important and longest celebration occurred in 1932, marking the two-hundredth anniversary of our first President's birth. Congress appointed a special commission to plan the program which continued from February 22 to Thanksgiving of that year. President Hoover issued a proclamation to honor Washington during this period.

On February 22, 1932, Congress held a joint session; choirs sang patriotic songs at the east front of the Capitol; President Hoover reviewed a parade at Alexandria and placed a wreath at Washington's tomb at Mount Vernon. That evening a fine masque with tableaux depicting historical events was accompanied by a chorus of singers.

During the months of celebration twelve stamps were issued with portraits of George Washington by such outstanding artists as Peale and Stuart. Many memorial trees were planted in schoolyards and parks. In forty foreign countries our first Chief Executive was honored; for his courage and leadership had inspired people in other lands to throw off the yokes of tyrants. In numerous places streets and squares were renamed for him. On November 24, 1932, after a wreath had been placed at the base of the Washington Monument in our national capital, the official ceremonies of the two-hundredth anniversary came to an end in the United States.

From the early days of its history, the West also had joined in observing Washington's birthday. After the American conquest of California and its entrance into the Union in 1850, the Yankees there promoted the observance of this holiday.

However, in the sleepy pueblo of Los Angeles one of the first of such festivities had some dire results. It took place in 1853 at El Palacio, the mansion built by Abel Stearns, an early Massachusetts settler. This home stood at the corner of Main and Arcadia streets;

here visitors were entertained and charmed by the gracious hospitality of Dona Arcadia, Don Abel's young California wife, of the noted
Bandini family.

The elite of the town had decided to have a ball to honor Washington's birthday, at the Stearns's home. But some of the rougher
element in the community considered this idea too exclusive; they
declared that all the Angelenos should celebrate together the anniversary of the Father of his Country.

That evening they dragged an old cannon from the nearby plaza
and placed it directly in front of El Palacio. At midnight when the
dance was at its height about two hundred members of the rowdy
element of the town determined to break up the party. Some fired
the cannon but missed the goal. Then several intruders tried to
force the door with a heavy piece of timber; when they finally succeeded and started to enter the home, one guest shot an assailant. In
the general fight that followed, several men were killed and others
wounded. For some time thereafter, there was bad feeling in the
pueblo; but gradually things quieted down.

This 1853 program was a marked contrast to a recent observance
in the same city. Six small boys of the Woodcraft Rangers met at
the statue of George Washington, at the east entrance of the Hall of
Records. There they held a contest to see who could give the best
delivery of sections of Washington's famous Farewell Address. The
winner was designated as the "Little George Washington of the
Year," and then fitted with an appropriate outfit.

Not long ago another group of about sixty boys and girls from
the organization, Children of the American Revolution, met at the
same statue and placed a wreath before it on February 22. In addition seventeen patriotic organizations of the county participated in
the county-wide observance.

In 1961 Washington's birthday was observed all over our land in
varying fashion. In many places public schools, banks, libraries, state,
county, and city offices were closed with the exception of police and
fire departments. Many municipal playgrounds staged patriotic activities.

At historic spots connected with the general, exercises are often
held. For example, in 1961 there was a re-enactment of the prayer
scene at Valley Forge. A military academy student, Robert W. Boar-
man, knelt in the snow, and nearby, holding his white horse, was his

aide, Joseph M. Gesker. It was a realistic scene with the young men in colonial dress; in the background was a log cabin like the one in which the Revolutionary soldiers lived that bitter winter.

A humorous touch has been added to the observance of the Washington's Birthday holiday in our national capital. Local merchants—and some in other cities as well—have made it the occasion for drastic price cutting. Some stores advertise February 22 as Cherry Tree Day, with all prices "chopped." One ad read:

> WE CANNOT TELL A LIE—FOR *WASHINGTON'S BIRTHDAY*
> WE REALLY CUT OUR PRICES

And another:

> *George Washington threw a silver dollar across the Potomac River, but you can make your dollars go farther during our Washington's Birthday celebration.*

In contrast to this sort of celebration there are dignified programs that pay homage to our first President. For instance, this year (1961) at the wreath-laying ceremony at the grave at Mount Vernon, President Kennedy's speech was read by an aide, and contained these passages:

> As time goes on, we realize more and more how deep is our debt to George Washington, and his strict sense of sacrifice and duty to his country. We are ever mindful of all he gave of himself in order that this country, in its infancy, might survive, grow, and prosper.
>
> As in the past, this anniversary of the birth of the father of our country inspires us anew with the strength for today's challenges.
>
> The spirit of George Washington is a living tradition, so that even today he serves his country well.

All over the United States we have honored him by naming for him our national capital, a state, and various communities. Each year patriotic programs keep his memory green; we recall with pride the character and deeds of this American hero, who, as Light Horse Harry Lee once declared was "First in war, first in peace, and first in the hearts of his countrymen."

Leap Year—February 29

Each four years, when leap year returns, with its 366 days, it is especially welcomed by those born on February 29; for then they can really celebrate their birth dates. Naturally, it should be the occasion for rejoicing by all unmarried females, for it has long been a woman's right to propose to the man of her choice during this year.

How did this extra day happen? Since it takes our globe 365 days, 5 hours, 48 minutes, and 45 seconds plus to make a complete solar journey, each year of 365 days gives us some leftover time. With the reformation of the Julian calendar and the adoption of the Gregorian in 1582, an extra day was added to each fourth year (with the exception of each hundredth year that is not divisible by 400). For example: 1600 and 2000 are leap years, but not 1700, 1800, or 1900. Pope Gregory also canceled ten days in order to solve the complicated problem. Result—people who went to bed on Thursday, October 4, 1582, awoke next morning to find it was a new date, Friday, October 15.

Why is the year with the extra day called leap year? The Encyclopaedia Britannica says: "The English name for the bisextile year is an allusion to the result of this interposition; for after February 29, a date 'leaps over' a day of the week." Another source suggests that since the date February 29 had no legal status in English courts, it was "leapt" over, as far as the records were concerned. For what happened on February 29 was dated as occurring on February 28.

According to one writer, leap year brings "the ideal excuse for a young lassie to pop the question to the gentleman of her choice." There are several reasons given for this belief. Some say it can be traced to an old legend about St. Patrick and St. Bridget in Ireland. At that time, it was not necessary for priests and nuns to remain unmarried.

Bridget headed a group of sisters, and one day she went to St. Patrick in tears. She told him of the unrest among her charges and declared they were unhappy because of the belief that only men could take the initiative in matrimony. St. Patrick was sympathetic and said he would allow the women to propose during each seventh year. This didn't satisfy Bridget; so she drove a better bargain, and obtained the right for every four years. When she started this custom by asking St. Patrick to marry her, he refused, saying he had taken vows of celibacy. To make it easier for her, St. Patrick gave her a kiss and a silken gown.

The story goes that for years it was an unwritten law in Britain that a man who didn't accept a woman's proposal during leap year had to pay her a forfeit of a silk dress. It was customary for each female, planning to take advantage of her special right in this year to let her intentions be known by wearing a scarlet petticoat whose edge was visible beneath her dress skirt.

In 1288 A.D. Scotland passed a law providing that every woman—no matter what her social class—had the prerogative to propose during leap year, and that if the man refused he had to pay her a pound—or less—unless he was already engaged to someone else. Laws of this type also existed on the Continent, in France, Switzerland, and Italy for example. Therefore, if an unattractive lady decided to propose to more than one man during this special year, she *might* add much to her bank account.

Leap year has long been "open season" on bachelors, but apparently it doesn't have much effect on marriage rates. The Institute of Life Insurance made a survey some time ago and checked marriage records over the past fifty years, reporting as follows:

> Nothing happens to the nation's marriage rate in leap year; it neither goes up very much, or down very much. If anything, as a matter of fact, it is apt to go down. It did, in any case, in five of the last leap years.

If we try to find the reason for this—why in the modern era, when women have taken a dominant place in the world—perhaps it stems from the fact, that, in spite of their new freedom, most women still prefer to be pursued rather than to pursue.

In one poll, of each 100 persons questioned, women opposed the idea of doing their own proposing nearly 2 to 1. More men favored women's proposing, and it was discovered that men with college educations were more receptive to the idea than males with less educational background. The president of one bachelors' club said he considered leap year proposals a good thing because they "present a wonderful opportunity to shy bachelors."

At the present time the chance of marriage for unmarried females is no laughing matter. At the beginning of 1960, the United States had 113 unmarried women to every 100 foot-loose men between the ages of twenty and sixty-four. Under age twenty, we learn that the males predominate—1,039 to 1,000.

Therefore, even though leap year returns with its special female privileges, there probably won't be a great increase in marriage rates during its twelve months' period. For no doubt most women will continue to want the man of their choice at least to *think* he did the proposing.

Purim—Adar 14

Since the ancient Jewish feast days are kept according to their ancient Hebrew calendar, these holidays vary, and do not always fall on the same dates in our calendar. Therefore, the dates on which they were observed in 1960 will give the approximate time when such festivals are celebrated. Purim fell on March 2 in 1960.

Purim is an occasion for feasting and gladness—"a festival of 'comic relief' "—and is considered the jolliest day of the year for Hebrew children. As the "carnival of the Jewish year," Purim is featured by much feasting, dancing, singing, and general merrymaking.

This festival is observed on the fourteenth day of the month Adar. Purim recalls the highly dramatic story told in the Book of Esther of how the Jews in Persia escaped annihilation at the hands of the haughty prime minister, Haman, during the reign of Ahasuerus (Xerxes 485–464 B.C.). Haman, in his anger that Mordecai would not bow to him, determined to exterminate him and his people.

Purim is often called the Feast of Lots because Haman cast lots to decide on the day for the destruction. However, Mordecai and Queen Esther were able to turn the plot against Haman and save themselves and the rest of the Jews. So, as Ben M. Edidin says, "On Purim they make merry to express their confidence that they will outlive every Haman."

This feast is observed not only in homes but also in the synagogues and community centers. There is a family reunion at the Purim feast —the Seudath-Purim—with everyone dressed in his best, seated around the festive table, sometimes with guests. There is a spirit of gaiety, and no mourning is allowed on this day.

Traditional foods are served; turkey is a popular main dish and there are cookies in special Purim shapes. Boys and girls enjoy the Hamanstaschen, or "Haman's ears," made with a filling of honey and poppy seeds. They are three-cornered in shape, a reminder of Haman's hat, so it is said.

Jewish people often keep open house on this day for rich, poor, young, and old. It is customary, too, to send gifts of food to friends, while the less fortunate receive many presents of money and edibles at this Feast of Purim.

At the family gathering gifts are exchanged with various members; they sing together and play Purim games. One of the favorite pastimes is for the youngsters to improvise little plays and present them before their parents. Of course these are based on the story of Queen Esther, Mordecai, and Haman. Sometimes the children, led by a clown, go from house to house, singing Purim songs or reciting funny verses. From the seventeenth century on, there were formerly groups of Purim spielers who roamed around giving productions about this Hebrew event.

Such dramatic presentations at the present time are popular for community gatherings at Jewish centers, etc. Purim is the time for dances, masquerades, charades, and games. Minstrel shows are often staged too, and everyone has a good time.

At the services in the temple or synagogue, attendants listen to the reading of the Megillah, a scroll that contains the story of Queen Esther and the Jews. During the first part, the room is quiet; then each time the name of Haman is mentioned, the children twirl noisemakers in derision. Adults too add to the din. Usually the rabbi preaches a short sermon on the significance of this festival. Then special contributions are accepted for the poor, and for the Jewish National Fund.

Although Hebrews celebrate Purim as a time of fun and merriment, it does have a deep meaning for them. As Ben M. Edidin states:

> Purim each year bids the Jew have courage and hope. There have been Hamans before; the Jews have suffered terribly, but they have survived them all. We shall survive the Hamans of this generation as well. We must not, however, depend on miracles, but must fight the evil on many fronts—by working for peace and democracy in the world; by re-building Palestine; by helping the victims of persecution to find new homes; by improving and strengthening Jewish life in every community; and by performing our duties as citizens loyally and intelligently.

St. Patrick's Day—March 17

On March 17, it's a good old American custom to wear something green—perhaps a blouse, scarf, or tie—to honor Patrick, Ireland's patron saint. Persons of various faiths celebrate this day, which is not his birthday but the date of his death in 493.

No saint is so good, Ireland's country adorning,
Then hail to St. Patrick, today in the morning.

St. Patrick, according to Roman Catholic authorities, was born in 387 A.D., not in Ireland but at Kilpatrick, near Dumbarton, Scotland. His father, Calphurnius, from a high Roman family, served as magistrate in his community.

When Patrick, whose original name was Maewyn, was sixteen, he was captured by Irish marauders and sold as a slave to a Druid chief, in what is now County Antrim, Ireland. There he spent six years as a swineherd, learned the Celtic language, and became familiar with Irish ways. These years influenced his later life and inspired him with a desire to convert the Irish from their pagan ways.

A legend tells that one day Patrick saw a vision and heard a voice say, "Behold, a ship is ready for thee." When he managed to escape from his master, he reached a vessel on the west coast of Ireland, and on it he went back to his former home.

At the age of twenty-two, Patrick decided to give his life to religion and studied at the monastery of St. Martin at Tours, France. During his eighteen years on the Continent, he finished his studies, became a priest, and later, a bishop.

In the year 431, Pope Celestine I named him Patricius and sent him to Ireland on a mission, where he landed in 432. Naturally, he met much opposition from the Druid priests, who resented his invading the land with his Christian ideas and converting their followers. When the Druids tried to stone him, Patrick escaped and reached his former master's home. He paid this Druid the price of his freedom and is said to have baptized the chief and his family in the Christian belief.

Several times Patrick and his followers were captured by Druids; once, when put in chains, he barely escaped death. On his missionary journeys, he was preceded by a drummer who announced his coming. This appealed to the imagination of the Irish, who firmly believed in spirits and all sorts of mysterious happenings. One story goes that, although it was contrary to his nature, St. Patrick sometimes used their own weapons against these Druids, and he would put a curse on their lands and streams.

Once he showed exceptional courage in disobeying the barbarian king at Tara. This monarch was an awe-inspiring sight with his great height of six and a half feet; he wore an animal skin slung over his shoulder and he was reputed to have the strength of a bull. The king planned to meet the Druid priests and he had ordered all lights extinguished until the signal was given from the castle. But St. Patrick defied the royal command by lighting a fire to proclaim that a new light had come—"the light of Christ's Gospel."

One of the Druid priests exclaimed prophetically: "O King, this fire, which has been lighted in defiance of the royal edict, will blaze forever in this land unless it be extinguished this very night."

And this prophecy came true; during the forty years that the saint worked "with apostolic zeal" in Ireland, he preached to countless persons in many places, baptized thousands of converts, established churches, schools, and at least one college, and consecrated two others.

In 433, after landing near Wicklow, St. Patrick was almost stoned to death, but nothing could diminish his missionary fervor. Still he begged the pagans to hear him. In trying to explain the difficult matter of the "Trinity in Unity," he realized that the people could not understand so he picked a trefoil or shamrock (this small white clover grows abundantly in Ireland and was employed by the Druids to cure diseases) and used its leaves to illustrate his meaning.

St. Patrick told his hearers that the three leaves of the shamrock represented the three members of the Trinity, that the stem was symbolic of the Godhead, and of the Three-in-One. And as one source has reported, he asked, "Is it not as possible for the Father,

Son, and Holy Ghost, as for these leaves to grow upon a single stalk?" Thus the saint explained and convinced his listeners of this truth.

So many legends have sprung up in connection with St. Patrick's life and works (also there's an air of mystery about him) that it is difficult to distinguish between truth and legend. Several miracles have been ascribed to him—that he raised some persons from the dead, including his own father; also, that once a crowd of demons in the shape of vultures, surrounded him. Immediately, the saint prayed, and the evil spirits perished in a nearby sea. And one cold day when he was traveling with some friends, they could find no fuel to make a fire. Patrick told them to make a heap of snow; when he breathed on it, a blaze sprang up and all could warm themselves.

Usually the main thing remembered about this saint is that he drove the snakes from Ireland. Tradition tells that he banished all venomous serpents, and caused the soil to be fatal to them the instant they touched it. He is said to have accomplished this feat by beating his drum. Once when he struck it too hard and made a hole in it, an angel appeared immediately and mended the drum.

There's a story that one old snake refused to leave Ireland. Therefore, St. Patrick made a box and asked the serpent to enter it. The creature objected, saying it was too small. The saint insisted it was big enough to accommodate him comfortably and urged him to try it. After some grumbling, the snake got into the box just to prove that it *was* too small; at once Patrick clapped down the lid and tossed the container, snake and all, into the sea.

Until his death, the saint visited and watched over all the churches he had founded, encouraged the pastors, and consecrated many bishops. When he became ill at Sabhall, he received the sacrament from his disciple, St. Tassach, before his death on March 17, 493.

Thousands of mourners came from long distances to his funeral. So many torches and candles were carried that it is said everything was as light as day. In a shroud made for him by St. Brigid Patrick was buried on the hill of Down, at Downpatrick, in Ireland. Later the Cathedral of Downpatrick was built there. Today, he is remembered by the many churches named for him, also by several towns, such as Kilpatrick, Dalpatrick, Kirkpatrick, and others. In addition, his name has long been a favorite one for boys. Therefore—

All hail to St. Patrick, who brought to our mountains,
The gift of God's faith, the sweet light of His love.

There was an old saying, in the Emerald Isle, "St. Patrick's Day, we'll all be gay." And for many years, the Irish, in Dublin for example, after attending Mass in the saint's honor, would parade proudly through the streets, carrying the green flag with the harp of Tara. Now this is displaced by the new ensign of orange, green, and white. It was customary, too, to get together in the evening of the feast day to dance Irish jigs and square dances and to sing gay airs like "Paddy Whack" and "Rocky Road to Dublin." Often there was an elaborate ball in St. Patrick's Hall where all "drowned the shamrock."

Recently, Thomas J. Fleming stated that nowadays Dublin does not have a parade or a noisy celebration; that the day is a holy one; the people go to Mass and all the public houses are closed.

Since Irishmen are adventurous souls, many of them emigrated and settled in various parts of the world; therefore, St. Patrick's Day has been observed round the globe.

It is said that the first celebration of this holiday in the United States took place in Boston. (General Washington had many Irishmen in his army.) The idea spread to other cities, including New York, and was sponsored by such groups as the Charitable Irish Society (founded in 1737), the Friendly Sons of St. Patrick (Philadelphia 1780), and the Ancient Order of Hibernians. The New York branch of the Friendly Sons of St. Patrick (founded 1784) was made up of both Roman Catholics and Presbyterians. The first president of this group was a Presbyterian.

There's a tradition that in 1762 a group of Irish celebrants met in a tavern near New York to celebrate St. Patrick's Day. They drank twenty toasts including this one: "May the enemies of Ireland never eat the bread or drink the whisky of it, but be tormented with itching, without benefit of scratching!"

By 1870 many Irish emigrants had settled in Los Angeles and had organized the St. Patrick's Benevolent Society. On his feast day, after attending Mass, the loyal sons of Ireland would seize their flags and join a parade in the saint's honor, with a band playing lively Irish tunes. In 1870, 150 members were served "a magnificent din-

ner" at the United States Hotel. Father O'Leary was the orator of
the day; humorous stories were told and many toasts were drunk.

As the band played "The Wearin' of the Green," this same organization paraded again the next year. Pupils of the school, directed
by the Sisters of Charity, sang "The Hymn to St. Patrick." At the
final celebration—a banquet—that evening, the speaker, John King,
extolled Ireland; all joined in such songs as "Through Erin's Isle"
and "The Twig of Shannon." When this organization celebrated in
1875, the chief speaker was Stephen M. White who later, as a United
States Senator, fought for a free harbor for Los Angeles.

Irish celebrations are still popular on the Pacific coast. They are
sponsored by such groups as the Ancient Order of Hibernians,
Irish-American clubs, Friendly Sons of St. Patrick, and the Ulster
Irish Associations of Southern California.

The festivities may consist of luncheons with top church officials
as speakers or banquets where awards are sometimes given to outstanding artists of Irish extraction in the entertainment field. In the
past these have included Dennis Day, Ann Blyth, George Murphy,
and Maureen O'Hara.

All over the United states the day is one of rejoicing and merrymaking. Houses and halls are gaily decorated with flags, dolls, clay
pipes, harps, and of course shamrocks. The sons of St. Patrick are a
warmhearted lot, and all are welcome on the saint's day. Guests are
expected to share the Irish stew and other refreshments, and to lend
their voices to the singing of "The Wearin' of the Green," "Where
the River Shannon Flows," "My Wild Irish Rose," and "When Irish
Eyes Are Smilin'."

New York has long been known for its elaborate parade on St.
Patrick's Day. It is said to have more Irishmen among its inhabitants
than Ireland itself. In accord with the proverbial luck of the Irish,
the weather usually is pleasant, bright, and clear. In 1959, a visitor,
Henry O'Mara, head of Ireland's National Police, declared, "I never
saw a parade like this in my life."

Today St. Patrick's Cathedral on Fifth Avenue, in New York, is
the central point of the observance. For many blocks, this famous
street is packed; usually more than a million persons turn out each
year to see a hundred thousand Irish—or semi-Irish—parade along the
avenue. There are many bands, with pipers, regiments of soldiers,
mounted police, social, civic, and other Irish organizations. The

paraders move jauntily along to the tune of such marching songs as "Garry Owen." Some dance jigs, and all of course wear something green. Bands play old favorites including "Come Haste t' th' Wedding," "Sprig o'Shillelagh," "Top o'Cork Road," or "Munster Buttermilk."

Cleveland, Ohio, has many Irish citizens, and they too stage parades on this popular holiday. In 1952, the city had a big, special celebration when the Ancient Order of Hibernians put on its eighty-fifth annual banquet.

Even down South, March 17 is a "great day for the Irish." Many such emigrants settled in that part of the United States during the potato famines in Ireland. In Savannah, Georgia, not long ago there was a parade with music by eighteen bands and a dinner given by the Hibernians. In the city of Atlanta, shamrock dust was recently spread along the famous Peachtree Street, and the fire chief in top hat and full dress led the parade. Whenever the Irish get together on St. Patrick's Day, you hear such expressions as *Erin go bragh* ("Ireland Forever") and *Beannact Dia leat* ("God bless you").

The shamrock, Ireland's chief emblem, has a town named for it in Florida. Each year many persons send letters there to be stamped with the "Shamrock" postmark. And annually, tons of shamrock plants, with "a bit of the auld soil clinging to them," are flown across the Atlantic for March 17.

County Cork is the center of this shamrock trade, and it sends millions of these plants all over the world. The small town of Rosscarberry, with only three hundred inhabitants, is engaged in this industry, which is presided over by Mrs. Catherine O'Keefe ("Mrs. Shamrock," herself). All the villagers, young and old, spend weeks gathering the plants in meadows or on rock-strewn acres. Also, most of the people grow shamrocks in their own homes and gardens. So it's not surprising that this "little sprig has saved a dying village."

The "wearin' of the green" has long been featured in our country on St. Patrick's Day. Even business houses in various parts of the United States have taken up the idea. One dry cleaner in Massachusetts offered to clean *free* any green garment; and "Glory be 'tis a a miracle" started an ad of the Muller Brothers, in Hollywood, California, that they would wash all green cars without charge on St. Patrick's Day.

In 1959 our national capital had a long-remembered celebration on this holiday, for smiling seventy-six-year-old President Sean O'Kelly of Eire was a guest there on March 17. He laid a wreath at the Tomb of the Unknown Soldier, addressed a joint session of Congress, had dinner with the Eisenhowers, and attended other functions.

During his visit Americans got a big surprise in regard to the association of the color green with the Irish. From the time the visitor arrived, he literally saw green everywhere. There was a long green carpet at the airport; President Eisenhower wore a green tie, and other officials, green socks. At the Congressional session, each member sported a green carnation.

Finally, at dinner that evening it was too much for the Irish President; he informed the guests that he and his countrymen do NOT like the color green. It is connected in their minds with too many unpleasant memories of the times when Ireland was not free. Now the old green flag is no longer the national ensign; also, the flag of the Irish President is blue with a white harp.

Since many Irishmen are outstanding citizens, not only here in the United States but all around the world, it is quite fitting for them to celebrate on March 17. And Robert Briscoe, the former Lord Mayor of Dublin, once said, "St. Patrick's Day for the Irish is one of the greatest milestones in its history. St. Patrick . . . brought to Ireland the great faith that Ireland still preserves and adheres to with such affection."

April Fool's Day—April 1

For unknown centuries the first day of April has been "consecrated to practical joking." From Latin we get the words "jovial" and "Jove" the name of the king of the gods (Jupiter) who enjoyed playing jokes on his fellow deities.

The first of April (All Fools' Day, or April Fool's Day) is not a real American holiday like the Fourth of July or Labor Day and is not observed by schools or the government. But no doubt even in our modern, sophisticated world some persons will continue each year to try to fool others on April 1.

This custom was not confined to any particular people or period and must have been of very early origin. Even though its beginning is uncertain, it still has widespread observance. Authorities have advanced several theories as to how "April fooling" got its start.

Some believe it came from the vernal equinox celebration, about March 21, the beginning of a new year for many peoples. There were several days of festivities with a gift exchange on the last day. Others trace the custom to an ancient pagan nature festival, observed by the Hindus, and termed the "Huli," also connected with the spring solstice. On its last day—April 1—unsuspecting persons were sent on foolish errands. This pastime was popular both with the higher and lower classes of society.

Another theory is that the idea started from the story of Proserpina, the beautiful daughter of Ceres. While she was gathering daffodils in the Elysian fields, Pluto, king of the underworld, suddenly appeared and carried her away. When Ceres heard her daughter's cries, she began her unsuccessful search for Proserpina's voice, a "fool's errand." So some declare that April fooling may be a relic of the Roman Feast of Cerealia.

It has also been said that this idea started with Noah, when he sent the dove out from the ark, before the waters had gone down. Another supposition—considered highly improbable by some—is that it came from an old miracle play, in which, when Christ was being tried (about April 1), in Jerusalem, he was sent from Annas to the high priest, Caiaphas, then to the Roman governor, Pilate, next to King Herod, and back to Pilate.

Certain sources believe that the observance of April Fool's Day began in France. At the time of an ancient spring festival, people noted there was an increase in the number of young fish in streams, and that they were more easily "hooked" than older ones. The custom of fooling in France may have become connected with April 1 when in 1564 Charles IX adopted the Gregorian calendar, which set January 1 as New Year's Day instead of April 1.

News traveled slowly in those days (also many objected to the change of date); so many Frenchmen continued to observe the holiday in the spring, to make New Year calls, and to send presents to relatives and friends. Gradually this evolved into a joke; mock gifts were sent and supposedly ceremonial calls were made.

Gradually all sorts of fooling became customary in France on the first of April. Such a victim was dubbed a *poisson d'Avril* ("April fish"). Therefore, most Frenchmen hesitated to begin anything of importance on this day. However, it did not stop Napoleon Bonaparte from marrying his second wife on the first of April, 1810; because of this, he was called a *poisson d'Avril*.

There's an amusing story showing how this date was once used to advantage by the Duke and Duchess of Lorraine. They were prisoners at Nantes and on the morning of April 1, dressed as peasants, they managed to pass through the prison gates. They had sent an informer ahead to tell the guards they were escaping. However, these soldiers, remembering what day it was, just laughed off the message, calling out "April Fool! April Fool!" and so the lucky pair escaped.

The first day of April is said to have been noted in ancient Britain "as a high and general festival, in which an unbounded hilarity reigned through every order of its inhabitants. . . ."

In the British Isles April fooling began later than in France. Gullible souls in Scotland were sent out on such expeditions as searching for hens' teeth, pigeons' milk, and other fantastic items.

The favorite April 1 prank of the Scots was "hunting the gowk (cuckoo)"; and anyone fooled on this holiday was termed an April gowk. For example, someone would give a person a letter to deliver at some distance. This was supposed to contain a request for information, or for a loan. When it was delivered, the receiver would say it was not for him, but for someone farther on. (Inside he had read the message, "This is the first of April. Hunt the gowk another mile.") Then after trudging on unsuccessfully, the weary victim finally reached home to find fellow townsmen waiting for the "gowk" to return.

Naturally this caused much fun for the spectators. "One fool exposed makes pastime for the rest—" so an old saying ran. This custom was mentioned in *Poor Robin's Almanac* in 1760:

> The first of April, some do say,
> Is set apart for All Fools' Day.
> But why the people call it so,
> Nor I, nor they themselves, do know.
> But on this day are people sent
> On purpose for pure merriment.

In the British Isles a man would sometimes be told that his girl friend wanted him to be at her home at a certain time. Then, when he reached there, he found he had not been invited and perhaps was not wanted.

A successful April fool hoax was "put over" in London in 1860. During the preceding month many people had been pleased to receive invitations, reading: "Tower of London, Admit Bearer and Friend" to the yearly "Washing of the White Lions." So great crowds made their way to see this much heralded affair, and the streets were filled with cabs and other vehicles carrying would-be spectators.

It is surprising to learn that adults, including some celebrities, took part in such April fooling. Even the great Dean Swift, the noted writer, once wrote in his diary of plans he and some friends had concocted to fool others on the next day.

In some places tricks were played only on the morning of the holiday. Then, if anyone tried to fool someone later that day, or on the next, he was jeered with these words:

> April Fool is past,
> And you're the biggest fool at last.

The custom of April fooling was brought to the New World by early settlers from England. Today youngsters and some adults enjoy the same worn-out devices that their ancestors used; and some people now fall for these ancient stunts.

They include pinning signs on people's backs, or coattails, with the words: "KICK ME," "PUNCH ME," or "PINCH ME"; putting pepper or salt in candy; or covering balls of cotton with chocolate to simulate candies. Children tell a grownup that he has a hole in his sock, or a black mark on his face, then yell "April Fool!" Sometimes a brick is placed under an old hat on a sidewalk for someone to stub his toe on. And there's the old purse trick; if a person tries to pick it up, it is snatched back by a string held by a hidden jokester. Or the purse may be filled with stones.

Not long ago some people who had passed up the worn purse on the sidewalk in one town, no doubt wished they had "fallen" for the old "gag." Finally a small boy did so and found it contained about $80. He was given a reward, and the April fool joke was on the persons who were afraid they would be fooled.

Thus tricks continue to follow former patterns, including false messages, and telephone calls. Recently eight senators at the California capital had red faces; on their desks they had found memoranda asking them to go at once to the governor's office; and this turned out to be a first of April antic.

One widespread joke often is played in cities with zoos and aquariums. These institutions receive "phony" calls for Mr. Campbell, Mr. Fish, Miss Katz, or Mr. Shepherd, and so forth. Some towns forestall this by having their telephones disconnected on the first of April.

And such pranks are also indulged in "Down Under," in Australia. It is said that on this holiday there are more calls for animals at the zoos than for people. The famous Botanic Gardens in Melbourne got ninety calls for "Mr. Gardiner" in one half day. And it happened that they *did* have two Mr. Gardiners working there as gardeners.

In Hawaii a disk jockey caused a sensation by broadcasting that because the bill for statehood had been passed, the islanders' taxes for the preceding year would be refunded. This caused much excitement; newspaper offices, radio stations, and the Internal Revenue Bureau were bombarded with telephone calls.

Since it's long been a world-wide custom for funmakers to celebrate on All Fools' Day, this date will doubtless continue to survive. And if you are fooled, just remember that other generations before you were also "taken in" on this annual fun-fest.

Pesach (Feast of the Passover) or (Feast of Unleavened Bread) Nisan 15

Pesach, or the Feast of the Passover, has been celebrated for more than three thousand years, and is said to be one of the oldest festivals in existence. It begins on the fifteenth day of the Hebrew month Nisan. (Pesach was noted April 1–8, in 1960.) This festival opens after the first full moon of the spring, and continues for seven days (eight for Orthodox Jews).

Moses had received instructions from God that the Jews in slavery in Egypt were to flee from their bondage on a certain night —one of full moon—the best time for their flight. The people were told to kill a lamb for each family, and to sprinkle their doorposts with some of the blood so that the angel would "pass over" their homes and not destroy their first-born children. Also God gave Moses this command:

And they shall eat the flesh in that night, roast with fire, and unleavened bread; and with bitter herbs they shall eat it.

The Passover is also called the "Feast of Unleavened Bread." Because of their hasty departure, the Israelites could take only this kind of bread with them. And the historian Josephus tells us:

. . . in memory of the want we were then in, we keep a feast for 8 days, which is called the feast of the unleavened bread.

The feast of the unleavened bread succeeds that of Passover and falls on the 15th day of the month and continues 7 days, wherein they eat unleavened bread; on every one of which 2 bulls are killed, 1 ram, and 7 lambs.

The Jews received instructions in Leviticus, chapter 23, verses 5 through 8 inclusive, in regard to the observance of this feast:

In the fourteenth day of the first month at even is the Lord's passover.

70

And on the fifteenth day of the same month is the feast of unleavened bread unto the Lord; seven days ye must eat unleavened bread.

In the first day ye shall have a holy convocation; ye shall do no servile work therein.

But ye shall offer an offering made by fire unto the Lord seven days; in the seventh day is a holy convocation; ye shall do no servile work therein.

The first observance of the Passover was the night the Jews departed from Egypt, and forty years later they celebrated it when they reached the Promised Land. During the time of the second temple in Jerusalem, great crowds thronged to the city for this feast; and many had to stay in tents outside the city walls. It is said that once 3 million Jews observed the festival with the slaying of 265,500 lambs.

During this feast, at their houses of worship, the Hebrews relive the escape from Egypt through the reading of Scriptures—for example, chapters from Exodus, Numbers, etc., with prayers, chants, and other exercises.

The Feast of Passover is closely associated with the "Seder," the family service, and the great Jewish family reunion of the year. Before the festival, houses are cleaned and traditional dishes are prepared. At the observance of the Seder, the father sits in the place of honor, with his wife on his right, and his children, guests, and servants seated around him, symbolizing the equality of all before God and man. A place is set and left vacant for the Prophet Elijah, in case he might care to come to the feast. Later the door is opened to make it easier for him to come in.

Three thin, flat cakes—the matzoth—are set before the father. These represent the unleavened bread of early times, "recalling the bread of affliction" eaten by their ancestors. In one dish is a roasted egg, with a shoulder or shank bone, representing the Paschal Lamb, while another contains the bitter herbs, reminder of the slavery days under the Pharaohs. After various ceremonies, the meal proper is served.

With the Orthodox it is said that the Passover is still the principal annual Jewish feast. Apart from the fact that the journey to Jerusalem is not possible and animal sacrifices are not offered, authorities say the Hebrew celebration of the Passover has remained basically the same for over three thousand years. According to one writer, Ben M. Edidin: "Pesach has come down to us as the most important Jewish festival of all, with the Seder as the dramatic event of the whole holiday."

Pan American Day—April 14

Pan American Day has been observed each year since 1931 on April 14, by the twenty-one American republics. In the United States our President makes a special proclamation for its observance. It is celebrated in Washington, D.C., and in many communities all over the country there are "ceremonies that express our cordial feelings of friendship for all our sister republics, and for the ideal of continental solidarity."

In 1889, at the instigation of James G. Blaine, Secretary of State (under President Benjamin Harrison), and often called the "Father of Pan-Americanism," the first International Conference of American States met in our national capital. Then on April 14, 1890, "setting a precedent in international cooperation as a mode of living," delegates from the North, Central, and South American republics passed a resolution that resulted in the formation of the Pan American Union.

This assembly made important history that day, which has since been observed as Pan American Day.

The purpose of the Union is "to promote peace, commerce, and friendship between the republics of the American continent by fostering economic, social, and cultural relations." This organization is supported by contributions from all the twenty-one republics; it is presided over by a director general, and an assistant director general. They are responsible to a governing board, made up of our Secretary of State and Washington representatives of the other republics. Owing to the generosity of Andrew Carnegie, the Pan American Union is housed in a distinctive building in our national capital.

On April 7, 1930 the board of the Pan American Union recommended that all the governments represented in the organization designate April 14 as Pan American Day, and display the various flags.

The purpose both of the Union and this holiday—to establish

more cordial relations between the United States and Latin America —and the significance of this movement have been well expressed by Hutton Webster:

> Pan-Americanism rests on the fact that the northern republic and her southern neighbors, however unlike in many respects, are one in their independence of Europe and detachment from European concerns, in their governmental systems, and in their political ideals.

On March 7, 1931, President Herbert Hoover issued a proclamation setting April 14 as Pan American Day; he urged that the Stars and Stripes be displayed everywhere, and that civic groups, schools, and the public in general celebrate the day in a way that would reveal "the sentiments of cordiality and friendly feeling which the government and people of the United States entertain toward the peoples and governments of the other republics of the American continent."

The first observance at our national capital took place in the handsome Pan American Building. It was attended by President Hoover, his Cabinet, and diplomatic representatives of the other American countries. There were addresses by the President, the Secretary of State, the Mexican and Cuban ambassadors, and two foreign students studying in this country. On the same date, local officials and foreign consuls took part in like programs in other communities.

Since Pan American Day falls when our schools are in session, there is opportunity to interest young people in this worthwhile project. Our students should be taught to become "hemisphere conscious" and to know about "the cultural and material achievements of our neighbors . . ." Since President Franklin D. Roosevelt put much emphasis on the Good Neighbor policy, our schools have been studying more than ever before the history, customs, and folklore of the other American republics.

In celebrating Pan American Day, schools have developed interesting and varied programs, including assemblies, with music and dancing of the various countries, with the participants in typical costumes. Often slides or moving pictures of travel in the other republics are shown; or pageants and skits are put on. Some schools have poster or doll-dressing contests. Social science classes emphasize the interdependence of the twenty-one republics in the matters of trade, travel, and industry. On this holiday, Spanish clubs take an important part in planning programs; also school papers give good publicity.

Each year, too, the community celebrations on this day are varied, some being quite simple, others elaborate. Often the governor or mayor makes a proclamation, and the beginning of the day (or of Pan American Week) takes place at the City Hall.

In some places gardens symbolizing Pan American friendship are started or "peace trees" are planted. Colorful parades feature marchers in costumes of the various republics, or a pageant may be staged. Store windows have displays of products, typical foods, dress, handicrafts, maps, posters, flags, coins, postage stamps, dolls, and jewelry. Sometimes libraries exhibit books by other American authors, while art galleries show their paintings. In churches sermons emphasize better understanding; a gala occasion is assured when a Pan American luncheon is put on with typical dishes, served by attendants in costumes, and musicians playing music from other American lands.

Among the noteworthy observances in recent years was a banquet and reception honoring Latin American diplomats and consuls, given at Miami, Florida; the ceremonial planting of twenty-one varieties of roses attended by foreign and local dignitaries at Portland, Oregon in 1950; and a special parade in New York City in 1951 which included ten thousand marchers and twenty-one floats representing the Pan American republics.

For several years, the city of Lakewood in California has put on a distinctive two-day celebration of Pan American Day. This is sponsored by several groups and includes a unique folk dance festival which shows typical costumes and dances of the twenty-one republics.

All these schools and communities have aided Americans throughout our great country to realize more and more the importance of Pan American Day and its significance, which President F. D. Roosevelt expressed in 1933 in these words:

> The essential qualities of true Pan Americanism must be the same as those which constitute a good neighbor, namely, mutual understanding, and through such understanding, a sympathetic appreciation of the other's point of view. It is only in this manner that we can hope to build up a system of which confidence, friendship, and goodwill are the cornerstones.

Patriots' Day—April 19

During the spring of 1775, General Gage, the British commander in Boston, learned that the colonists had assembled military supplies at Concord, sixteen miles away. Therefore, he planned a secret expedition to seize these stores. However, the Americans heard of his intention and decided to forestall it.

Near midnight of April 18, 1775, General Gage sent eight hundred men under Major Pitcairn and Lieutenant Colonel Smith to carry out the affair. When these forces got on their way, Paul Revere rode through the night and roused the people of the countryside.

At dawn the British soldiers reached Lexington, six miles from Concord, and found seventy armed men drawn up on the village green. When they refused Major Pitcairn's order to disperse, his men fired on them and several were killed, and others wounded. The survivors had to retreat; but under the leadersip of Major Buttrick and Adjutant Hosmer, another skirmish took place at Concord Bridge, with losses on both sides.

These encounters were important because they aroused the Americans to action, both in Massachusetts and other colonies. Troops were raised; the people set up provincial congresses; and by the end of the summer of 1775, the power of the royal governors was ended.

This date—April 19, 1775—is a vital one in our history; for it was the opening of the American Revolution that won us our freedom from the mother country.

Today, the date of April 19 commemorates the Battles of Lexington and Concord; and the day is a legal holiday in Massachusetts and Maine. Varied celebrations take place; historic scenes, including the famous ride of Paul Revere, are staged, and remind younger generations of these important events.

When you visit Lexington and Concord, you see the noted monument that was placed at Old North Bridge to honor the minutemen of Revolutionary times. On the base of the statue is the famous poem, written by Ralph Waldo Emerson, whose grandfather watched the battle from the nearby Old Manse.

The monument was dedicated on July 4, 1837; and today many visitors pause to read the poem written for this occasion. For it contains the well-known lines

> Here once the embattled farmers stood
> And fired the shot heard round the world.

Emerson concluded with this stanza:

> Spirit, that made these heroes dare
> To die and leave their children free,
> Bid time and nature gently spare
> The shaft we raise to them and thee.

Shrove Tuesday, Ash Wednesday,
and Lent

The important church festival Easter is a movable one and occurs between March 22 and April 25. The Council of Christian Churches fixed the date for this annual observance at a meeting in Nicea, Asia Minor, in 325 A.D.

Easter is celebrated on the first Sunday after the first full moon, following the spring equinox. (If the Paschal full moon happens on a Sunday, Easter is observed on the next Sunday.) One source states that the reason for this particular date was the need for moonlight, for travelers coming from a distance to observe the holiday.

During this present century—according to a chart giving dates of all Easter Sundays occurring in it—about one-fourth will fall in the month of March, and three-fourths, in April.

Lent, the lengthy fast preceding Easter, may begin in February or March, depending upon the date of Easter Sunday.

PRE-LENTEN CARNIVALS

A time of merrymaking known as the carnival, just before Lent begins, has long been a custom. In some places it started at Epiphany, January 6. However, now the official Mardi gras season is usually ten days. The climax comes on the last day—Mardi gras ("Fat Tuesday") or Shrove Tuesday.

Early Egyptians and the Romans celebrated at this time; the carnival idea spread from Rome and survives today. Some authorities say that the Christian observance was just another case in which the church "attempted to regulate and sanctify what it could not entirely suppress." Some of the popes, it is said, tried to curb these activities, while others encouraged them.

In Rome there were parades of costumed maskers and races of

riderless horses. Revelers bombarded each other with confetti. Some carried lighted tapers and tried to put out other persons' candles, while keeping their own lighted. Venice and Florence also were famous for their carnival revelry, and the splendor of their costumes and floats. Venice received special acclaim for her garlanded gondolas, and the extravagance of her masquerade balls. The end, or death, of the carnival was portrayed in Italy by burning a huge effigy.

Although the Spanish cities of Madrid, Seville, Cadiz, and Valencia staged outstanding carnivals, Barcelona had the most distinctive processions, and really sumptuous balls. Citizens in Portugal indulged in confetti battles and attended floral balls during the pre-Lenten season.

From the fifteenth century on, the French too put on elaborate costumed dances; these were suppressed during the French Revolution but revived by Napoleon Bonaparte. Parisians had an old custom of having a fat ox lead the procession. Following the animal, in a triumphal car, was a child, designated the "King of the Butchers." French celebrants delighted in throwing confetti, sweetmeats, and flowers, or in blowing horns. Their long parades included floats decorated with allegorical figures.

Nowadays, as in other Roman Catholic lands, countries in South America observe this pre-Lenten gaiety both in the large and small communities. There are "gay doings" in places like Buenos Aires and Montevideo. On the final evening of the carnival, the streets are thronged with gaily costumed singers, dancers, drummers, and other musicians. Both participants and observers are showered with confetti, and unless the latter are careful to stay out of range they are likely to be sprayed with perfumed water as well, for almost any prank is tolerated on the last night of Mardi gras.

Rio de Janeiro is noted for her carnival spirit, and the festivities begin on the Saturday before Ash Wednesday. There are parades with beautifully created floats and an annual musical contest when the composers of the best songs for the year's fiesta are awarded prizes, in addition to the traditional balls.

In the United States, carnivals or pre-Lenten festivities are usually observed in the sections of the South with a French or Spanish heritage. The last day before Lent—Shrove Tuesday—is a legal holiday in Alabama, the Canal Zone, in some places in Florida, and in the Louisiana parishes. And the date is also observed in Pennsylvania, where some people, of German origin especially, eat fried crullers— *Fastnacht Kuchen.*

Southern cities, acclaimed for their carnivals with much varied entertainment, include New Orleans, Mobile, Memphis, Galveston, Shreveport, and Pensacola. Mobile, for instance, "carries on" for five days before Ash Wednesday, and a fine parade on Tuesday evening climaxes the observance. This originated in 1704 and was suspended during the Civil War but since 1869 has been an annual affair.

However, the most joyous Mardi gras celebration at this season of merriment occurs in New Orleans. This festive observance ends on the night of "Fat Tuesday," and is attended by thousands of visitors, many from foreign countries.

It is said that this carnival idea was brought to New Orleans by a group of young men sent to Europe to complete their education. As early as 1827, maskers paraded through the streets of the "Crescent City" and by 1838 pageants were being staged.

In 1857, an organization known as the "Mystic Krew of Comus" originated a torchlight parade. Its theme was "The Demon Actors" in Milton's *Paradise Lost.* This continued until the Civil War; it was revived from 1866 to 1884; and started again in 1910.

For 1961 plans were made for six parades on Mardi gras Day, and for seventeen others the week before the Grand Finale. The entire city is under the rule of Rex. He first appeared in a parade in 1872. He is accompanied by his bodyguard, the Mystic Krew of Comus; there are carloads of masked attendants; many local military and visiting groups take part in long parades through streets thronged with spectators.

Often pageants are given, with brilliantly lighted floats on which historical scenes are depicted. The Mardi Gras spirit prevails at the magnificent balls.

There is much merriment in the celebrated French Quarter—of ninety blocks—where there are elegant French restaurants, old Creole mansions, and night clubs "with blaring Dixieland bands." On the narrow crowded streets, people of all types and stations in life jostle each other—"debutantes, dowagers, writers, artists, bankers, and collegians."

This yearly celebration in New Orleans is sponsored by societies of leading business and professional men. Next day—Ash Wednesday—the people go to church, and then back to their work. With the beginning of Lent, all look forward to another important holiday—Easter Sunday.

SHROVE TUESDAY

Let glad Shrove Tuesday bring the pancake thin,
Or fritter rich, with apples stored within.

Since the date of Shrove Tuesday, the climax of pre-Lenten festivities, depends upon that of Easter, it comes at no set time. During early centuries the churches observed Shrovetide on the three days between the evening of the Saturday before Quinquagesima Sunday, the last before Easter, and the morning of Ash Wednesday. At first this period was a solemn one; adherents went to church to make their confessions and to receive absolution. Since the priests "shrove" them, in anticipation of the coming Lenten season, the last day was known as Shrove Tuesday.

Then the rest of the day was given over to feasting and other pastimes. It was only natural for thrifty souls to want to use up the meats and fats which were forbidden in Lent. This holiday in Italy was called "carnival" or "farewell-to-meat" day; in Germany, *Fastnacht*, where often a play of this name was given.

In England and Scotland, Shrove Tuesday was a merry event. Bells pealed, there were football games, and much horseplay was indulged in. Sometimes people beat cocks to death—perhaps in punishment of the one heard by Peter.

One early writer related that on Shrove Tuesday "men ate and drank, and abandoned themselves to every kind of sportive foolery." All feasted, reveled, and played dice and cards. In addition there was "an immensity of mumming." Since this was the most important holiday for apprentices, these young people looked forward to the day.

According to the ancient Shepherds' Calendar of 1676 it appears that there was a weather superstition, connected with Shrove Tuesday, as with Candlemas (or Groundhog Day, on February 2).

"Some say thunder on Shrove Tuesday foretelleth wind, store of fruit, and plenty. Others affirm that so much as the sun shineth on that day, the like will shine every day in Lent."

It was a custom for young boys to go out begging. Here is a song they often sang on this day, before various homes:

> A-shrovin, a-shrovin,
> I be come a-shrovin,
> A bit of bread, a piece of cheese,
> A bit of your fat bacon,
> Or a dish of doughnuts,
> All of your own makin!

Or perhaps some made this plea:

> Shrovetide is near at hand
> And I come a-shroving,
> Pray, dame, something,
> An apple, or a dumpling.

If the neighbor did not give them some bread and cheese, the boys retaliated by throwing clods or other missiles against the house.

Shrove Tuesday has also been known as Pancake Tuesday because of the custom of making and eating pancakes on this holiday. In Pasquil's "Palinodia"—1634—the poet declared that on Shrove Tuesday every stomach

> . . . till it can hold no more
> Is fritter filled, as well as heart can wish;
> And every man and maid doe take their turne,
> And toss their pancakes up for feare they burne;
> And all the kitchen doth with laughter sound
> To see the pancakes fall upon the ground.

Often there were contests as to who could throw the cake up into the air after it had been baked on one side and return it properly to the pan. And the word flapjack is still current today.

In the village of Huddleston, in Hertfordshire, an old curfew bell rang at 4 A.M. on the morning of Shrove Tuesday, and again at 8 P.M. that evening. This allowed the people to bake and eat pancakes between these hours.

One British writer stated that at eleven o'clock in the morning the "pancake bell" sounded:

> Then there is a thing called wheaten flour which the cooks do mingle with water, eggs, spices, etc. . . . then they put it little by little into a frying pan of boiling suet . . . until at last by the skill of the cook, it

is transformed into the form of a flipjack, called a pancake, which ominous incantation the ignorant people do devour very greedily.

And some unknown versifier of early times composed this bit of verse:

> But hark, I hear a pancake bell,
> And fritters make a gallant smell . . .
> The cooks are baking, frying, boiling,
> Stewing, mincing, cutting, broiling,
> Carving, gormandizing, roasting . . .

At the noted Westminster School for boys in London, at 11 A.M. the cook came in from the kitchen. The boys gathered around, expectantly, to watch him twirl a pancake in a frying pan. When it was baked, he tossed it out; and all scrambled to get a taste of it.

At the present time many Americans bake and serve various kinds of pancakes to their families and friends on Shrove Tuesday. And one locality at least, Liberal, Kansas, has become known internationally for its unusual activity on this day. It is said that the first pancake race was staged in 1445, at Olney, England; in this contest participants run and flip the cakes at the same time. Since 1950 the women of Olney and Liberal have put on such a yearly competition; to date the honors are about evenly divided.

LENT

The Lenten period may begin in February or March, as its date is dependent on the time that Easter occurs. The name Lent comes from the Anglo-Saxon "lencten," meaning "spring" or "vernal feast." (One source says it is derived from "lengthentide," "springtime.")

Lent was described by Pope Gregory I as "the spiritual tithing of the year"; and it is considered "pre-eminently a season of special self-denial" in preparation for Easter. It is believed to have started to commemorate Christ's fasting in the wilderness, as well as that of Elijah and Moses. Lent is a forty-day fast, not including Sundays; it begins forty-six days before Easter, on Ash Wednesday, and ends on the Saturday before Easter Sunday. This feast is observed by the Roman Catholic, Eastern, and Anglican churches.

There is some evidence that, before the third century the last two days of Holy Week were observed by Christians. Later they included the entire week. This annual feast of Lent was recognized by the Nicean Council in 325 A.D.; and Athanasius urged a forty-day fast for the adherents in Alexandria. One authority credits St. Telesphorus, bishop of Rome, as the founder of the Lenten observance.

According to Johannes Cassianus, Lent in 420 A.D. lasted six or seven weeks, with not more than thirty-six days of fasting. Much latitude was permitted in regard to eating during this season. Chrysostom is said to have recommended fasting but did not enforce it; also he insisted on "the prior necessity of good works and almsgiving."

The early church is said to have stressed penitence rather than fasting; but during the medieval period, rules for abstinence became strict. Then it was the custom to refrain from all meats, milk, and its various products, and eggs; also a person was supposed to eat only in the evening. Today—according to one source—fasting "is more nominal than real"; another source asserts that the Lenten observance "in its present form dates from the ninth century."

ASH WEDNESDAY—FIRST DAY OF LENT

Ash Wednesday, a day of solemn repentance, occurs forty days before Easter (not counting the intervening Sundays).

Its Latin name, *Dies Cinerum,* originated from an ancient custom —the use of ashes as a symbol of repentance. It is a ceremony of great antiquity and was used first for those doing public penance, and later applied to all penitents.

One Anglo-Saxon wrote in the tenth century that his people followed the Bible example of strewing ashes on their heads to show repentance. In 1191, Pope Celestine III recommended the use of this rite in all the churches. Therefore, since the officials wished to remind their parishioners that all are mortal, this ceremony came into popular use.

And today, in Rome, after an Introit and four collects, the priest sprinkles with holy water the ashes that are the remains of the palms of the last year's Palm Sunday services. Then he dips his finger in the ashes, makes the sign of the cross on the forehead of each kneeling penitent. At the same time, he says in Latin, "Remember, man, that thou art dust, and shalt return to dust."

In addition to the Roman Catholic Church, the various branches of the Church of England, including the Protestant Episcopal Church in the United States observe Ash Wednesday. Some Protestant reformers gave up the old custom. In England, for instance, instead of using the ashes, a series of denunciations against sin, based on the twenty-eighth chapter of Deuteronomy, were made. These are still read, along with penitential prayers on Ash Wednesday. Thus, some Protestants still observe this fast day without using the rites that gave it its name.

Palm Sunday, Holy Week,
and Easter

Palm Sunday, the one before Easter, is the first day of Holy Week. Its name came from the ancient custom of carrying palm branches on this feast day, in commemoration of Christ's triumphal entry into Jerusalem.

The palm is mentioned several times in the Bible. Its Hebrew name is *tamar*, symbolic of elegance and grace. It was a favorite name for Jewish women. For example, Absolom had a sister and also a daughter by this name. We read in Exodus 15:27 that the Israelites reached Elim, which had "three score and ten palm trees." And Revelation 7:9 tells that people stood before the throne of God "with palms in their hands."

In the New Testament the palm was considered an emblem of victory and peace. In Zechariah 9:9 the prophet had uttered these well-known words: "Rejoice greatly, O daughter of Zion; shout, O daughter of Jerusalem; behold thy King cometh unto thee . . . lowly, and riding upon an ass . . ."

This prophecy was fulfilled when Christ rode into the city of Jerusalem, and was greeted by great crowds. St. John, in his gospel, John 12:12, 13, wrote:

> On the next day much people that were come to the feast, when they heard that Jesus was coming to Jerusalem,
> Took branches of palm trees, and went forth to meet him, and cried Hosanna; Blessed is the King of Israel that cometh in the name of the Lord.

And in Matthew 21:8 we read that some spread their garments in the way, and others cut down branches; Mark does not mention the strewing of palms, but Luke tells that some clothes were placed in Christ's path.

One minister, Dr. J. Richard Sneed, has pointed out that this Palm

Sunday happening was described by all four Gospel writers. Mark emphasized the excited acclaim of the throngs; Matthew, the curiosity Jesus aroused, for some asked, "Who is this?"; Luke related his weeping over the city of Jerusalem; while John pictured him as a king entering in triumph.

Early Christians did not observe Palm Sunday until about the fourth century. Then, at church, they held up unblessed olive twigs; for the rite of blessing the palm trees came four hundred years afterwards. By the tenth century, Palm Sunday was well established; and now this feast day is "rooted in fifteen hundred years of history."

During the Middle Ages, the holiday was a popular festival and had such different names as "Blossom Sunday" in Germany, and the "Sunday of the Willow Boughs." In various lands of Europe, including England, worshipers used olive, willow, or other tree branches. After the priests had blessed the boughs and sprinkled them with holy water, attendants carried them through the town in a joyous procession, in memory of Christ's entry into Jerusalem. The branches were then taken back to the altar to be burned; the ashes were saved for use on the next Ash Wednesday.

Henry VIII made changes in regard to church matters; however, he did not forbid the custom of carrying boughs on Palm Sunday. He allowed church officials to make their own decisions in regard to the rite. On the Saturday before Easter or early on that Sunday, people went out and brought in willow slips or other boughs. And it is said that in some parts of rural England even today branches are placed in churches.

At an early date the Roman Catholics in Rome and elsewhere accepted a special observance for Palm Sunday. The palms were blessed at a church outside Rome. Then a group carried them solemnly to the Basilica of the Lateran, or to St. Peter's, where the Pope sang a second Mass; later, the first service was discontinued.

Today only the liturgy texts are preserved; and the blessing of the boughs and the procession take place within the church, or on its grounds. The cardinal and his assistants wear purple vestments; after he or a priest blesses the branches and sprinkles them with holy water and incense, they are given to priests, altar boys, and members of the congregation.

The procession goes to the main door; church officials remain outside, while inside chanters sing a hymn. The latter are symbolic of angels, singing praises of the Lord, and those who march represent Christians in attendance upon Christ. When a sub-deacon raps on the door, those outside re-enter the building.

On Palm Sunday 1961, there was an unusual service at St. Peter's in Rome. This, the largest church in the world, was chosen instead of St. Paul's outside the walls so that more pilgrims could attend the rites.

Pope John XXIII, who headed the yearly procession, was the first pontiff to attend this ceremony since 1870. More than fifty thousand persons crowded into the great church. The square outside was filled as the Pope passed by on his portable throne. Then inside the sanctuary, he blessed a large pile of a hundred and eighty palm branches; he personally gave them to eighteen cardinals, bishops, archbishops, and other church dignitaries.

In the Holy Land, at Jerusalem, on this same Palm Sunday, the Latin Patriarch, Alberto Gori, opened the Holy Week observance by leading the twenty-five thousand pilgrims who had gathered from round the globe. They started the three-hour walk (covering about two miles) at Bethphage, where centuries ago people hailed Christ as he started His triumphal entry into Jerusalem.

These modern pilgrims passed the Mount of Olives, Gethsemane, and the valley of the Kidron. When they reached the walls of the Holy City, they entered at St. Stephen's Gate, and proceeded to the convent of St. Anne. Then the solemn pontifical Mass was celebrated in the Basilica.

In connection with Palm Sunday, as with some other feast days, several quaint customs and superstitions arose. In some localities in Europe, there was a parade in which a figure of Christ riding on a donkey (mounted on wheels) was the central feature. This procession originally used to go through the town, but later the paraders simply walked around the church or its grounds. On Palm Sunday graves in the churchyard were sprinkled; this ceremony has continued in some places until the present time.

As the donkey passed, spectators shouted and threw down willow branches. Then they gathered these boughs which they believed were "infallible protection against storm and lightning in the ensuing year." Also priests made small crosses from palm leaves for their parishioners as "safeguards against disease."

In the city of Monaco on the Mediterranean, on Palm Sunday visitors came from long distances to see a mystery play staged by members of a brotherhood. These men acted the parts of those present at the trial and crucifixion of Jesus, and performed their drama in the old narrow streets of Monaco. For lights there were torches and candles, priests chanted, and drums sounded. The spectators enjoyed such performances which had taken the place of old Greek plays.

At the town of Caistor, in Lincolnshire, England, a strange custom prevailed on Palm Sunday. A man came into the church with a long whip which he cracked three times, then folded. Later, while holding the whip upright, he went to the minister. At the upper end of the whip was a purse containing thirty pieces of silver. Some believe this custom originated from the procession in which the wooden donkey was featured.

Nowadays, Palm Sunday is observed by almost all churches, Anglican, Roman Catholic, and Protestant. The buildings are decorated with greenery; in some places there are choral processions of palm-bearing singers. Often ancient ceremonies are carried out, while some sects favor less elaborate rites centered around a sermon suitable for this occasion.

On Palm Sunday attendance is large; that favorite anthem, "The Palms" is sung. In the Episcopal churches sometimes the choir boys carry palm branches, and often the congregation receives small palm leaf crosses.

Dr. J. Richard Sneed of Los Angeles has well expressed the significance of Palm Sunday in these words:

> Today, Christians in every land wave their palm branches and shout Hosannas. Palm Sunday offers the means for renewed loyalty to Jesus' leadership; it provides a climactic time for re-dedication to His service.

MAUNDY THURSDAY OR HOLY THURSDAY

The Thursday before Easter is Holy Thursday in Rome and in Roman Catholic countries. Once it was termed "Sheer Thursday" in England. Now in the British Isles and in the United States it is Maundy Thursday.

The word Maundy—according to some authorities—is derived from *mande* (Old French, from the Latin, *mandatum*, meaning "a command.") In John 13:34 Jesus said, "A new commandment I give unto you" (In Latin, *mandatum novum do nobis*).

Other sources believe that Maundy stemmed from an Anglo-Saxon word, "Mand" (later "Maund") denoting a basket. "A thousand favors from her maund she drew."—Shakespeare.

Proponents of the second derivation declare the word Maundy originated from the fact that English monarchs distributed gifts to the poor from a basket or maund.

The annual holy day—Maundy Thursday—arose from the incident of Christ's washing the feet of His disciples, and his command to them to follow His example, as told in John 13:4, 5:

> He riseth from supper and laid aside his garments; and took a towel and girded himself.
> After that he poured water into a basin, and began to wash the disciples' feet, and to wipe them with the towel wherewith he was girded.

This meal, partaken by Christ and His disciples, was the initiation of one of the most important ceremonies of the church, the Lord's Supper, or Holy Communion.

For many years it was customary for the Pope to wash the feet of thirteen men, representing the twelve apostles and an angel; afterwards he served them at a supper. Also there was a group of men and women in Rome who devoted themselves to this rite and other charitable acts. They performed the foot-washing ceremony for pilgrims who had made their way to the city for Maundy Thursday from a distance of over sixty miles, serving men and women in separate rooms.

English kings observed this ceremony from the time of the twelfth century, sometimes washing the feet of one individual for each year of their own lives. Afterwards they distributed "maunds"—gifts of food, clothing, and money.

Occasionally members of the nobility followed the monarch's example. For instance, the Duke of Northumberland performed the rite, as did Cardinal Wolsey at Peterborough Abbey in 1530:

> And upon Maundy Thursday, he made his Maundy there, in our Lady's Chapel, having 59 poor men whose feet he washed and kissed, and after he had wiped them, he gave everyone of the said poor men 12 pence in money, 3 ells of good canvas to make them shirts, a pair of

new shoes, a cast of red herrings, 3 white herrings, and one of these had 2 shillings.

At the age of thirty-nine, Queen Elizabeth I received thirty-nine men and thirty-nine women at Greenwich on Maundy Thursday. Her attendants washed the visitors' feet, but the Queen marked each foot with a cross above the toes and kissed it.

British rulers performed this rite through the reign of James II. In April 1731, the King, then forty-eight years old, gave money, clothing, and food to ninety-six poor persons. At the royal chapel at Whitehall, the Archbishop of York on this occasion washed the feet of the recipients, "in imitation of our Saviour's pattern of humility."

On Maundy Thursday, William IV distributed royal gifts at the Chapel Royal:

> A quantity of salt, fish consisting of cod, pieces of very fine beef, 5 loaves of bread, and some ale to drink the King's health.

A yeoman of the guard carried 150 bags, each with 75 silver pennies in it. On this feast day the people also received woolen cloth, linen, shoes, and stockings.

Since the beginning of Queen Victoria's reign, money rather than food and clothing has been given to the poor persons. When George VI was fifty-four, he presided at the annual observance for 108 people. The Bishop of Lichfield, his Lord High Almoner, presented the specially coined money, in green and white, and red and white purses.

During her father's illness, Princess Elizabeth took his place. She attended the ceremony at Wesminster Abbey "clutching a nosegay of daffodils, roses, and violets, to ward off the plague," as was customary on Maundy Thursday. However, she did not present the money, as only the ruler or the Lord High Almoner can do this.

In 1957 when Queen Elizabeth II was thirty-one, she broke a long tradition (the first time since the reign of Charles II) by presenting these alms outside of London. That year the Maundy Thursday rites were observed in the great St. Albans Abbey, in Hertfordshire. The Queen and Prince Philip, both carrying bouquets of sweet herbs, walked in a procession. There was no foot washing, even though the Lord High Almoner and his assistants carried towels. The Queen herself distributed the coins, in green and white purses, to 31 women and a like number of men. Each man received 2 pounds, 5 shillings (about $6.30) while a woman got 1 pound, 15 shillings ($4.90).

Today churches all around the globe hold Maundy Thursday services; Christians meet together on this evening to meditate about the coming Good Friday and Easter, to recall the act of humility Christ performed for His disciples centuries ago, and to partake of the Lord's Supper.

It is customary for various churches to hold communion services on this sacred day. Sometimes this is done in an unusual way. In one California church, a room is prepared with a table and thirteen chairs, with the central one left vacant. Then twelve persons come in from the auditorium, and take communion together, in a setting similar to that of the "Last Supper" as painted by da Vinci.

GOOD FRIDAY

Good Friday—just preceding Easter Sunday—the day that commemorates Christ's suffering and crucifixion, has been observed for centuries as an important church holy day. The events of this momentous occasion can be found in the various gospels: the story of Jesus' trial, in Luke 22; his examination by Pilate, in John 18; and the final sentence and crucifixion at Golgotha, in John 19 and 20, and in Luke 23.

Good Friday is a legal holiday in England (one of two, the other being Christmas), and in Ireland, where all business is suspended. In several of our states, it is also a legal holiday. According to the World Almanac, these are:

> Arkansas (a memorial day), Connecticut, Delaware, Florida, Illinois, Indiana, Louisiana, Maryland, Minnesota, New Jersey, North Dakota, Pennsylvania, Tennessee, Canal Zone, Virgin Islands. In California, from 12 noon to 3 P.M. In Wisconsin from 11 A.M. to 3 P.M.

Authorities seem uncertain as to how the day got the name of Good Friday; one writer asserts it came from "God's Friday," while another thinks it refers to "the good which came to the world through the life and death of Jesus." Floyd K. Basquette suggests that, since crucifixion was the most degrading form of punishment, probably early Christians turned this into victory, and termed the day of the crucifixion "Good Friday."

It has had several names, such as "Holy Friday" or "Great Friday," while the Anglo-Saxons called it "Long Friday," perhaps in reference to the long hours of torment suffered by Jesus. In some lands it is always spoken of as "Holy Friday."

At first, Christians had no special ceremonies for this occasion, but observed it as part of Easter and as a time of mourning and fasting. Later, Good Friday became an independent feast—the Festival of the Crucifixion, or the Day of Salvation. Constantine the Great forbade markets and courts to open on this day.

At Rome on Good Friday, priests were clad in black vestments. At first the altar was bare and no candles were lighted. Then came the adoration of the cross, followed by the symbolical burial of Christ in a tomb, back of the altar. Before the time of Henry VIII churches in England had similar rites, with a figure of Jesus on the cross, the mourning, and burial.

Various legends, beliefs, and customs became associated with Good Friday. One was that bread baked on this day should be kept throughout the year and that a few crumbs from it, taken in water, could cure sicknesses.

In ancient England, with much pomp and ceremony, the kings hallowed rings to be worn as a preventive of the "falling sickness." This idea is believed to have originated with a ring brought to King Edward from Jerusalem. The monarch gave it to a poor man; it was subsequently returned to his possession, and eventually it was preserved with veneration at Westminster Abbey. Often rings blessed by the English kings were called "cramp rings" and given to persons suffering from this malady.

In Spain ladies dressed in black went out on Good Friday to collect funds for the poor. In Palermo, Italy, there was a strange custom: penitents, wearing hoods with eye openings, and having crowns of thorns on their heads and ropes around their necks, marched around the town under the guidance of a monk or priest. In some localities there were processions or mystery plays on this church day.

There was an annual event in Portugal and Spain that made its way to Mexico, and then into Southern California. Los Angeles was founded in 1781 by families from Mexico, who brought Spanish traditions with them. Most of the settlers were Roman Catholics, and on their feast days they staged colorful celebrations.

On Good Friday, the Angelenos engaged in a ceremony that gave the spectators and participants much pleasure. This was the punishment of Judas Iscariot. Beforehand, some of the men had made a straw effigy of the traitor. On Good Friday afternoon they placed this image in a cart and drove it around the historic old plaza. While onlookers peered at Judas and made fun of him, they accused him of such crimes as cheating at cards, or of stealing chickens and cattle.

After an orator had given a lengthy speech denouncing Judas, the whole town gathered for the public hanging. Next a company of soldiers fired several rounds of ammunition into the "body." The spectators had fun shooting at what was left of the figure, or hurling bottles and other missiles at it. Each year the people of Los Angeles looked forward to this piece of horseplay, which apparently they did not consider unsuitable for this solemn day.

Today in Rome on Good Friday there are services in the Sistine Chapel, with the Pope, cardinals, and other church dignitaries taking part. After the final chant is sung in the Sistine, the Pope goes to St. Peter's.

Now it has come about that most churches of varied beliefs observe Good Friday with appropriate services as at Christmas and Easter Sunday. In the United States, members of different denominations sometimes join in a three-hour service, lasting from twelve noon until three o'clock in the afternoon, commemorating the hours Christ spent on the cross. Such assemblies are simple and reverent; there are prayers by the ministers, suitable musical numbers, talks on the "Seven last words from the cross," with intervals of silent prayer and meditation.

Many churches also have evening services when fine oratorios, by the world's best composers, are sung. These include such masterpieces as "The Crucifixion," "The Messiah," "Requiem," or the "Seven Last Words."

Good Friday is of vital importance to the Christian world, and it has been well said: "Good Friday should be reserved as a sacred and solemn occasion, commemorating the crucifixion of our Lord and Christ."

A food long connected with Good Friday is the hot cross bun. At first these sweet, fruity buns, flavored with allspice, and decorated with crosses of white icing, were eaten only on this particular day. But now, in many places, they are featured throughout Lent.

Several stories are told of their origin. One relates that eating this food goes back to the ancient pagan custom of worshiping the Queen of Heaven with offerings of cakes, marked with her image. It is said that the Egyptians made buns with two horns on them to offer to the moon goddess, and that the Greeks changed the symbol to a cross so the bun could be more easily divided. Anglo-Saxons marked theirs with a cross to honor the goddess of light.

With the Christian Era, the followers of Christ attached a new meaning to the decoration. A legend is told of St. Clare, daughter of a nobleman, in Assisi, Italy. She wanted to be a teacher of the Christian faith, but, knowing of her parents' opposition to such a plan, fled to a small chapel where St. Francis was preaching.

At its altar she donned a brown robe and became the first abbess of a convent. One day the Pope visited her convent and asked St. Clare to bless the small buns they were about to eat. As soon as she had made the sign of the cross, this emblem appeared on each of the buns the Pope was holding. One writer states: "The hot cross bun is the most popular symbol of the Roman Catholic religion in England that the Reformation has left."

Someone has said that the bakers became jealous of the profits made by the churches; therefore they made hot cross buns to increase their own revenue. These products became very popular in London and all over England, and it was the custom to eat them for breakfast on Good Friday.

Early on this day many vendors went out to sell the buns, with their distinctive crosses. Streets resounded with the cries, "Hot Cross Buns! Hot Cross Buns!" Often a man would call out bits of verse like these:

> One a penny, *buns,*
> Two a penny, *buns,*
> One a penny, two a penny,
> *Hot cross buns!*

> One a penny, two a penny,
> *Hot cross buns,*
> If you have no daughters, give them to your sons;
> But if you have none of these merry little elves,
> Then you may keep them all for yourselves.

In addition to the street sellers of buns, several bakers opened houses for their sale during the eighteenth century. The two most fashionable and famous ones were in the Chelsea district of London. It is said that on Good Friday morning sometimes fifty thousand people would flock to the Old Chelsea Bun House and buy as many as a hundred and fifty thousand buns. King George III preferred the Old Chelsea to a newer establishment and went personally to get his own supply.

Since it was considered "the thing" to buy them in this part of London, often members of middle-class families would walk several miles to purchase the Chelsea products. Then, tired from the long jaunt, some sat down on benches under the roof that protruded out over the pavement and consumed hot cross buns to their hearts' content.

Some people carried out the custom of hanging a hot cross bun in their homes; they believed it could keep out evil spirits, prevent the home from catching on fire, and also cure certain diseases. This bun remained up until replaced by one the following year.

The English brought this Good Friday eating custom with them when they settled in the New World. At the present time hot cross buns continue to be popular at the Easter season.

HOLY SATURDAY

The Saturday before Easter (*Sabado de Gloria*) was a sad one for Christ's disciples. Their Master had been put to death, and as soon as Pilate allowed Joseph of Arimathea and Nicodemus to take His body away, they, with the women, prepared it for burial and laid it in Joseph's tomb. Even though the three Marys were hesitant to leave this place finally, as darkness came on, they went silently to their homes not dreaming of the great joy that would be theirs on the next day.

Holy Saturday is observed with special ceremonies in some localities; for instance, in Roman Catholic lands like Lebanon and Honduras, the church bells which had been silent all week peal out joyously at 11 A.M. on this day. After attending church services, people feast together and look forward to the coming of Easter.

In at least one place in the United States on Easter Saturday an unusual observance takes place. It is the annual "Blessing of the Animals," started several decades ago at the old plaza church, Our Lady of the Angels, in Los Angeles. A colorful event, it attracts numerous visitors.

From the time man started to domesticate the beasts, he has looked after their welfare. One writer said that "the early Roman Catholics regarded no beasts, birds, or fish, as hateful." St. Anthony of Padua was "especially solicitous about animals," for he considered "all God's creatures worthy of protection." One painter, Salvatore Rosa, painted St. Anthony preaching to animals. The saint was credited with having cured beasts of the plague.

It is asserted that the rite of blessing animals first was observed on St. Anthony's Day. During the nineteenth century a Lady Morgan wrote of the yearly ceremony in Rome at a church dedicated to St. Anthony:

> . . . for not only every Roman, from the Pope to the peasant, who has a horse, a mule, or an ass, sends his cattle to be blessed at St. Anthony's shrine, but all the English go with their job horses and favorite dogs; and for the small offering of a couple of paoli get them sprinkled, sanctified, and placed under the protection of this saint. Coach after coach draws up. Strings of mules mix with carts and barouches, while the officiating priest comes forward from his little chapel, dips a brush into water, sprinkles and prays over the beasts, pockets his fee, and retires.

The custom of blessing animals reached Los Angeles through Mexico, from Spain. Mrs. Christine Sterling who "saved" Olvera Street revived the idea. At first it took place on St. Anthony's Day; but as rain often interfered, about 1938 the event was set on Holy Saturday.

Each year, on this day, many youthful owners gather on Olvera Street, with their pets gaily decorated with ribbons or flowers. You may see a handsome, well-groomed cow with a saddle of gardenias, a donkey wearing a lei of pink carnations, ponies, dogs of all sizes and descriptions, rabbits, birds, mice, fluffy chickens, doves, lambs, turtles, goldfish, just to mention a few. Of course it is a field day for photographers.

When the parade is ready to move, it proceeds along Sunset Boulevard, where all traffic is stopped, and enters the patio of the old church through the rear gate. On a platform are a Claretian father and some altar boys. The patio is filled with sightseers, as the father gives a brief history of the event, sprinkles each animal as it passes him, and says this prayer:

Almighty Father, we bless the animals for all they have done for us in supplying our food, in carrying our burdens, and providing companionship, and rendering a service to mankind since the world began.

He also prays that they will be kept in bodily health, and free from disease so they may be used for good purposes; that they may be blessed with fertility, and their kind preserved through the ages.

Most of the pets behave well; one white horse kneels to receive his blessing; but sometimes Pancho the donkey refuses to budge and embarrasses his young master. After the religious ceremony is over, white doves are released, as Mexican musicians play gay airs. Then the animals go back to Olvera Street for a special treat; and this ends another celebration of the ancient rite of the "Blessing of the Animals" on Holy Saturday.

EASTER SUNDAY

Easter Sunday, the Christian festival honoring Christ's resurrection, is considered by most people the world's greatest religious observance. For without Easter, "Christmas would have no meaning." It is a day of much rejoicing and is so welcomed by millions all around the earth. All four gospels give accounts of this notable day: Matthew, in Chapter 28; Mark, Chapter 16; Luke, Chapter 24; and John, Chapter 20.

According to the Venerable Bede (672 to 735 A.D.), the name Easter comes from that of the Teutonic goddess, Eostre, or Eastre. She is said to have opened the gate of Valhalla, when Baldur, the sun god, was killed by an arrow, and condemned to spend half of each year in the lower regions. Eostre was the deity of both the dawn and spring, and "the pagan symbol of fertility." At her festival in April, sacred fires were lighted on the hills, especially in Nordic lands. (At this same season, ancient Romans observed the Feast of the Vernal Equinox.)

The word Easter—first applied to this time of spring—was transferred to the day itself when the Saxons began to commemorate Christ's rising from the dead.

Among early Christians there was some controversy about when Easter should be observed. Christ rose on the first day of the week, at the time of the Jewish Passover. The Christians converted from Judaism celebrated Easter on the same date as the Passover, regardless of the day of the week. However, the Gentile converts wanted the date of Easter to fall upon a Sunday.

The matter finally was settled at the Church Council at Nicea, in 325 A.D., where the date for the spring equinox was placed on March 21. As stated before, Easter varies over a period of thirty-five days, and can fall between March 22 and April 25. There has been repeated discussion through the centuries about having a fixed and uniform date for this church feast. However, no "secularly established date" has ever been accepted, even though the matter was brought up before the League of Nations in 1923. In England the date of Easter is quite important; for the English courts open following this holiday.

Christians at first took little note of Easter until some Gentile adherents started a joyful celebration with garlands, processions, and general rejoicing, reminiscent of the pagan spring festivals that had always welcomed the return of that happy season.

Perhaps it was Constantine the Great who originated the Easter parade when he ordered the court to wear their finest garments to honor this feast day. Gradually many churches developed elaborate rituals; and it was easy to transfer the old heathen time of rejoicing to one that honored Christ's return to life.

In the Roman Catholic Church, High Mass was celebrated on Easter. Often there were dramatic representations in the churches; a tomb was erected near the altar; three deacons represented Mary Magdalene, Mary of Naim, and Mary of Bethlehem, seeking Christ at the tomb. Then His reappearance was featured, and the service closed with the *Te Deum*.

As usual, certain traditions and customs arose in connection with this holy day. In Italy and Greece, it was the time for athletic contests. Many attended church services; then fasted together and engaged in games, in playing ball or dancing. In Germany, children and parents tried to surprise each other in bed by striking the "victims" with switches. In prewar Russia, anyone could go into a church and ring the bell on Easter. When a Russian met someone on the street, he would say, "Christ is risen!" The other replied, "He is risen, indeed."

When Puritanism came into prominence in England, its followers did not celebrate Easter or any other holy days such as Christmas, for these adherents abhorred all rituals. This was true, also, of the Puritans, who emigrated to New England.

There is an old belief that on Easter morning the sun dances, and those who rise early can see this performance. One authority says that the first Easter sunrise service occurred at Herrnhut, Germany, in 1732. The night before, some young men decided to go to the cemetery on Easter before dawn, to sing hymns and to meditate on Christ's resurrection.

The first of such meetings in the United States took place at Bethlehem, Pennsylvania, in 1741. The Moravians there and also those at Winston-Salem, North Carolina, continue this custom to-day. About half an hour before sunrise, the trombone choir, singers, clergy, and church members leave the Bethlehem church and go to the cemetery, where they greet the sun with the playing of trombones and the singing of a traditional hymn.

Today sunrise services are featured all over the United States. An early western one occurred at Easter in 1770, just 11 years before Los Angeles was founded. Father Crespi, a Franciscan monk who had gone north from Mexico to San Francisco Bay with Gaspar de Portola, kept a detailed diary of the expedition. It started southward in January 1770, and by Easter had reached the wooded rim of the Arroyo Seco, where South Pasadena now stands.

Father Crespi hung a bell on a branch of a tall oak, and called worshipers together. So an audience of red-skinned Indians and swarthy Spanish soldiers united in the first California tribute to Easter, a sunrise service. For many years this tree—the "Cathedral Oak"—stood there, and in 1932 was marked with this plaque:

> UNDER THIS OAK, THE LEGEND RUNS, THE FIRST EASTER SERVICES
> IN CALIFORNIA WERE HELD BY FATHER CRESPI IN 1770. MARKED
> BY ONEONTA CHAPTER, D.A.R., MRS. STANLEY H. BENT, REGENT

Finally the stately tree had to be cut down, but part of the trunk, and the plaque still mark the spot.

In 1849, about eighty years later, a German, who was visiting at Mission Dolores at San Francisco, wrote of the Easter season there:

> Easter was approaching; and all sorts of preparations were made
> at the Mission, especially a thorough cleaning and ventilating of

the church took place . . . an old settler informed me that "today is the Resurrection of the Lord" . . . Even the Indians seemed to feel the influence of the festival to be celebrated. At all events, they were cleanly washed; and all wore blue waterlilies. . . . Thus ornamented they formed a procession, and to the tune of a violin, they marched into the church . . .

About fifty years later (1909) the famous "first" sunrise service was held on Mount Rubidoux. It was really inspired by two great Americans, Theodore Roosevelt and Jacob Riis. The former, when a visitor to Riverside in 1903, had suggested his friend Riis as a speaker. Then in 1907 when a roadway was completed to the summit, the great philanthropist, Jacob Riis, advanced the idea that a cross, honoring Father Junipero Serra and other Franciscan padres, be placed on the mountain; this was done later that same year.

On another visit to the noted Mission Inn owned by Frank Miller, Riis suggested that the Millers sponsor a pilgrimage with torches up the slope at Christmas. However, they decided on an Easter service instead.

For that first service in 1909 about a hundred persons went to the top of Mount Rubidoux, where, to the accompaniment by Allis Miller on a portable organ, the crowd sang "In the Cross of Christ I Glory." A cornetist played "The Holy City," and then all joined in the Lord's Prayer.

Four years later, Henry van Dyke, the well-known poet, read his poem, "The God of the Open Air"; when he again took part in this distinctive service in 1927, he had added this special stanza to the poem:

> And then on Easter morn, His victory won,
> Breaking the mortal bars that sealed the tomb
> In a fair garden filled with flowers abloom,
> The risen Jesus met the rising sun.

Carrie Jacobs Bond attended these ceremonies, and at the Mission Inn, from which she had a view of Mount Rubidoux, composed her favorite song, "At the End of a Perfect Day." John Steven McGroarty, author of the famous "Mission Play," often visited here and gained inspiration. By 1922, at least twenty thousand visitors were in attendance on Easter, even though by that time several other such services, including the one at Hollywood, were being given in California.

At the Hollywood Bowl at Easter 1959, there was a capacity audience when Ezra Taft Benson gave the Easter message. Such film stars as Dale Evans, Roy Rogers, and Vincent Price took part, the last named reading the "Salutation to the Dawn." This service at the Bowl is known for its beauty; and on this occasion, the stage was decorated with more than a hundred thousand calla lilies. Also there was the beautiful and inspiring traditional feature—a cross made up of two hundred teen-agers.

In New York in 1960, about seven thousand persons attended the forty-first annual Easter dawn service in Radio City Music Hall, in an appropriate setting, "The Glory of Easter." And at nearby St. Patrick's Cathedral, Cardinal Spellman celebrated pontifical Mass.

After church, New York has its annual Easter parade. Originally this consisted of a dignified stroll by parishioners of St. Thomas, St. Bartholomew, and other fashionable churches as they emerged after the services and turned up Fifth or Park Avenue for a brief walk in the spring sunshine. However, in recent years a growing commercialism has changed the character of the parade. The fashionable are seen no more, but name milliners vie with each other for months in creating startling hats. Some dog outfitters, not to be outdone, dream up jeweled collars, leashes, and dog jackets, some mink-trimmed. New York's pampered pets get into the spirit of the occasion and strut proudly along the avenue with Easter costumes to match or complement those of their owners, some poodles wearing corsages of fresh flowers in the shape of hats. One recent year a famous actress turned out for the Easter parade with her tame cheetah on a leash.

So after observing the appropriate religious rites of the day, New York kicks up its heels and reverts to type with the lighthearted gaiety for which it is famous. Each year people gather from near and far, often braving dense crowds and chill winds to spend Easter in New York. Others watch the performance on their television screens and listen to the on-the-scene reports of the news services.

At Natchez, Mississippi, an old Indian mound once used for sun worship is the site of a well-attended sunrise gathering. And students from the University of the Pacific sing on the shores of Mirror Lake in Yosemite National Park, while down in St. Augustine, Florida, many persons gather for the annual sunrise service atop an old Spanish stronghold.

These assemblies are just a few of the many that take place every year, all across our wide land. They are well attended by countless modern pilgrims, who get much inspiration from such meetings in "God's great outdoors."

Besides going to these early events, millions attend later services at their own churches. At first, the Protestants in the United States did not have any special rites for Easter. But after so many men died in the Civil War, and homes were in mourning, ministers tried to comfort the families by conducting suitable services at this time. The Presbyterian Church is said to have taken the lead in this movement. Churches were decorated with greenery and flowers, often with Bermuda lilies, known as "Easter lilies"; choirs sang special musical numbers; and the pastors preached inspiring sermons.

Nowadays, even with our outstanding Easter services, there are some who feel that we have lost the true meaning of this Christian holiday. In many cases, donning fashionable new clothes and joining in the Easter parade seem to be of prime importance. However, one source believes that in doing this, human beings are simply fulfilling "the age-old desire to spruce up when nature is blooming with new life." And another writer declares that the new clothes, the rabbit, chicks, lilies, and other Easter accessories are merely symbols of the "great Easter meaning, the resurrection and life everlasting."

Eggs have become closely associated with Easter, and are regarded as a symbol of resurrection. For they hold the seeds of life, and represent the revival of fertility upon the earth. However, the egg as a life emblem is much older than Christianity.

As people were forbidden to eat eggs during Lent, they saved them, and served them at Easter. There was an old belief in some districts of France that if one didn't eat eggs on Easter, he would be bitten by snakes in the ensuing year. In medieval England, at Easter, priests blessed the eggs, which were then eaten "in thankfulness of the resurrection of our Lord."

The hare, too, has been sacred to this holiday. And from Germany came the idea that the Easter rabbit, or bunny, laid the eggs for which children searched in the grass. This originated, it is said, from the fact that rabbits are prolific—hence a symbol of fertility. In France, children were told that the hare had to run to Rome to bring back their Easter eggs.

Among the ancients, eggs were scarce and the gift of an egg was gratefully received. As they became more common, people began to color them. This goes back to the early Egyptians, Persians, Phoenicians, Assyrians, Greeks, Romans, Gauls, Goths, and Norsemen. All these peoples dyed eggs for their spring festivals; and from an early period eggs were eaten at this particular season.

Several reasons have been given for coloring them: one to suggest joy; another to fulfill the longing for bright colors as spring arrived; to imitate the hues of the aurora borealis; or to symbolize Christ's blood—this last reason accounted for those stained by Christians hiding in the catacombs. Very wisely, church officials took over the pagan idea of coloring eggs and turned it into an association with Christ's blood and His resurrection.

The giving of fancy, highly decorated eggs is an old custom. An account book of Edward I (who ruled from 1272 to 1307) shows that four hundred eggs were bought to be boiled, stained, or covered with gold, as presents for members of the royal household. In many European countries egg decorating is a fine art, with Russia and the Ukraine especially noted along this line. One person often spent several days on ornamenting just one egg. Sometimes they were designed by real artists; in the time of the czars, many were set with precious stones.

When the Easter season comes on, here in the United States, handsomely decorated eggs are on sale along with cheaper ones. Much business, too, is done at this season in the preparation of fancy eggs and Easter baskets.

Easter Monday has long been a holiday in various lands. Years ago there was a great annual fair on Easter Monday, at Greenwich, England. It lasted all day, was largely attended, and continued till late at night. Easter Monday is still a holiday in many places around the world, and business does not resume until the Tuesday after Easter.

In several European countries varied games were played with colored eggs on Easter Monday. Sometimes opponents knocked eggs together in the attempt to "nick" them. In medieval England it is related that bishops and the clergy used Easter eggs in playing handball with members of lower ranks.

Egg rolling, too, was a popular pastime in England, especially in Yorkshire, which had been settled by the Danes. It is said that this game was based on the idea of rolling away the stone from Christ's tomb. The custom of rolling hard-boiled eggs down a hill was brought to the New World by British settlers and is still continued.

Sometimes a community or perhaps a service club stages such a party, often for underprivileged children. Recently a men's group in Los Angeles gave $120 in prizes to twelve boys and girls at their annual egg rolling at Pershing Square. A clown distributed candy eggs and balloons to all present. The local country club has sponsored this kind of event each year since 1898.

At a ranch in Dallas, Texas, in 1959, three hundred youngsters on horseback took part in hunting twenty-five hundred eggs which had been hidden in tree branches. In Houston, in the same state, more than a hundred and fifty children joined the younger members of the Jamail family in searching for fifteen hundred colored eggs hidden on the J. J. Jamail estate.

Red Cloud, Nebraska, claims to have the biggest Easter egg in the world; it is 12½ feet long and 9 feet wide. This is exhibited at their annual egg rolling, often attended by three thousand boys and girls.

Naturally the most highly publicized egg rolling in our country is the one that takes place on Easter Monday on the White House lawn. The custom is said to have begun during the term of James Madison. His stepson, John Payne Todd, told his mother that Egyptian children had rolled eggs against the pyramids.

So Dolly Madison allowed the children to start this Easter pastime on the Capitol grounds. It continued there, except for the Civil War period, until the administration of President Hayes when officials decided it was ruining the grass. Mrs. Hayes came to the rescue and saved the game for the small fry by inviting them to the White House lawn.

The yearly Easter egg rolling (followed by a Marine band concert) was carried on until World War I and later revived by President Harding. Omitted during the Second World War, it was brought back by the Eisenhowers in 1953. Adults are admitted if accompanied by a child. Many tourists visit the grounds on this day, the only one of the year when the public can enter. The gates are open from 9 A.M. to 4 P.M.; the youngsters, twelve or under, bring their own eggs, and at a given signal roll them down a slope.

In 1960 President Eisenhower thrilled his visitors by stepping out onto the south portico of the White House and smiling and waving to the throng of more than two thousand gathered on the lawn below. Although the ground was soggy from a recent rain, the sun came out later, and the band played stirring tunes as adults and children, many of them in Easter bunny costumes, wandered around. It was a field day for the camera addicts as well. They dashed about making a record of the colorful scene for posterity in both moving pictures and stills.

Arbor Day

Once President Theodore Roosevelt declared: "A people without children would face a hopeless future; a country without trees is almost as hopeless."

One of our most important holidays, Arbor Day, is devoted to tree planting; the occasion is sponsored by civic organizations and especially noted by our public schools. The date varies widely in different states.

Most Americans realize the need to teach children the value of conserving our forests and reforesting denuded areas. At this holiday, pupils are impressed with the beauty of trees, their importance for shade and as bird sanctuaries, and the dangers of flooding in deforested sections. They also are taught the various uses of lumber, for home building, paper making, and for other vital products. On Arbor Day, schools participate in the actual planting of trees on their own grounds, parks, or other recreational centers.

While Arbor Day is a comparatively new holiday in the United States, for centuries special tree planting has been carried on in other parts of the globe. For instance, among the ancient Aztecs whenever a child was born a tree was planted and named for the new arrival. In Mexico some of the Indians still observe this rite, and set out a sapling at the first new moon after the child's birth.

Long ago in Switzerland when villagers wanted an oak grove near their town, each man went out and brought in a young tree and planted it in a designated spot. Tree planting has also been a custom in Spain on their Arbor Day (*Fiesta del Arbol*). Spanish boys were encouraged to water and carefully tend their individual saplings. Even the young monarch, King Alphonso XIII, set out a tree in April 1896.

In England numerous trees have been planted, often to commemorate noted personages or events. For example, when Queen

Victoria observed her Diamond Jubilee in 1897, people in the town of Eynsford planted trees in the form of an acrostic.

In some places during Colonial times, it was customary for the bride to take a tree from her father's garden and replant it at her new home. It then became her duty to water and watch over it so that no harm came from the transplanting.

As Americans have since realized, in clearing lands for cultivation, many early settlers were quite wasteful and so denuded regions and invited flooding. This practice continued until farsighted individuals saw the seriousness of the situation and the urgent need for reforestation in various localities.

For this vision much credit belongs to George P. March. When acting as Minister to Italy and to Turkey, he studied those countries' methods and also those of the rest of Europe. In 1864 he wrote a book, called *Man and Nature,* and in his chapter on woods Mr. March stressed the fact that the United States should start and encourage systematic reforestation.

Dr. Birdsey G. Northrup, secretary of the Board of Education in Connecticut, traveled in this country and in Asia and Europe lecturing on the importance of planting trees, not only for their commercial value but to make the world more beautiful. Dr. Northrup organized village improvement societies. He urged all states to set out more trees and in 1876 offered prizes of one dollar each to all children who planted five centennial trees. In 1883 he was instrumental in getting a resolution passed by the American Forestry Association that Arbor Day be observed in all schools.

However, the man to whom we must give the honor of having promoted the *first* formal observance of Arbor Day in this country, in April 1872, was J. Sterling Morton, of Nebraska.

Not long after his graduation from college, Mr. Morton homesteaded in a treeless section of Nebraska. He soon realized the need for lumber for homes, barns, fence posts, and as a protection against blizzards.

He founded a newspaper, wrote articles about trees, and talked with many people about the idea of starting a tree-planting day. Mr. Morton served in the territorial legislature, and for a time as governor, but he failed to win the election as head of Nebraska when it entered the Union. Later he was Secretary of Agriculture in President Cleveland's second Cabinet, and was also one of the United

States Commissioners for the Louisiana Purchase Exposition. After Mr. Morton's death in 1902, the Arbor Day Memorial Association erected a monument in his honor, at his old home, "Arbor Lodge," near Nebraska City.

Realizing the great need that future generations in his state would have for wood and its products—also to conserve their soil—J. Sterling Morton, when a state Commissioner of Agriculture, placed the following resolution before the legislature:

> Resolved that April 10, 1873 be, and the same is hereby especially set apart and consecrated for tree planting in the State of Nebraska, and that the State Board of Agriculture hereby names it Arbor Day. . . .

The resolution passed and a prize of $100 offered to the county agricultural society that planted the largest number of trees. Also a $25 library of farm books was given to the individual with the highest score.

The Arbor Day idea soon spread through Nebraska; in 1885 the state legislature made the day a legal holiday, and chose for its annual observance April 22, J. Sterling Morton's birthday. By 1895 this one state had planted so many trees it won the name, "Tree Planters' State." Within sixteen years, 600 million had been set out; and 100,000 acres of waste lands had been turned into forested areas.

The observance of Arbor Day soon became prevalent in other states. Kansas, Tennessee, Minnesota, and Ohio soon followed Nebraska's example; now all states, territories, and the District of Columbia take note of it. Some states publish a special manual each year to assist in its celebration. In 1922, President Harding urged all states to adopt an annual tree-planting plan.

The time of Arbor Day varies in different places; most observe a date in March or April (according to local traditions and climatic conditions). In some localities it occurs in January, February, May, November, or December. West Virginia has two such days, one in the spring, the other in the fall. In three states Arbor Day is a legal holiday: Florida (third Friday in January); Nebraska (April 22); and Utah (second Monday in April).

Unsuccessful attempts have been made for a uniform observance. In 1949, for example, it was suggested that as many trees as possible be planted on the third Friday of that April.

However, no matter what the date, this holiday has played an important role in reforestation, also in calling attention to the need for conserving national resources, so strongly urged by Theodore Roosevelt. It has been estimated that since Nebraska's first Arbor Day *billions* of trees have been set out on this holiday.

Once the famous plant wizard, Luther Burbank, said, "Do not build me a monument—plant a tree." And his good advice has been accepted by countless individuals, schools, and clubs, all over the country. One man, Frank Fields, living at Nebraska City, planted his first tree in 1902, and has planted one each year since.

One of the earliest schoolmen to promote Arbor Day was J. B. Peaslee, superintendent of the Cincinnati, Ohio schools. In Eden Park, on April 27, 1882, he sponsored the planting of a grove—each tree marked with the name of a soldier, author, or other distinguished person—by the school children. In April 1889, in recognition of his work, a tree—"Peaslee's Oak"—was set out in Philadelphia.

In various American communities—and in other places—trees ("living monuments to fallen heroes") commemorate men who died in wars. In Ballarat, in Australia (formerly a noted gold rush town) now called the "Garden City" I saw a memorial arch at the end of three-mile-long Sturt Street; thirty-six hundred trees have been planted on each side of this road, each one recalling the name of a soldier who made the supreme sacrifice. There can be no finer memorial than a beautiful tree. Some schools feature the planting of trees to honor such men as Audubon, Muir, Burroughs, Theodore Roosevelt, or Johnny Appleseed.

Often women's organizations have taken an active part in promoting the beauty of their communities by adding more trees. One woman's group plants a tree each year, and their attractive grove by this time contains varied specimens, including camphor, live oak, weeping elm, acacia, Jeffrey's pine, plane, pepper, Chinese maple, red eucalyptus, sycamore, jacaranda, shamel ash from Mexico, and an elm, "a grandchild" of the noted tree, under which General Washington took command of the Continental Army in Cambridge, Massachusetts.

From East to West, and North to South, towns and cities plan extensive tree-planting projects for Arbor Day. In California the celebration occurs on March 7, Luther Burbank's birthday. There it is a combination of Bird Day and Conservation Day, and the children take this pledge:

I give my pledge as an American to save and faithfully defend from waste the natural resources of my country, its soil and minerals, its forests, waters, and wild life.

Tree planting takes place at schools all over the United States with youngsters planning for the enjoyment of future generations. Such a scene is delightfully portrayed by the famous artist, Grant Wood, whose canvas, "Arbor Day," is well known. In it, as someone has said, Wood has "captured the spirit of Arbor Day as he visualized teacher and children laboring enthusiastically to beautify an Iowa country schoolyard."

Thus one generation plants for another in the same spirit in which Martin Luther declared, "If I knew that tomorrow the world would go to pieces, I would still plant my tree." Washington Irving expressed a similar feeling when he wrote:

He who plants a tree cannot expect to sit in its shade, or enjoy its shelter; but he exults in the idea that the acorn shall grow to benefit mankind long after he is gone.

May Day—May 1

Ancient Romans observed their spring festival, the Floralia, to honor Flora, the goddess of flowers, by staging floral games with blossoms used in processions and dances. The festivities ran from April 28 to May 3. With the return of spring, flowers were abundant so everyone went out to the fields and meadows to gather them. Lovers brought back blossoming boughs to place in the houses of their sweethearts, while some young men raced to see who could be first to crown Flora's statue with a wreath and entwine garlands around the columns of her temple.

On May Day, Roman slaves were allowed to say and do as they pleased; the only stipulation was that they return to their master's house that evening.

Some sources trace our May Day rites to the Druids, who worshiped the sun. On this holiday, they lighted fires on hilltops to honor the sun; this was called "Belten" (or "Beltane") meaning Bel's Fire and was also associated with human sacrifices.

Peasants in Sweden, Czechoslovakia, Finland, and some other European countries kindled bonfires to celebrate the return of light after the long winter. Many believed such fires would drive the witches away from their ceremonies. Men often liked to jump over the blazing fires or drive cattle between them. Among the rural folk of Ireland, the Isle of Man, and the Scottish Highlands, such old customs continued for many years. During the medieval and Tudor periods May Day was one of the most important holidays of the year and a time of great rejoicing at the arrival of spring. Hawthorn was termed the "May"; and on this date, rich and poor, young and old, went "a-Maying"—that is, to gather great boughs of hawthorn.

Such excursions started before sunrise, and on the way home there was singing, accompanied by horns and the tabor. Then the happy crowd made wreaths and garlands of the May and added festive decorations to their homes. Chaucer wrote of such an expedition into the woods:

> Forth goes all the court, by most and least,
> To fetch the flowers fresh.

Even the King and his courtiers mingled with the lower classes of society on May Day. Henry VIII and his Queen, Katherine of Aragon, left their palace at Greenwich to meet the heads of the Corporation of London at Shooter's Hill. After returning from the woods, everyone spent the rest of the day in merriment; the popular poet, Robert Herrick, asked,

> Can such delights be in the streets,
> And open fields, and we not see it? . . .
> But, my Corinna, come, let's go a-Maying.

Early on the morning of this holiday, many women went out where no one could see them to bathe their faces in the dew to improve their complexions. In his famous *Diary* Samuel Pepys says that his wife got up about three in the morning "to go with her coach abroad, to gather May-dew. . . ." It is said that as late as 1791 such before-sunrise excursions were still made.

When the people of an English village had gathered the "May," they assembled at the green. A May queen had been selected (some trace this back to the worship of Flora); and she, surrounded by her attendants, sat in a bower covered with flowers and greenery. Apparently as someone remarked, she had nothing to do "but smell flowers, eat sweets, sip ale, and be admired by all the village lads." Sometimes queens from different places went to London; there was one chosen to rule there as Queen of London.

There were varied contests, sports, and races staged on the village green, before the fair monarch. Jesters rode around on hobby horses; morris dancers performed in fantastic costumes with bells jingling; Robin Hood and his men, dressed in green, Maid Marian, Friar Tuck, and others were on hand, while the spectators enjoyed the archery contests. It was customary, too, to sing special May Day carols about the coming of spring. Often children carrying a doll dressed in white—"The Lady of the May"—went around singing and giving away flowers, for which they received small gifts.

Besides adorning their own homes, townspeople set up a Maypole, and decorated it with colored ribbons, wreaths, branches, and garlands. Sometimes eight oxen brought in the pole, often of birch. To the Puritans, "the enemies of mirth and good humor," Maypoles were "eyesores" or "styncking ideas" around which people "leape and dance as the heathen did." Towns vied with each other as to who could have the tallest pole. Sometimes one was erected in front of a church; for many thought that evil spirits were around, as at Halloween, and that this would prevent their entering the sacred building.

Usually the pole stood just for May Day; however, some towns had permanent ones. London had several noted poles, which were adorned with flags, gay ribbons or strings, and golden or brightly painted balls. A smith whose daughter married General Monk (who later became the Duke of Albermarle) set up a Maypole at the end of Drury Lane to celebrate his daughter's good fortune. Each year at the Church of St. Andrew in Leaden-Hall Street, a Maypole taller than the church steeple was erected.

Naturally the Puritans were against such revelry and frivolity as holding ribbons and dancing around Maypoles; they termed these activities "licentious" and put an end to this gaiety. On April 6, 1644, Parliament declared:

> The Lords and Commons do further order and ordain, that all and singular Maypoles that are, or shall be erected, shall be taken down, and removed by the constables, tithing men, petty constables, and churchwardens of the parishes, where the same be, and that no Maypole be hereafter set up, erected, or suffered to be set up within this Kingdom of England . . . the said officers to be fined 5 shillings weekly until the said Maypoles be taken down.

But with the return of the Stuarts, Maypoles were again set up though it is said that the revelry was more restrained; also after the Restoration more young people than adults participated in the festivities.

On the return of Charles II to London in 1661, a 134-foot pole—the tallest ever seen in the city—was brought from Scotland Yard by 12 seamen. They dragged it in triumphantly, while flags waved, drums sounded, and music was heard. Then it was "reared with great ceremony and rejoicing" in the Strand. This pole was adorned with three gilt crowns, "streamers, flags, garlands of flowers, and other ornaments," and became the talk of the town. Pope once wrote of it: "Where the tall Maypole o'erlooked the Strand."

Later, in 1717, when this great pole decayed, Sir Isaac Newton bought it and set it up in a park in Essex. There it was used to support a 124-foot telescope, the largest one in the world at that time. This insrument had been given to the Royal Society by a French scientist, Monsieur Hugon.

After the return of Maypoles to England, one objector commented in these words:

> The country, as well as the town, abounds with vanities, now the reigns of liberty and licentiousness are let loose. Maypoles and plays and jugglers and all things else now pass current; sin now appears with a brazen face.

In contrast to this criticism, other writers praised the custom of observing May Day around the Maypole. Washington Irving (1783–1859) visited England and wrote:

> I shall never forget the delight I felt on first seeing a Maypole. It was on the banks of the Dee, close to the picturesque old bridge that stretches across the river from the quaint little city of Chester. . . . The mere sight of this Maypole gave a glow to my feelings and spread a charm over the country for the rest of the day. . . . One can readily imagine what a gay scene it must have been in jolly old London, when the doors were decorated with flowering branches, when every hat was decked with hawthorn, and Robin Hood, Friar Tuck, Maid Marian, the morris dancers and all the other fantastic maskers and revelers were performing their antics about the Maypole, in every part of the city.

And an early poet (name not given) wrote verses in which he gave his reaction to this old custom:

THE COUNTRY MAYPOLE

It is a pleasant sight to see
A little village company
Drawn out upon the first of May
To have their annual holiday;
The pole hung round with garlands gay,
The young ones footing it away,
The aged cheering their old souls,
With recollections of their bowls,
Or, on the mirth and dancing failing,
Their oft-times-told old tales re-taleing.

On May Day the chimney sweeps played special roles. One fellow called "Jack-in-the-Green" was concealed in a bower of foliage and flowers, and carried about the streets to the accompaniment of music by fifes and drums. In some towns, milkmaids in grotesque costumes headed the procession leading a decorated cow. Usually there was also a man wearing a frame so studded with silver dishes and flagons set in flowers that only his legs were visible as he joined in the dancing.

When the Pilgrims reached America, they found the trailing arbutus, which they called "Mayflower." (One source says there is "no one universally recognized Mayflower," for various blooms have been given this name." The Canadian Mayflower, for example, is the wild lily of the valley.)

The Puritans naturally brought with them to the New World their dislike for May Day and other gay celebrations. On May 1, 1627, the inhabitants of Plymouth Colony were "scandalized" when an Anglican, Thomas Morton, set up a Maypole at his nearby Merry Mount Plantation. It is said that he and his men danced with the Indian squaws. This made Governor Endicott so angry that he went to Merry Mount, had the pole chopped down, and stopped the festivities. The governor accused Morton, who loved "cakes, ale, and the gay life," of having traded arms to the Indians and shipped him back to England.

A custom which came here from Great Britain and still exists is that of giving May baskets. It was customary to hang little flower-filled baskets on doorknobs on the eve of May Day and call out, "May basket!" The idea was to get away without being discovered. (This custom stemmed from the old belief that the baskets would keep evil spirits away.)

For some time this custom died out; but in recent years it has been revived by schools where the youngsters fashion the baskets, then fill them with flowers or other little gifts, and hang them at their friends' doors. Today, the children apparently *want* to be discovered, and to get something in return. In some localities, boys and girls are urged to make such baskets for shut-ins or for those in hospitals.

Instead of lessening in the United States, the observance of May Day has increased in recent years. This is due both to the schools, and to playgrounds in parks, with trained directors. Often May Queens are chosen; Maypoles are set up and decorated; and dancing takes place around them. May Day is welcomed with "dancing on the green," the dances including old numbers like the English Ribbon Dance.

In some places, after queens are chosen at the different playgrounds, all are crowned together; a dozen or more Maypoles are erected so that all the children can dance at one time, and this makes a beautiful scene. Some clubs or churches stage pageants with the young actors in appropriate costumes and with musical accompaniment. Such plays as "The Enchanted Garden" or "The Princess and the Players" are presented before the May queen and her court.

On some American college campuses, it is customary to revel in spring's return by putting on old or modern pageants. Recently, in the West, at Scripps College, the girls gave one with an unusual setting—a tenement. The queen, dressed as a scrubwoman, with a mop for a scepter, was crowned, sitting on an ashcan. This was a decided contrast to the long-established Eastern affair at Wellesley College, where the annual hoop rolling takes place on May Day. In their caps and gowns, the seniors roll hoops down a slope to the chapel. The winner receives a bridal bouquet and is supposed to be the first girl of the class to be married.

In Hawaii, our newest state, May Day has long been observed as Lei Day, one of the world's most colorful and fragrant celebrations. The word, "lei," refers to a garland of flowers worn round one's neck. Each island has it own special type. Leis are fashioned from such popular blooms as vanda orchids, carnations, ginger flowers, tuberoses, or bougainvillea. Sometimes a lei of small orchids has as many as three hundred flowers in it.

Hawaiians wear leis at any time, but the garlands are featured at weddings, birthday feasts, and hula graduations. The early Polynesians loved nature and were surrounded by lovely flowers, so it was natural for them to decorate themselves with them. Each year, on May Day or Lei Day countless attractive garlands are worn, and there is music together with pageantry, and dancing.

When one leaves the islands by ship, he is supposed to wear the lei until the vessel rounds Diamond Head. Then he casts it into the sea. It is believed that if the flowers float back to the shore, the wearer also will return.

To many workers around the globe May Day is not the time

for merrymaking, but it is a serious one—a day devoted to working-men and their interests. The Second Internationale, at the suggestion of a German socialist, adopted May 1 as its political holiday. Its object was to stop a world war if it should start. It failed to do so, and was then dissolved by Lenin and his group.

In March 1919, the Third Internationale was formed. Now many foreign labor organizations commemorate May 1 as symbolic of "the international solidarity of workingmen." Some observe it in memory of the eight-hour day that came into being in 1866.

In various countries, May Day is the time for labor demonstrations, which at times have led to violence. In Moscow, the Russians put on a great show of military might; however, in recent years they have "played this down" and emphasized sports. Not long ago over a million civilians paraded in Moscow on May Day. In the United States, in New York for example, loyalty parades have been staged on this date, but our *real* workers' day comes in September, on Labor Day.

In recent years, a new way of celebrating May Day has come about through the efforts of the American Bar Association, which sponsors "Law Day" on May 1.

The observance in 1961 was the fourth, but in fact the *first* "official" celebration. For Congress by a joint resolution established this day; and President Kennedy in his proclamation asked all Americans to display the Stars and Stripes, and to observe the date "with suitable ceremonies."

There had been about 75,000 local celebrations in 1960, but the number was expected to increase greatly in the years following the official sanctioning of the occasion.

In 1961 Law Day was observed in varied fashion. In New York, the president of the American Bar Association spoke at the opening of the exhibits at the interchurch center; in Pittsburgh, two "top" students from each high school visited community officials to observe "government in action." Chicago held its largest naturalization ceremony in McCormick Place; in our national capital there was another such affair in a room where the Supreme Court used to meet. In Long Beach, California, 15 high school students, finalists in the annual Long Beach Bar Association's scholarship competition, received awards, totaling $1,000. Detroit, and many other places throughout the nation, observed the day with "mock trials, school assemblies, radio and television programs, essay contests, sermons, and exhibits."

All of these are excellent ways to call attention to this worthwhile observance of Law Day, on May 1, "a day set aside for Americans to rededicate themselves to the principle of individual freedom under law."

Cinco de Mayo—The Fifth of May

A very important date in Mexican history is May 5, *Cinco de Mayo*. It is *not* their national Independence Day, as some think; that day occurs in September. However, May 5, 1862 was the day when the Mexicans succeeded—if only for a time—in opposing the French invasion of the country.

The following events led up to that decisive battle: Since Mexico had defaulted in her payments to France, Spain, and England, the three lands decided "to make a joint naval demonstration against her" to force her to settle with the bondholders. The fleets reached Vera Cruz late in 1861; but the English and Spanish ships left, after some preliminary arrangements had been made. Then the French repudiated the contract and started a war of conquest.

On May 5, 1862, under General Ignacio Zaragoza, 2,000 Mexicans repulsed about 6,000 French soldiers. After Napoleon III had sent re-enforcements, Maximilian was placed on the throne of Mexico. (Later he was executed, and the Mexicans took over control again.)

The people were so thrilled by the Fifth of May victory that they changed the name of the place where it occurred (Puebla de los Angeles) to Puebla de Zaragoza to honor their beloved leader. And ever since that time, all over Mexico, and wherever natives of this country happen to be on May 5, they gaily celebrate *Cinco de Mayo*.

There are many people of Mexican extraction in Southern California, with over 500,000 in the Los Angeles area. This is said to be the largest such group in one community on the North American continent, with the exception of Mexico City itself. So, naturally, when May 5 comes around these people enjoy gay festivities. The Americans join with them; for Angelenos also love fiestas, a heritage from the days of the early California dons.

Various colorful events are planned for *Cinco de Mayo* by the city officials and a group of Mexican leaders. Distinguished Mexicans, such as cabinet members, or governors, arrive to be guests of honor. They give speeches in which the friendship between the United States and our "South-of-the-Border" neighbors is stressed.

In 1959 the Mexican consul general received a scroll with these words: "The two great republics walk down the road of destiny on the way to peace." At one program the Under Secretary of Foreign Affairs declared: "The very fact that our countries live happily side by side is an example to the rest of the world." On such occasions the mayor of Los Angeles usually gives part of his speech in Spanish; this pleases the Mexicans and adds to the "Good Neighbor" idea.

The main celebration of the day occurs on the steps of the City Hall; and the Mexican Tipica orchestra vies with a Los Angeles band in furnishing musical numbers. On the decorated platform there is a picture of General Zaragoza; and the red, white, and green Mexican flag flies along with the Stars and Stripes.

Thousands of Mexicans, Angelenos, and visitors gather to hear the music, an address of welcome, and speeches of visiting dignitaries. Many Mexican men wear beautifully braided native suits, while the women wear gay ruffled dresses and lace mantillas. The little girls have similar costumes, and often boys walk proudly around in their *caballero* outfits.

Mexican celebrities of stage and screen furnish the entertainment. Senoritas in colorful costumes click their castanets as they swing and sway their graceful skirts in the performance of intricate dance steps to the music of strumming guitars, and the singing of songs like "La Golondrina" or "La Cucaracha."

Later, the celebrants scatter to various places to enjoy the rest of the holiday. Some throng to quaint Olvera Street, or roam around the old plaza, where the city was founded in 1781. At several city parks there are special *Cinco de Mayo* fiestas, with picnic dinners, sports events, instrumental music, singing and dancing. Also gala luncheons, with distinctive Mexican foods, are served at such places as the well-known La Golondrina Cafe on Olvera Street.

There is an annual banquet at the Biltmore Hotel where honored guests are entertained by the city fathers. After a day filled with the fiesta spirit, large numbers of people gather at the plaza, for a final fling—a program of music and dancing.

Thus the Mexicans and United States residents observe this day together. For, as the personal representative of the Mexican President once said in Los Angeles on *Cinco de Mayo:*

> It celebrates a symbol. *Cinco de Mayo* is a symbol that all people of the world—yesterday, today, tomorrow—will fight curtailment of the most beloved principle of freedom and liberty.

Mother's Day—Second Sunday
in May

On the second Sunday in May, mothers are the center of attention and, being human, of course they enjoy it. They listen to sermons and other tributes, and are guests of honor at luncheons and dinners. This American holiday has been observed nationally since 1914, when President Woodrow Wilson proclaimed the day as "a public expression of our love and reverence for the mothers of our country."

However, this idea of honoring mothers was not new; in fact, it goes back to antiquity. According to ancient mythology, a yearly spring festival was dedicated to Rhea (wife of the Titan, Cronus) mother of the gods Jupiter, Pluto, Neptune, and the goddesses, Vesta, Ceres, and Juno. In Phrygia, Rhea became identified with Cybele, and the worship of Rhea, as mother of the gods, reached Rome from Greece, about 250 B.C. The Romans began her three-day festival, the Hilaria, on the Ides of March.

Early Christians set apart the fourth Sunday before Easter to honor Mary, the mother of Christ. On that day, many visited her shrine or took flowers to altars of churches where they had been baptized. Sometimes expensive presents of jewels and rich metals were given to honor the Virgin, and also many mothers received gifts from their children.

For years "Mothering Sunday" was observed by an ecclesiastical order on St. Anne's Day (mother of the Virgin Mary). At first it came on the fourth Sunday in Lent; later the "gentry" discontinued its celebration, although the clergy encouraged its observance.

This holiday, Mothering Sunday, was especially popular with servants and apprentices, who looked forward to the day when they were permitted to "go a-mothering," to visit their homes and mothers. Many walked long distances to such family reunions, for to be at home on this holiday was a great treat. This celebration was popular in western England, especially in Gloucestershire and Bristol. In Lancashire, children gave their mothers bunches of primroses as tokens of affection.

Usually on Mothering Sunday the oldest son took his mother a special present, "a mothering cake," which was cut and shared by the family. At first it was just a "wheaten cake," later a "plum cake," rich with fruits, and skillfully decorated with wreaths or other ornaments. Sometimes small hard cookies, or "simnel cakes" were eaten on such occasions. The British poet, Robert Herrick mentions this custom.

> I'll to thee a simnel bring
> Gainst thou go'st a-mothering
> So that when she blesseth thee
> Half that blessing thou'lt give me

Also in some parts of England waffle-like cakes were baked on special irons, handed down from one generation to another.

On Mothering Sunday, it was necessary for the sons and daughters to attend to the household duties and to prepare the dinner so that the mother could go to the morning church service. A popular song about this holiday by George Hare Leonard began:

> It is the day of all the year,
> Of all the year the one day
> When I shall see my mother dear
> And bring her cheer,
> A-mothering on Sunday.

He tells that he will take her a cake, while his sister, Jane, will cook the midday meal.

> For Mother'll come to church you see
> Of all the year it's the day
> "The one," she'll say, "that's made for me."
> And so it be.
> It's every mother's free day.

Thus England was really observing a Mother's Day, long before we were. In some other countries, too, people took note of this holiday. In Yugoslavia, for instance, such an occasion was celebrated just before the Christmas season. However, when the movement started in the United States, many persons probably did not know it was really a revival of an old custom.

On November 24, 1948, Anna M. Jarvis, penniless and almost sightless, died in a quiet sanitarium in West Chester, Pennsylvania at the age of eighty-four. Although she is given credit as the originator of our modern American Mother's Day and was acclaimed throughout the world for this achievement, unfortunately much of her life was filled with strife and bitterness.

Anna M. Jarvis was born May 1, 1864, in Webster, West Virginia. Soon her family moved to Grafton, where she attended elementary schools. After her graduation from the Female Seminary in Wheeling, Anna became a teacher in Grafton; later she went to Philadelphia with her family.

Her mother, Anna Reese Jarvis, daughter of a minister, taught classes in the Andrews Methodist Church Sunday school in Grafton for more than twenty years. During that period, her daughter had often heard her say that there should be an annual day honoring mothers.

Although Anna M. Jarvis was an attractive, intelligent young woman, she never married, but cared for her blind sister, Elsinore. When their mother died, on May 9, 1905, Anna felt her loss deeply.

Two years later, on the second Sunday in May, she invited some friends to her Philadelphia home and told them of her plan to start a "Mother's Day." She was much concerned because too many adults neglected their mothers, and did not appreciate them until it was too late. Miss Jarvis also noticed the lack of deference toward parents, and believed that the hectic pace of modern life caused home ties to be neglected.

John Wanamaker, to whom Anna Jarvis went for advice, urged her to begin her campaign at once for a national observance of a day devoted to mothers. She did so and wrote countless letters to people in all walks of life. Many agreed that it was a worthwhile project. Wilbur Chapman, the noted evangelist, declared it one of the finest suggestions he had heard in years. At once he incorporated it as a feature of his religious campaigns. Anna also wrote to members of Congress asking for their aid.

Before the third anniversary of her mother's death, Anna Jarvis had asked the church in Grafton, West Virginia, to arrange a "Mother's Day" service to honor Mrs. Jarvis. This was carried out with fitting ceremonies. The minister, Dr. H. C. Howard, used this text: "Woman, behold thy Son; Son, behold thy mother." A similar program was held on that same date, May 10, 1908, in Philadelphia.

That Sunday in Grafton, carnations (her mother's favorite flower), furnished by Miss Jarvis, were given to those in attendance. A neighbor said this of Mrs. Jarvis: "She loved the old-fashioned pinks that bloomed in the great beds in front of her house, and that is why we wear carnations on Mother's Day."

At first only white flowers were worn; later these became symbolic of mothers who had died. Then the custom arose of using red carnations for living mothers. One writer, Ruth Baird, has said: "To wear a carnation this Mother's Day, whether red, or white, is to symbolize the purity, fidelity, prayers and enduring love of mothers."

Soon the idea of observing Mother's Day spread through our country; and one Philadelphia editor asserted that it would become world-wide. In 1910 the governor of West Virginia issued the first Mother's Day proclamation; Oklahoma followed suit; and in 1912, Governor Hay, of Washington, asked his people to attend church, to visit or write their mothers on this holiday, or if their mothers were not living to wear white carnations, "symbolic of sweetness, purity, and endurance" in their memory. By this time all our states were observing Mother's Day, as were several foreign lands.

In December 1912, the Mother's Day International Association came into existence. On May 7, 1914, Thomas J. Heflin of Alabama and Senator Sheppard of Texas introduced into Congress a resolution to set aside the second Sunday in each May as "Mother's Day": "Whereas the service rendered by the American mothers is the greatest source of the country's strength and inspiration. . . ." Two days afterward, President Wilson issued his proclamation, and urged that the Stars and Stripes be flown on this holiday.

Naturally, Anna Jarvis was honored for her work in promoting this project; she was chosen as a delegate to the seventh World's Sunday School Convention at Zurich in 1913. Japan praised her idea as "a great American gift to Japan."

Although the celebration at first was carried out by church programs, as Miss Jarvis wished it to be, the scope of the observance was broadened to include demonstrations of affection by sending gifts, writing letters, and making visits. With this widespread celebration, commercialism began to play its part; and Miss Jarvis was dismayed at this turn of events. She disliked the advertisements stressing the giving of presents, such as those of the telegraph companies, florists, candy makers, and others. (It is said that at this holiday in 1961, more than 55 million families bought Mother's Day gifts, totaling more than $875 million.)

In her vigorous struggle to keep Mother's Day free from commercialism, Anna Jarvis became more bitter with the years. She also became involved in litigation, then shut herself away from the world, becoming almost a hermit.

For many years people had urged the postmaster general to issue a stamp commemorating Mother's Day. Finally, in 1934, James A. Farley ordered a three-cent stamp made, carrying the famous portrait of Whistler's Mother. One critic stated that this picture had "caught the spirit of eternal and immortal motherhood." After the artist had completed the painting, called "Arrangement in Black and Grey," the French government bought it, and it was sent to the United States for the art exhibit at the Chicago Fair of 1934.

When the stamp with the Whistler portrait was issued, Anna Jarvis protested strongly, and even went to Washington to see the postmaster general himself. His department apologized to her, but citizens all over the United States welcomed the distinctive stamp.

During the years that Mother's Day was growing in importance, Miss Jarvis lost her sister and her property, and became almost blind. One cold day in November 1944, she entered the general hospital and asked for treatment, as she had no funds. At once a group of friends provided for her, and placed her in a West Chester sanitarium.

After Miss Jarvis had begun her lifelong devotion to this cause, some sources asserted that others before her had worked along the same lines. For example, one authority states that Julia Ward Howe, author of "The Battle Hymn of the Republic," was the first to promote the idea. During the Civil War she suggested that the Fourth of July be made a holiday devoted to peace, by recognizing it as "Mother's Day," but the proposal was rejected.

Another declares the event really began in 1887, in Henderson, Kentucky, when a teacher, Mary Towles Sasseen, invited her pupils' mothers to attend a musical affair in their honor. This became a yearly event; also Miss Sasseen spent much time organizing

Mother's Day programs in neighboring schools and localities. She died just two years before Miss Jarvis sponsored her first observance.

According to a third source, the honor of starting this holiday should go to Frank E. Herring of the Fraternal Order of Eagles in Indiana, who, in an address to his lodge in February 1904, urged that a day be set apart each year to honor mothers and that the event should be nationwide.

But no matter who began it, Mother's Day has proved its worth and is a good thing, both for mothers and children. On this holiday we hear eulogies of mothers; and literature and history contain many expressions of gratitude to them. Lamartine, a noted Frenchman, was pleased that his mother had not been overly ambitious for him, but had allowed him to develop naturally. Susannah Wesley, mother of nineteen children, including John, the founder of Methodism, and Samuel, the hymn writer, was praised for giving "pleasant commands; when scolding was necessary, she did not do it in anger, but as the remonstrance of a tender mother."

Thomas Carlyle remembered that his mother was confident that he would finally make good. John Ruskin's mother had him learn Bible passages each day; he later affirmed that this had made him develop the habit of "taking pains"; and best of all, she introduced him to good literature. Oliver Cromwell's mother did the same for him; she also stressed right principles of living so strongly that Oliver "understood perfectly his duties to God and man."

Several American celebrities have also paid tributes to their mothers: Thomas Edison, for example, maintained that his mother had encouraged him in his struggle for success, even though others (including one teacher) had thought him "addlepated." And in spite of dire poverty, Nancy Hanks, the mother of Abraham Lincoln, succeeded in inspiring her children. In after years her famous son declared that her prayers had followed him all his life; and he gave her full credit for his success.

Although Eugene Field's mother had died when he was only six, all his life he carried the memory of "her gentle voice and soothing touch." Mrs. Beecher, whose sons, and daughters, Harriet and Catherine, became noted, was "a restful person," around whom all seemed to find peace and comfort, just from being in her presence.

Frances Willard wrote that her mother was free from "pettiness" of character, always so busy with worthwhile things that she had no time for gossip. William Cullen Bryant recalled that his mother was quite broad-minded; that she took much interest in local and national affairs; and that she was not only devoted to her own family, but was ever ready to help her neighbors.

For centuries in England it was customary to place complimentary remarks on a person's tombstone; and many mothers were so honored. A famous example can be seen in the churchyard of St. Giles Church at Stoke Poges not far from the ancient yew tree under which Thomas Gray is said to have composed his famous poem, "Elegy Written in a Country Churchyard." At the tomb in which his aunt, Mary Antrobus, and his mother, Dorothy Gray are interred, you can read these words:

In the Vault beneath are deposited
In Hope of a joyful Resurrection,
the remains of

❀ MARY ANTROBUS *❀*

She died, unmarried, November 5, 1749,
Aged 66.

In the same pious confidence,
beside her friend and sister
here sleep the remains of

❀ DOROTHY GRAY *❀*

Widow, the careful, tender Mother
of many children, one of whom alone
had the misfortune to survive her.
She died March 11, 1753,
Aged 67.

Thomas Gray in accordance with his wish was buried "in the same tomb upon which he so feelingly inscribed his grief at the loss of a beloved parent."

Here in the United States, in old burying places, one comes

across like inscriptions. In the Old Granary Burial Ground, in the heart of Boston, Benjamin Franklin erected a monument to his father and mother, bearing these words:

> JOSIAH FRANKLIN, and ABIAH, his wife, lie here interred. They lived lovingly in wedlock 55 years. Without estate or any gainful employment, by constant labor and honest industry, maintained a large family, and brought up 13 children respectably. From this distance, Reader, be encouraged to diligence in thy calling, and distrust not Providence. He was a pious and prudent man, she, a discreet and virtuous woman. Their youngest son, in filial regard to their memory, places this stone. ☙

Also, down in St. John's churchyard, in Richmond, Virginia, you can read Poe's eulogy to his mother, who died when she was only twenty-four. (He lost his father, too, at an early age; after the little boy, Edgar, had gone to live with the Allans, they often found him crying at his mother's grave.)

Some years ago the Raven Society of the University of Virginia placed a memorial to her in this churchyard. Her profile is on a copper plate; and below it are words written by her famous son, Edgar Allan Poe, and published in the *Broadway Journal*, July 19, 1845.

At that time actors and actresses were not considered too highly by some persons; however, Poe wanted the world to know how proud he was of his mother:

> The artist of talent is poor indeed, if he does not look with contempt upon the mediocrity of a king. The writer of this article is himself the son of an actress—has invariably made it his boast—and no earl was ever prouder of his earldom than he of his descent from a woman, who, although well-born, hesitated not to consecrate to the drama her brief career of genius and beauty.

Armed Forces Day—Third Saturday in May

The third Saturday in May was named Armed Forces Day by Presidential proclamation in 1947. This was to replace Army Day, April 6; Navy Day, October 27 (the birthday of Theodore Roosevelt); and Air Force Day, the second Saturday in September.

On May 21, 1960, President Dwight D. Eisenhower announced from the White House:

> It is America's hope and purpose to work continually toward the peaceful adjustment of international differences, and it is fitting that Armed Forces Day again emphasize the fact that our strength is dedicated to keeping the peace.

Army Day had been set aside to show respect to the Army of the United States and its component parts, the Reserve, the National Guard, and the veterans who are now civilians. This anniversary celebration was started by the Military Order of the World Wars, on April 6, 1928. It was recognized by Congress in 1937. Until 1948 it was observed all over the country by civilian and military ceremonies, usually featuring parades, with army components and veterans' organizations taking part. However, since Armed Forces Day was established, there has been less observance of Army Day.

(On November 10, the Marine Corps pays tribute to its establishment in 1775; and August 4 is Coast Guard Day. Its purpose is "To commemorate the founding on this day, in 1790, of the Coast Guard, an armed force serving as our foremost agency for promoting maritime safety and law enforcement.")

Armed Forces Day is a reminder of the setting up of our Department of Defense in 1947, and according to one source has "to some extent" taken the place of Army Day and Navy Day. Since 1953, the keynote of the observance has been expressed by the slogan, "Power for Peace."

The Department of Defense, in cooperation with civilian communities, has designated Armed Forces Day to pay respect to the role of the United States Government in promoting the general welfare of the entire country. Although this date is not a legal or public holiday, it is observed in many localities.

In certain places where there are defense installations, the week preceding the third Saturday in May is known as Armed Forces Week; the observance culminates usually with an elaborate parade on Armed Forces Day, in which our military might is proudly displayed with "the steady cadence of marching boots, the rumble of tanks and armored vehicles, and blaring bands."

Naturally, the ceremonies on this holiday vary; but in some communities city officials, service clubs, and other groups honor at luncheons or banquets men and women from various branches of the Service. Sometimes there is a gala dance, where "Miss Armed Forces" and her attendants preside. Not long ago New York featured five Armed Forces queens, representing the Air Force, Navy, Army, Coast Guard, and the Marine Corps.

On Armed Forces Day jets fly overhead; naval vessels in ports are open to the public. At various bases and military establishments, and on ships, there are exhibits and demonstrations of new weapons and other equipment. Also, the different branches hold open house and welcome civilians. Therefore, Armed Forces Day is the time when citizens should take advantage of the chance to see at first hand the latest developments in our national defense.

In Southern California during Armed Forces Week in 1960, countless visitors thronged through the Space Technology Laboratories, Army Nike sites, and Fort MacArthur, where the latest army equipment was displayed. Many went aboard the heavy cruiser, *Los Angeles*, the carrier, *Kearsarge*, and other Navy craft. Civilians viewed jet fighter and helicopter demonstrations and missile exhibits.

"A giant B52 bomber, the big punch of the Strategic Air Command," was exhibited at the Long Beach Air Force Base, along with the "Hound Dog guided missile, designed to be launched from the B52 against targets on the ground."

In one of his Armed Forces Day proclamations, President Eisenhower declared that this time is to be "devoted to paying special tribute to those whose constancy and courage constitute one of the bulwarks guarding the freedom of the nation and the peace of the free world." The Chief Executive urged the state governors to plan for the observance of Armed Forces Day in a suitable manner. In addition he appealed to private citizens to display the Stars and Stripes and "to show their recognition of the gallantry, sacrifice, and devotion to duty of the men and women of the armed forces."

Shavuoth (Pentecost) (Feast of Weeks)—Sivan 6

Shavuoth, also called Pentecost (because it occurs on the fiftieth day after the second day of Passover) falls on the sixth of the month, Sivan. In 1960 it was observed on June I. This festival is also known as the Feast of Weeks; for it came at the end of a "week of weeks," or seven weeks. In Deuteronomy XVI, verses 9 and 10 we read:

> Seven weeks shalt thou number unto thee; begin to number the seven weeks from such time as thou beginnest to put the sickle to the corn.
>
> And thou shalt keep the feast of weeks unto the Lord thy God with a tribute of a freewill offering of thine hand, which thou shalt give unto the Lord thy God, according as the Lord hath blessed thee.

According to Webster Pentecost is also: "A Christian festival commemorating on the seventh Sunday after Easter the descent of the Holy Spirit on the Apostles; hence, Whitsunday."

Two additional names given to this Jewish festival were the Feast of Harvest, or Day of First Fruits. Originally this was an agricultural feast; in Biblical times, it celebrated the wheat and barley harvests and the first appearance of fruits after the spring plantings. Following the early harvest in Palestine the people carried offerings of their first fruits to the temple in Jerusalem. Pentecost, or the Feast of Weeks, was one of three occasions when all male Jews were commanded to visit Jerusalem and "to draw near to the Shekinah Glory which dwelt in the Temple in the Holy of Holies."

This day, one of the most colorful in the Jewish calendar, also commemorated the giving of the Ten Commandments to Moses on Mount Sinai. Among Reform Jews it is said that the historical aspect of the festival has supplanted the older agricultural one. The idea grew after the destruction of the temple and the dispersion of the Jews.

There are still some traces of the ancient rural aspect for on this feast day, homes and places of worship are decorated with flowers and grains. The agricultural characteristic is further emphasized in the traditional foods eaten at this time, which are chiefly dairy products.

The Book of Ruth is read in the synagogues. Not only was Ruth the widow whose loyalty to her husband's people did not end with his death, but with the beautiful words, ". . . thy people shall be my people, and thy God my God" she accompanied her mother-in-law on her journey back to Bethlehem, where she embraced the Jewish faith, worked in the fields, and was accepted as a "sojourner," not a "foreigner," even before her marriage to Boaz.

During the passage of centuries, the importance of the feast lessened, but in recent years it is again playing an important role. Now Pentecost marks the time of religious dedication of the boys and girls who have finished their elementary religious education.

The service of confirmation, at the end of the ninth or tenth grade of religious school, began—so it is claimed—in 1831 in Germany. At first it was not favorably received by non-Reform Jews; but now both Conservative and Reform congregations use the day for confirmation. Therefore, Pentecost is an important time in the American Jewish calendar.

There are colorful rites on this occasion. The graduates put on a program of special prayers and songs; they present a floral tribute to the temple; and all recite the Ten Commandments together. At the close of the service, the spiritual leaders bless the youthful group, and the new adherents promise to live their lives according to the principles of Judaism.

National Maritime Day—May 22

On May 2, 1933, President Franklin D. Roosevelt issued a proclamation, designating May 22 as National Maritime Day, "to stimulate public awareness of the American Merchant Marine." He urged everyone to display the flag on this date, both on their homes and public buildings.

Congress had just passed a resolution recommending the observance of such a day on May 22. For it was on this date, back in 1819, that the steamer, *Savannah*, left Savannah, Georgia, for Europe. She was the first vessel to try steam propulsion on such a crossing. Even though she used her sails most of the time, she really pioneered with steam on this history-making voyage.

This was a hazardous undertaking; for the *Savannah* was only 98.5 feet in length, with a beam of 25.8 feet, and gross tonnage of 319.7. She was built in New York as a three-masted vessel, for use as a sailing packet between New York and Le Havre.

Captain Moses Rogers, a river pilot, with experience on inland waters, had been the skipper of the *Clermont*, on which Robert Fulton made the first successful steam voyage up the Hudson. So Rogers became interested in the new packet being constructed at a shipyard on the East River. He believed she could be equipped with steam power as auxiliary to her sails, and that such power would shorten the Atlantic crossing.

Finally he was able to persuade some Savannah capitalists to finance the addition of the necessary machinery. Then the vessel was named the *Savannah*. Besides her full complement of sails, she was fitted with an inclined steam engine. Her paddle wheels of wrought iron were made in such a way that they could be folded up like a fan and hauled on deck when the *Savannah* moved under sail.

When the new craft reached Georgia, "after a boisterous voyage" from New York, she was received by large, cheering crowds. At that time President Polk was visiting in Savannah and he took a ride on her to see how her engine performed. A newspaper advertised that passengers could be accommodated, but as no one offered to go, the *Savannah* sailed without cargo or passengers.

Today the ship's log book can be seen in the United States National Museum in Washington, D.C.; and it gives an interesting account of that first journey.

> At 7 A.M. got steam up, winded ship and hove up the anchor, and at 9 A.M. started with steam from Savannah.

Ten days later, an American schooner sighted the ship, headed for Europe, with smoke pouring from her funnel. As he thought she was afire, the skipper stood by. But when he discovered she was actually running by steam, he declared her action "a proud moment of Yankee skill."

As the *Savannah* neared the coast of Ireland, authorities reported her as a ship in distress, and sent out the cutter *Kite* to aid her. But they were not able to overtake her even though she was traveling "with bare poles." When they fired at her, the *Savannah* stopped; then the men in the *Kite* were surprised to learn of her new motive power.

When the vessel moved up the Mersey River at Liverpool, the house roofs and piers were filled with excited spectators. The *London Times* noted briefly that an American ship, the *Savannah*, "the first vessel of its kind, which ever crossed the Atlantic" had been taken for a ship on fire.

During the twenty-five days she was in port British authorities kept a close watch on her movements, for they suspected she might be trying to get the large reward Jerome Bonaparte had offered to anyone who could rescue his brother Napoleon from St. Helena.

The American ambassador to Great Britain, Richard Rush, was delighted with the *Savannah*'s accomplishment, and in a letter to John Quincy Adams, then Secretary of State, he declared:

> She excited admiration as she entered port under power of her steam. She is a fine ship and exhibits in her construction, no less than in her navigation across the Atlantic, a signal triumph of American enterprise and skill upon the ocean.

The *Savannah* next proceeded to Denmark and Russia. At ports in both countries, members of the royal families, nobility, and high officials visited her and made short trips on her. For ten days of the thirty-three from Liverpool to St. Petersburg, she operated under steam.

However, on the return voyage to Georgia, because of coal shortage, the vessel had to use her sails all the way. But as she entered her home port, the *Savannah* gave the citizens of that southern city a thrill by moving proudly to her anchorage with clouds of smoke pouring from her funnel. Later, because of financial losses in a great fire in Savannah, the owners were forced to sell the vessel. After serving as a sailing packet between Georgia and New York, the *Savannah* reached the end of her career when she was wrecked in a heavy storm off Long Island.

Since this ship had actually operated only eighty hours by steam during her thirty days' Atlantic crossing, some authorities believe she should not be credited with the honor of having been the first to sail with steam propulsion. Even though she did not attain the complete success her confident captain, Moses Rogers, had hoped for, she did play an important role in our steamship history.

Therefore, it is fitting to remember the little *Savannah* on May 22 —our National Maritime Day—when we pay honor to our American ships and those who man them.

Memorial Day—May 30

Soldier, rest, thy warfare o'er,
Dream of fighting fields no more.
Sleep the sleep that knows not breaking,
Morn of toil, nor night of waking.
                                        —Sir Walter Scott

Each year, on May 30, when we honor our war heroes, it is indeed "a day to remember their sacrifices and deeds." And we Americans are continuing a custom almost as old as time itself.

For history reveals that older civilizations such as the Greek and Roman honored the dead by decorating their graves. The Druids observed a memorial day about the first of November; in Japan, people paid homage to their departed relatives and friends at the "Feast of Lanterns."

At Whitsuntide, during the Middle Ages, monasteries held memorials for the brothers who had died; and in France and Italy it was customary to visit cemeteries on the eve of All Saints' Day to pay tribute to the dead. Today, almost everywhere around the globe people observe a time of remembering, not only for those who gave their lives in battle, but it has come to be "a day of personal and family commemoration."

The origin of Memorial Day in the United States has been attributed to different persons and to various localities. Some credit Cassandra Oliver Moncure, of Virginia; others believe the day really started in Boalsburg, Pennsylvania.

Here it is claimed Miss Emma Hunter instituted the idea in 1864, when she carried flowers to the tomb of her father, Colonel James Hunter. He commanded the 49th Pennsylvania Regiment that took part in the Battle of Gettysburg. That day, while Miss Hunter was in the cemetery, she met a Mrs. Meyer, whose son had been killed in the war. The two women then decided to meet the next year to decorate the graves again.

Gradually other townspeople took up the idea; and some time ago they erected this sign on Route 322:

> BOALSBURG
>
> AN AMERICAN VILLAGE
>
> BIRTHPLACE OF MEMORIAL DAY

Another story, crediting southern women of Columbus, Mississippi, is perhaps better known. On April 26, 1866, these Confederate ladies went out to decorate their soldiers' graves. (Four years before, after the Battle of Shiloh, about 1500 southern and a hundred northern men had been buried in the plot, now known as Friendship Cemetery.)

This was during the Reconstruction. The South was impoverished, and under military occupation, and some leaders in Washington were not dealing too wisely with southern problems. Fortunately, these ladies of Columbus had kindly feelings, even toward their enemies. After scattering flowers on the graves of the Confederate dead, they placed magnolia blossoms on the Union men's resting places.

The news of this unselfish act reached the North; in the *New York Herald Tribune*, edited by Horace Greeley, this tribute appeared:

> The women of Columbus, Mississippi, have shown themselves impartial in their offerings to the memory of the dead. They strewed flowers alike on the graves of the Confederate and of the National soldiers.

This kindly act touched many northern hearts; and a beautiful reaction was the poem, "The Blue and the Gray," by a young lawyer, Francis Miles Finch, of Ithaca, New York. This appeared in the September 1867 issue of the *Atlantic Monthly*, and soon became popular reading all over the country.

> Sadly, but not with upbraiding,
> The generous deed was done:
> In the storm of the years that are fading
> No braver battle was won;
> Under the sod and the dew,
> Waiting the judgment day;

Under the blossoms, the Blue,
Under the garlands, the Gray.

According to one writer, the first Memorial Day service took place on Belle Isle in the James River, at Richmond, Virginia. The school superintendent, Andrew Washburn, and F. B. May, the mayor, planned a program for May 30, 1866. Several teachers, and Miss Gibson, a nurse, went to the burial ground of Union soldiers, who had died during the war in a Confederate prison located there.

It was raining when Mr. May set up a cross and placed bouquets at each headboard, Miss Gibson sang a hymn, and the others joined in the refrain. R. R. Wilson, who described the scene, in the *New York Tribune*, stated that suddenly the clouds parted and a bright ray of sunshine shone on the cross.

According to the *History of the Grand Army of the Republic* (the Union veterans' organization), Adjutant-General N. P. Chapman had received a letter from a Union soldier of German origin (his daughter later said it was her father, Captain Joseph Rudolph), saying that in Germany it was the custom each spring to decorate the graves of fallen soldiers, and he suggested that the Grand Army adopt this idea.

The adjutant-general spoke to General J. A. Logan (the national commander) about this; and the general was so impressed that he issued an order naming May 30, 1868

> . . . for the purpose of strewing with flowers or otherwise decorating the graves of the comrades who died in defense of their country during the late rebellion and whose bodies lie in almost every city, village, or hamlet churchyard in the land. It is the purpose of the commander-in-chief to inaugurate this observance with the hope that it will be kept from year to year while a survivor of the war remains to honor the memory of the departed. . . . Let no ravages of time testify to coming generations that we have forgotten, as a people, the cost of a free and undivided Republic.

After the first observance in 1868, when there was a program at the National Cemetery at Arlington and memorial services in various communities, the idea gradually spread around the country. In 1873 New York was the first state to make the day a legal holiday; and others soon followed. Now the occasion is set by Presidential proclamation.

May 30 as Memorial Day is a legal holiday in the District of
Columbia, Canal Zone, Guam, Puerto Rico, the Virgin Islands, and
all states with the exception of Alabama, Georgia, Mississippi, North
and South Carolina, and Texas. (In Florida May 30 is a memorial
day for veterans of all wars; in Virginia it is Confederate Memorial
Day.)

Nine states of the former Confederacy have independent observances, sponsored by the Daughters of the Confederacy. Alabama, Georgia, Mississippi, and Florida celebrate the Confederate
Memorial Day on April 26. It is said that this day was chosen because it was the first anniversary of the "last-ditch" surrender of
General Joseph E. Johnston, at Durham Station, South Carolina,
seventeen days after the surrender of General Lee at Appomattox.
North and South Carolina observe the day on May 10; Virginia,
May 30; Louisiana and Tennessee, on June 3, the birthday of Jefferson Davis ("by present custom held on the Sunday nearest the
date").

At these southern Memorial Day services such songs are sung as
"Dixie," "The Conquered Banner," and the favorite hymn of General Robert E. Lee, "How Firm a Foundation."

The term Decoration Day at first was the official name since the
chief idea was to decorate on that day the graves of the dead
soldiers who fought to preserve the Union. Finally the name became Memorial Day as the members of the Grand Army of the Republic and many private citizens thought the latter name more
suitable. However, the term Decoration Day is still more popular in
some places.

Gradually regulations were adopted by branches of the Armed
Forces to be followed on this holiday. For many years the Grand
Army of the Republic was in charge of local ceremonies. Usually
there was a parade of veterans and citizens; the town band played
patriotic and Civil War music; and after the procession had reached
the cemetery, flowers and flags were placed on graves of the "Men
in Blue." In the early celebrations there was much "oratorical
glorification of the victory of the Northern armies."

However, as years went by and men both of the North and South
fought side by side in later years, Memorial Day became a time to
honor all who had lost their lives in such conflicts. Today flags fly
at half-mast; there are parades with massed colors, with military and

local bands, fife and bugle corps, servicemen, civic organizations, Boy Scouts, and school children. At some places planes fly overhead and scatter flowers over cemeteries or on the sea.

At Arlington National Cemetery there is always an impressive tribute to our war dead. At Vicksburg, both southern and northern soldiers are honored, for several states have erected distinctive memorials to their soldiers there.

In 1938, at Gettysburg, 1800 Civil War veterans from all over the United States met together to honor their brothers on the seventy-fifth anniversary of the Battle of Gettysburg. An audience of 150,-000 saw President Franklin D. Roosevelt dedicate a memorial—"The Eternal Light Monument"—on Oak Hill.

Together a Confederate soldier and a Grand Army veteran unveiled the memorial on which these words are inscribed:

AN ENDURING LIGHT TO GUIDE US IN UNITY AND FELLOWSHIP

On the shaft is a flame that burns continually which can be seen for twenty miles. In his address that day the President included these words:

On these hills of Gettysburg two brave armies of Americans met in combat. . . . Surely this is all holy ground. . . . Two subsequent wars, both with foreign nations, measurably allayed and softened the ancient passions. It has been left to us of this generation to see the healing made permanent. We are all brothers now in a new understanding.

Twenty years later on Memorial Day 1958, another distinctive event took place in Arlington National Cemetery, at the Tomb of the Unknown Soldier of World War I. Two unidentified men, one representing those of World War II and the other those of the Korean conflict, were interred beside the soldier whose casket had been placed there on Armistice Day in 1921.

There were preliminary selections for the two new Unknown Soldiers. Early in May at Épinal, France, thirteen caskets with bodies of men from all the American cemeteries in Europe and Africa waited side by side. General Edward O'Neill, with battle decorations for three assault landings, walked along solemnly. After pausing with bowed head, the general laid a red and white wreath on the fifth casket from the left. A bugler sounded taps; the selected body was flown to Naples and placed aboard the United States destroyer *Blandy*.

A similar event occurred at Hickam Air Force Base near Honolulu, when Air Force Colonel Glenn T. Eagleston, a veteran of ninety-six combat missions in World War II, selected the unknown man from the Pacific theater. He did so by placing a Hawaiian lei of white carnations on top of one of the six flag-draped coffins. The body of a Korean fighting man was selected at the National Cemetery near Honolulu, and the two caskets were carried home on the cruiser, *Boston.*

At sea off the Virginia capes, the *Blandy* and *Boston* met the *Canberra*, to which the three bodies were transferred. The final choice between the two bodies from the Pacific area was made by a navy hospitalman third class, William R. Charette (a medal of honor winner), who laid a wreath on the coffin at his right. The *Canberra* steamed farther out to sea, and four chaplains, in robes of different faiths, said prayers. When the bearers tilted the platform, the shrouded body of an Unknown Soldier slipped into the waves.

The *Blandy* bore the other two bronze caskets up the Potomac River; a composite guard of honor from the Army, Navy, and Air Force escorted the hearses along the way to the Capitol where many citizens had gathered to honor these dead heroes. As soon as the bodies were taken up the Capitol steps, the Stars and Stripes flew at half-mast over the building. For one day the caskets lay in state in the rotunda while countless Americans passed by in silent tribute.

The two Unknowns were conveyed to Arlington, on Memorial Day, May 30, 1958, followed by units of the Armed Forces, many civilian officials, and members of the diplomatic corps. There was subdued band music along the way; artillery salutes sounded, and jets flew overhead. The two caskets were placed above open crypts, flanking that of the original Unknown Soldier of the First World War.

The ceremonies reached a climax when President Dwight D. Eisenhower conferred medals of honor on the two men, in these simple but meaningful words:

> On behalf of a grateful people, I now present medals of honor to these two unknowns, who gave their lives for the United States of America.

On Memorial Day, in 1960, "The nation's capital today honored in speeches, in the booming of cannon, and with floral tributes the memory of all Americans who died in war."

White House aides placed the Presidential wreath on the Tomb of the Unknowns as an honor guard composed of members of the Army, Navy, Marine Corps, and Air Force stood at attention. From Fort Meade, Maryland, a battery of howitzers gave a twenty-one gun salute to the dead; and the annual ceremony in memory of the Grand Army of the Republic was held in the Arlington Amphitheatre, where Undersecretary of the Navy, Hugh H. Milton, gave the address.

Another special ceremony that day in Washington honored the late Lieutenant General Claire L. Chennault. AMVETS also placed a wreath on the grave of General John A. Logan, commander-in-chief of the G.A.R., who had issued the order that Memorial Day be observed on May 30, 1868.

At the National Cemetery in Memphis, Tennessee, on May 29, 1960, under sponsorship of the American Legion and Veterans of Foreign Wars more than four thousand people gathered. Gold Star mothers placed wreaths at the cemetery's flag; a navy bugler sounded taps, and an eight-man Marine Corps squad fired a salute. Music was supplied by the navy choir from the Memphis Naval Air Station.

The speaker of the day, Dr. C. C. Humphreys, president of Memphis State University, spoke of our pride in material things, and warned against a new kind of warfare waged by the Communists in this country: "Not with guns and marching men, necessarily. They prefer other means: the corruption of our philosophy, the robbing of our native birthright."

Meanwhile across the country audiences heard admonitions regarding our future. Rear Admiral John R. McKinney declared:

> We must not allow our riches to make of us satiated citizens of weak physical characteristics, loose morals, and decreased mentality. If we do so, we are not honoring those departed war heroes whom we memorialized today. They will have died in vain.

At one veterans' cemetery "some 35,000 crosses, row on row were decorated in a floral tribute."

Throughout the world, wherever American soldiers are buried, Memorial Day is observed, in cemeteries in Alaska, Hawaii, Puerto Rico, Holland, Luxembourg, France, Belgium, Italy, the Philippines, and in many South Pacific Islands. It is the time not only for honoring those who made the supreme sacrifice, but for stressing the futility of war and expressing our hopes for a lasting world peace. B. Y. Williams in his inspiring poem, "I Heard the Drums," asks:

> What is the truth mankind must learn
> Before all wars shall cease?

Children's Day—Second Sunday
in June

The second Sunday in June has long been noted by many Protestant churches in the United States as Children's Day. While there had been from time to time Sunday school anniversary days or children's programs at churches, it is not known who originally had the idea of devoting one Sunday service to the interests of boys and girls.

It is believed that the custom may go back to the Old World May Day rite when children carried flowers or tree branches to their churches. On this day boys and girls were confirmed in Lutheran and Roman Catholic churches. At first, the occasion was called Flower Day or Rose Day. Later it was shifted to June, since more flowers were available at that time in northern lands.

The earliest known celebration of a special Children's Day, it is said, took place in Chelsea, Massachusetts, on the second Sunday of June, 1856. This program was arranged by the Reverend Charles H. Leonard of the Universalist Church of the Redeemer, in Chelsea. At this event, which the minister called Rose Day, he baptized boys and girls of the congregation. Later such a program was called Children's Day.

Usually the Methodist Church is given credit for first *formally* recognizing the observance. Its adoption was recommended in 1865. When the General Conference met in 1868 (it convenes every four years), a resolution was passed that Children's Day be celebrated in all Methodist churches on the second Sunday in June. That same year, such a program was conducted in Camden, New Jersey.

At their general convention the preceding year, 1867, the Universalists had established the day as the time for the baptism of boys and girls.

For years, before the setting of a special date for Children's Day, many Presbyterian ministers, and those of other denominations, had devoted much time to training children in Christian living; and on certain Sundays had devoted the day to their interests. In 1883 the General Assembly of Presbyterian Churches declared:

> It thereby designates the second Sunday in June as Children's Day, on which special services for children shall be held, and the vital topics of the Christian nurture and the conversion of the young shall be pressed upon the thought of the entire congregation.

Two years later, leaders at the General Assembly spoke with approval of the way the churches were observing Children's Day and of the hearty support given this project by laymen of Presbyterian churches.

Today Children's Day is observed by various denominations, and their publishing houses usually furnish materials for programs, and for ways to make the day effective. In some places the date is the end of the Bible school term and time for advancing to higher classes. Therefore, the children receive promotion certificates; and some are baptized and taken into church membership.

At the morning service the minister may preach a "sermonette," especially for the boys and girls. However, the children themselves usually furnish the exercises. Churches are decorated with flowers and greenery, and the youth choirs march in carrying flowers or branches. These groups furnish musical numbers; perhaps a cantata is performed or a pageant is staged. Programs often include poems and Scripture readings relating to children, and showing Christ's attitude toward them. In one congregation more than a hundred boys and girls—some dressed in costumes of other lands—went up to the altar where a globe had been placed. There they added flags of many countries, and prayed for world peace.

In recent years Children's Day has taken on added significance, since this special date often coincides with that of the baccalaureate or vesper services for high school and college graduates. As a result, various churches have adopted the idea of having not only the younger boys and girls honored but also the youth who are completing their public school or college work. These graduates appear in the caps and gowns of their individual institutions, receive recognition for their accomplishments, and are given Bibles as mementoes of this occasion. Some pastors have used the following texts: "Children of God," "Children Are Everyone's Business," and "Building Tomorrow's World Today."

In some churches Children's Day is a special time for boys and girls to learn the joy of giving to some particular missionary project, or to student aid funds. One denomination has especially stressed this point; and annually on this day gathers funds to help young men and women complete their college courses. Some who have proved their college ability by outstanding work may be given outright scholarships, while others may borrow from a student loan fund. This money is to be repaid in a few years so that others may have the benefit of its use.

So this institution of Children's Day has proved to be a worthwhile church festival—the time when the importance of young people as the future supporters of the church is recognized and emphasized.

Flag Day—June 14

It's rather strange that, although the United States is among the world's youngest *great* nations, our flag is one of the oldest of the national emblems. In fact, it is older than the present Union Jack of Great Britain and the French and Italian ensigns.

Each year on June 14, the Stars and Stripes are flown and especially honored, for on this date we celebrate the birthday of "Old Glory." This popular nickname is credited to a sea captain, William Driver, of Salem, Massachusetts.

Before Captain Driver sailed for a round-the-globe voyage in 1824, a group of ladies went aboard his ship and presented him with a beautiful 12 by 24 foot flag which they had made. As it waved from the masthead, the captain was so impressed that he exclaimed proudly, "Old Glory! Old Glory!" And ever since that time, this name has been used and has become symbolic of love for our national emblem.

During the Revolutionary War, before our present ensign was designed and accepted, several different ones had been used by colonial fighting units. These included the Liberty Tree banner of New England, which showed a green pine tree on a field of white, with the words: "An Appeal to God."

The Culpeper County (Virginia) flag with a coiled rattlesnake, carried the warning: "Don't Tread on Me!" Also stars and stripes had been seen on some early colonial flags. For example, there were thirteen alternate red and white stripes on the "Grand Union" (with the British Union Jack in the upper left-hand corner). This ensign was raised by General Washington over his headquarters at Cambridge, Massachusetts, on January 1, 1776. During the preceding month—on December 3, 1775—Captain John Paul Jones had flown this on his ship, *Alfred*.

In 1775, the Continental Congress named a committee composed of Benjamin Franklin, Thomas Lynch, and Benjamin Harrison, to suggest a design for a new national emblem. Later, at Philadelphia, on June 14, 1777, Congress resolved:

> That the flag of the thirteen United States be thirteen stripes, alternate red and white; that the union be thirteen stars, white in a blue field, representing a new constellation.

It is said that George Washington thus described the make-up of the new banner:

> We take the stars from heaven, the red from our mother country, separating it by white stripes, thus showing that we have separated from her, and the white stripes shall go down to posterity, representing liberty.

Also a contemporary writer declared that the blue was "taken from the edge of the Covenanters Banner of Scotland" and denoted the covenant of the new country against oppression; that the stars placed in a circle signified eternity; and that the red was a symbol of daring, and the white, of purity.

The five-pointed star—instead of the British six-pointed one—*may* have been chosen because of its likeness to that of our ally, France. Early flags were not always uniform about the way the stars in the Union were arranged. They appeared in a circle in the first banner raised and saluted by American troops. This event occurred at Fort Stanwix, New York, August 2, 1777. "Old Glory," so history tells us, was first under fire at the Battle of the Brandywine, on September 11 of that same year.

At once the new ensign was raised on our naval vessels. In the fall of 1777, Captain John Paul Jones sailed for France to inform our minister, Benjamin Franklin, that the British general, Burgoyne, had surrendered to the Continental Army at Saratoga. Franklin was trying to persuade the French government to help us with men, money, ships, and arms. The news carried by Captain Jones influenced them to give us aid. As the American ship left Quiberon Bay in February 1778, the French men-of-war gave the new American flag flying on the *Ranger* a nine-gun salute. This was the first time foreign vessels saluted the Stars and Stripes.

Vermont entered the Union in 1791, and Kentucky the following year. Two stripes and two stars were added to the flag to represent them. Such a fifteen-star and fifteen-stripe ensign was flying over Fort McHenry that September night in 1814 when Francis Scott

Key was inspired to write our national anthem, "The Star Spangled Banner."

When five more states became part of the country, there were many arguments about the additional stars and stripes. Members of Congress realized that if a stripe were added for each new state, the flag would either be too large, or the stripes so narrow they couldn't be easily distinguished. Consequently, it was decided to return to the thirteen stripes, to honor the original colonies, and to add a new star for each state. In 1818 President Monroe signed a bill, including these sections:

> That from and after the Fourth of July next, the flag of the United States be thirteen horizontal stripes, alternate red and white; that the union be twenty stars in a blue field.
>
> That on the admission of every new state into the Union one star be added to the union of the flag, and that such addition shall take effect on the Fourth of July next succeeding such admission.

With the rapid entrance of more states, our flag underwent many changes in the number of stars and their arrangement. Then with the admission of Arizona, the forty-eighth state, in 1912, the banner remained the same until 1959. Two stars have since been added for Alaska and Hawaii, the latter's becoming official on July 4, 1960. In August 1959 President Eisenhower displayed a copy of our latest flag; now the Union contains fifty stars in nine rows. Five rows have six stars each, the other four, five each.

Since our flag was adopted on June 14, 1777, it has been seen in many parts of the world. Various American flags are still preserved in national museums because of the roles they played in historical events. These include flags borne in various wars in which we have engaged.

It is said that the largest United States banner ever made was created for the J. L. Hudson Department Store in the city of Detroit. It was ordered in 1923 to commemorate the fifth anniversary of Armistice Day. This banner is 270 by 90 feet and required 2,800 yards of bunting, at a cost of about $4,000.

Another flag that has a story connected with it was fashioned in California in 1846 during the Mexican War, not by an American woman but by a gracious Spanish senora, Dona Refugio Bandini. Her husband, Juan, owned a big ranch in Lower California, also extensive holdings near San Diego. Their town house in this port was the center of local social life.

In this conflict—the Mexican War—Juan Bandini favored the American cause. (Later, his lands in Mexico were confiscated because he had aided the Americans.) When Major Hensley landed at Ensenada, Mexico, with two hundred men to march northward to meet Commodore Stockton for the attack on Los Angeles, the Bandinis were at their ranch below the border. There Don Juan Bandini furnished the major hundreds of horses and cattle and eight ox-drawn carts.

The Bandini family traveled northward with the soldiers. When they were about fifteen miles from San Diego, Major Hensley expressed his regret that he had no American flag to head his column when entering San Diego. At once Dona Refugio Bandini came to the officer's rescue. The procession stopped; and from the clothes worn by her little daughters she managed to assemble the necessary red, white, and blue materials. When the improvised ensign was finished, the group moved on toward the town with the new flag fluttering triumphantly in the breeze.

That evening in San Diego the band serenaded the Bandini family. Commodore Stockton and his officers thanked the senora and gave her this promise: "Whatever you ask of the United States, it shall be granted."

This same banner was used in the march of the six hundred Marines under Commodore Stockton and Kearney's Dragoons as they entered and took over the pueblo of Los Angeles. It was a good omen that the first American flag here was made by a native Californian; and soon the settlers from the East and Californians were living happily together under the Stars and Stripes.

In 1877, just a century after our flag had been agreed upon, Congress declared that it should be flown over public buildings on June 14. A school principal, George Balch, of New York City, instituted a patriotic program to celebrate the day in 1889. Soon afterward the Board of Education urged all schools to have special exercises on Flag Day. In 1893, the mayor of Philadelphia asked that the Stars and Stripes be flown over all civic buildings and that schools, too, take note of this anniversary. Four years later, New York followed suit, and the idea soon spread to other communities.

The first school in our country over which the American flag is said to have flown was a small log building in the Catamount Hills in Massachusetts. This occurred in 1812, but the practice did not become general until many years later.

In 1916 President Woodrow Wilson proclaimed that Flag Day be observed each year on June 14. (Now it is celebrated throughout the land, but is not a legal holiday except in Pennsylvania.)

A year later, in an address to the people to explain our entering World War I, the President said:

> We celebrate the day of its [the flag's] birth and from its birth until now it has witnessed great history, has floated on high, the symbol of great events, of a great plan of life, worked out by a great people.

Many clubs and organizations stress the importance of Flag Day and sponsor patriotic programs on June 14. Dr. Bernard J. Cigrand, of Chicago, is said to have founded the American Flag Day Association, and promoted the first public observance in 1906. As a young man, he had taught school at Waubeka, Wisconsin, and there he conducted yearly flag ceremonies. The old schoolhouse has been restored, and a bronze tablet placed there, honoring Dr. Cigrand.

The first Flag Week (May 23–30, 1926) was started "to inculcate and promote greater love and respect for the Stars and Stripes."

The Fraternal Order of Elks has long made a study of our flag and what it has contributed to our history. The members have a special ritual in which they present various ensigns used in the United States. In 1908, at their national convention, the Elks pledged themselves to hold yearly observances on June 14.

On such occasions there is a procession of patriotic organizations, with massing of the colors, the Pledge of Allegiance to the Flag, a prayer, the history of Old Glory, a tribute to it, various appropriate selections by the Elks band and their Choraleers, ending with all singing the national anthem. These all make up a beautiful and inspiring program.

Naturally, in connection with the American flag and Flag Day, we think of the Pledge of Allegiance to it. The original one read:

> I pledge allegiance to my flag and the Republic for which it stands— one nation indivisible—with liberty and justice for all.

Some years ago, the words, "of the United States of America," were added to make it more specific; and in 1954 the insertion of "under God" reaffirmed "the transcendance of religious faith in America's heritage and future." Now we say:

I pledge allegiance to the flag of the United States of America and to the Republic for which it stands, one Nation under God, indivisible, with liberty and justice for all.

Beliefs seem to vary as to who actually should be given credit for the original pledge. In 1892, the personnel of the *Youth's Companion* editorial staff wanted to lead a "re-dedication to Americanism." One plan was to raise the national flag over all public schools on Columbus Day 1892. The head of the *Youth's Companion,* James B. Upham, spoke of a new flag salute which Francis Bellamy, a former minister, thought should be "a warm, human, simple pledge," rather than a stiff, formal one.

According to Margarette S. Miller (who has done much research on this matter), Francis Bellamy is the real author of the pledge. On the other hand, the Upham family and others maintain it was the work of James B. Upham. Miss Miller states that Mr. Upham had praised Mr. Bellamy for this work, which the latter always regarded as the best thing he had ever written. The *Youth's Companion* published a history of the Pledge of Allegiance, giving Mr. Upham credit for the first draft, "afterwards condensed and perfected by him and his associates of the *Companion* staff."

Today Flag Day is observed on June 14 by Presidential Proclamation. Recently, because of troubled world conditions, patriotic leaders in many communities have been urging greater participation in these ceremonies on the part of all citizens.

For example, in 1960, in Memphis, Tennessee, the committee asked that "now, as seldom before, the true colors of every citizen shall be displayed before every home, on the national emblem's birthday." Some interesting contests were put on to stimulate interest; young people went out to get pledges from householders that they would display the flag on June 14; and the winner received a fifty dollar savings bond and a fifty star flag. Home owners also had the chance to get a new flag by guessing the number of homes that were cooperating in this project.

This Flag Day observance was sponsored by the American Legion Post No. 1. The ceremonies took place at Court Square, with "a concert by the Admiral's Band from the Memphis Naval Air Station, and exhibitions by an Army color guard, Navy drill team, Marine Corps drum and bugle corps, and a flyover of Air Force planes." Boy Scouts and other local groups also took part in the celebration.

It is interesting to note, too, that many Americans reverence our flag and show this not only on this special holiday, but on other occasions. On September 19, 1960, the *New York Mirror* had a picture of Old Glory on its front page. This happened during the time that many foreign celebrities were in the city to attend sessions of the United Nations. The picture of the flag brought such interesting reactions as the following. Lillian Waugher of Brooklyn wrote:

It thrilled me when I saw that photograph of Old Glory on the front page of the *Mirror*. Why give our enemies headlines? I'd minimize their presence to the last degree.

Edward Bruder of Roselle, New Jersey, commented:

The *Mirror* did itself proud by printing a picture of Old Glory, the symbol of unity, truth, and peace. The Reds couldn't have been ignored in a better way. Well done, *Mirror*.

And it was Robert Brown of New York City who declared:

Patriotism is not dead. Yet there is hardly one U.S. Flag flying here in New York. All businesses, institutions, and private individuals should display the Flag at least for the duration of the UN sessions to remind all foreign visitors—K. etc.—that the American people are united in this world crisis.

Father's Day—Third Sunday in June

The third Sunday in June is Father's Day in this country, the time when the man of the house gets unusual attention and is really "King for a Day." This holiday is not so old as others, but it has a worthwhile object—to cherish "the honor and dignity of fatherhood."

In various nations round the globe, the father's role in the family differs, just as it has since ancient days. In some places the father "rules the roost"; in Japan, for example, he demands and receives respect from every member of the family. He walks ahead of his wife when they go out together, is the first served at meals, and makes decisions for his family. Here in the United States the father is supposedly the head, although if he has an especially strong-minded wife, he may take a second place.

Often when such a project as Father's Day starts, in a land as big as ours, more than one person may think of the idea at about the same time. As in the case of Mother's Day, there are conflicting accounts as to who really initiated Father's Day.

For example; Mrs. Charles Clayton of Fairmont, West Virginia, believed that honoring fathers was a good thing. At her request, at the Central Church in her town, the minister, Dr. Robert T. Webb, conducted a Father's Day service on July 5, 1908. Another source claims that the observance started in Vancouver, Washington, for in 1912 the Reverend J. H. Harrington, of the Irvington Methodist Church, had a day for honoring fathers. (It had been suggested in the *Portland Oregonian* during the previous year.)

Mrs. Walter H. Burgess, of Miami, Florida, stated that in 1919, when she was a young girl of fifteen living in Drewry's Bluff, Virginia, she had written to a newspaper suggesting that fathers be given tributes. In June 1921, she persuaded the governor to proclaim a Father's Day. Then, in 1932, Mrs. Burgess registered the name, "National Father's Day Association," with the U.S. Patent Office.

One source states that at the time she had not heard of Mrs. John Bruce Dodd's work in Spokane; so later Mrs. Burgess withdrew her claims to priority in establishing the day.

When he was president of the Uptown Lions Club Harry C. Meek, of Chicago, promoted the project of Father's Day. He says he first thought of it on Mother's Day, in 1915, when visiting his boyhood home at Carrollton, Kentucky. At once he began to talk about the idea before different Lions Clubs; members helped him promote it by setting the third Sunday in June (nearest his birthday, which came on June 25) as the date. Mr. Meek received a gold watch from the Lions Clubs of America inscribed:

To Harry C. Meek, Originator of Father's Day
June 25, 1920

He called on President Harding and President Coolidge and asked them to proclaim a national Father's Day. However, both refused to do so, fearing that commercialism might become connected with it. Congress failed to pass such a resolution, and to date has not done so. Mr. Meek spent more than twenty years promoting the project and has always refused to endorse any products for Father's Day gifts. He had promised President Harding he would never commercialize the day.

No doubt these are all valid claims; however, according to several sources, Mrs. John Bruce Dodd of Spokane, Washington, "was primarily responsible" for furthering this holiday.

As she listened to a Mother's Day sermon in Spokane, Washington, in 1909, her thoughts kept turning to her father, William Jackson Smart, known as "Billy Buttons." Now that she was married and had a child of her own, she could appreciate more keenly than ever the sort of courage it took for her father to face the tragic early loss of her mother and shoulder the full responsibility of bringing up his six children—five boys and a girl, singlehanded. The more she thought of it, the more she became convinced that fathers, too, should have a day.

After the sermon, Mrs. Dodd spoke to Dr. Rasmus about her idea. He was enthusiastic about it and promised to help her get the project started.

During the year, she discussed the plan with others and it was well received. In the spring of 1910, Mrs. Dodd presented a petition to the Reverend Conrad Bluhm, president of the Spokane Ministerial Association, asking that he suggest to the members of the association that they select one Sunday in June (the month of her father's birthday) to remind their parishioners of the appreciation owed to fathers. The ministers agreed to preach on this theme, and the YMCA also helped to sponsor the event. The mayor of Spokane issued the first Father's Day proclamation; soon Governor M. E. Hay became interested; and he set the third Sunday in June for the state-wide observance.

In Spokane, during the week before the celebration, many merchants arranged window displays, calling attention to the day. For instance, John Matthieson showed the portrait of George Washington, the Father of his Country, with the caption, "Remember Father."

On that first Father's Day (June 19, 1910), when Mrs. Dodd attended the Centenary Presbyterian Church, she was pleased by the tribute Mr. Bluhm paid fathers. He used the topic, "The Knighthood that never retreats." She considered this an appropriate text as her father had truly lived by the Golden Rule and had never flinched in his duties.

After this initial observance in Spokane, newspapers carried the story, and soon other communities made plans for such services. That noted orator, William Jennings Bryan, was one of the first to congratulate Mrs. Dodd for promoting this worthwhile project; he endorsed the idea, saying, "Too much emphasis cannot be placed on the relation between parent and child."

In 1916 from his desk in the White House, President Wilson pressed a button to begin the observance; this unfurled a flag at a celebration in Spokane. Eight years later, in 1924, Calvin Coolidge recommended that Father's Day be noted in all the states, declaring that such an occasion would bring about a clearer relationship between fathers and their children, and also impress upon the former their obligations.

At present, the movement is sponsored by the National Father's Day Committee, founded in 1935. It is a nonprofit public service organization, "dedicated to building a democratic world through wholesome child upbringing." The group emphasizes the need for closer home relations and suggests ten commandments for fathers to follow in building their children's future.

These include responsibility for the boys' and girls' behavior and security, for their mental and spiritual development, and for the home as their haven. A real father shares the youngsters' activities, wins their confidence, recognizes their weaknesses, and helps them correct them, aids in solving their problems, wins their respect and devotion (doesn't demand it), and finally—"He tries to be what his child thinks he is."

Each year the National Father's Day Committee stresses a certain theme. In 1960 the special purpose was to inculcate this idea: "Juvenile integrity starts in the home."

The committee also gives citations to outstanding fathers in various lines of work. Its highest award carries the title, Father of the Year. It has been given to such men as former President Eisenhower and President Truman, General Mark Clark and General Mac-Arthur, Marine hero, Al Schmid, Henry Cabot Lodge, Jr., Drew Pearson, General Sarnoff, Warren Austin, Dr. Ralph Bunche, Paul Hoffman, Senator Estes Kefauver, and Justice William O. Douglas.

Senator Kefauver emphasized the importance of Father's Day by saying:

> With the exception of setting the right example, I think the next most important element in instilling a genuine respect for law and order in our children is that of being real comrades to our children. Often the improper "bending of the twig" comes when we are so busy with our own interests that we leave our children to the influence of others.

Of course Mrs. Dodd has been thrilled by the wide spread of this yearly observance; she believes its great popularity is due to its emphasis on safeguarding marriage, the father's place in the home, and the right training of children. She suggested wearing a red rose for a living father, and a white one for the deceased. Mrs. Dodd was pleased that her father (who died in 1919, at the age of seventy-seven), lived to see nine Father's Day celebrations. Her husband, John Bruce Dodd, helped her promote the holiday until his death in 1945.

Mrs. Dodd is a graduate of the Chicago Art Institute, "a home-maker, author, artist, poet, song writer, grandmother, and business woman, all with much success." However, her major interest has been Father's Day. She declares the project has developed far beyond her greatest hopes. "In my heart," she says, "I cannot reckon the riches in happiness that I have realized through Father's Day." She is very proud of the excellent work done by the National Father's Day Committee.

Her only child, John Bruce Dodd, Jr., (associated with the National Park Service in Washington, D.C.) not long ago was named the "Ideal Father" for the District of Columbia. Of this his mother remarked: "I was thrilled but not surprised, for John was an ideal son to his father. And ideal sons are the material from which ideal fathers are made."

The "mother of Father's Day" has never attempted to cash in on her idea, and she has refused hundreds of offers to endorse products in connection with the observance. This does not mean that she is opposed to giving gifts at this time or thinks the day too commercial. Mrs. Dodd recalls that back in 1910 she asked Spokane merchants to display gifts. "After all," she asks, "why should the greatest giver of gifts not be on the receiving end at least once a year?"

And even though some decry the commercial side of the occasion, Mrs. Dodd asserted:

> The gift idea was included in the original program and is as old as the day itself. I'm convinced that it's a sacred part of the holiday, as the giver is spiritually enriched in the tribute paid his father.

In various communities it has become a custom for a committee to select a local "Father of the Year." Nominations giving the person's qualifications are sent to the committee; after studying the entries, the group makes its selection. Of course, it is a great honor for a father to be chosen for this award; in addition, the local merchants also contribute worthwhile gifts to the winner of the citation.

Mrs. Dodd, when asked in 1953 how Father's Day should be spent, voiced the same thoughts she had, years ago: "It should include family attendance at church, a little gift for Dad, and some tender words you've always longed to say to him."

We Americans should be grateful to the various persons who promulgated the idea of this holiday, and especially to Mrs. Dodd, whose love for her devoted father, Billy Smart, inspired her to carry on this distinctive project.

American Independence Day— July 4

On July 4, 1776, the Continental Congress, assembled in Philadelphia, announced that it had adopted the Declaration of Independence from the mother country, England.

Therefore, our proudest secular holiday commemorates the birth of our nation. It is a legal one in all states and possessions; and no matter in what part of the globe Americans find themselves, they observe this important date.

July 4 is noted too for other reasons. It is the birth date of such people as Nathaniel Hawthorne, Calvin Coolidge, Stephen Foster, and the Italian patriot, Garibaldi; also several important events have occurred on July 4.

Providence, Rhode Island, was founded in 1636 by Roger Williams; in 1777 John Paul Jones raised the Stars and Stripes over his ship, the *Ranger;* July 4, 1802 was the opening day of the United States Military Academy at West Point. By a strange coincidence, while the country was joyously celebrating the semi-centennial observance of our independence, two former Presidents, John Adams and Thomas Jefferson, died on July 4, 1826.

Two years later in 1828—the last surviving signer of the Declaration of Independence, Charles Carroll of Carrollton, turned up the first shovelful of dirt to start construction of our earliest important railroad, the Baltimore and Ohio. A third President, James Monroe, died July 4, 1831; and the cornerstone of the Washington Monument (the first to honor the Father of his Country) was laid on this date, in 1848. The surrender of Vicksburg occurred on our Independence Day in 1863.

Just after the beginning of this century, in 1903, President Theodore Roosevelt opened the new Pacific cable via Hawaii by sending a message to the Philippines; and forty-three years later, on July 4, those islands became a free and independent republic.

During that hot summer of 1776, when the members of the Continental Congress were debating the matter of whether to declare their independence from Great Britain, it was a dark and dangerous time for the colonists. Howe's army was expected at any time in New York; in Canada, Burgoyne's men had driven the Continentals into swamps, where many died of smallpox. Several of the colonies had failed to send their quotas of ammunition; and more and more Tories were joining the British regulars.

On June 7, 1776, Richard Henry Lee (who for some time had been advocating Colonial independence) introduced into Congress a resolution declaring:

> That these United Colonies are, and of right ought to be, free and independent states, that they are absolved from all allegiance to the British Crown, and that all political connection between them and the state of Great Britain is, and ought to be totally dissolved.

This resolution came up again on June 10, when a committee of five men, headed by Thomas Jefferson, and including John Adams, Benjamin Franklin, Philip Livingston, and Roger Sherman, was selected. This group, working in Philadelphia, was asked to "embody the spirit and purpose of the resolution in a Declaration of Independence."

(Its consideration was postponed for three weeks, as not all the representatives of the thirteen colonies were ready to vote for independence; also the proponents hoped "to bring the doubters into line.")

When the committee was about to begin its work, Thomas Jefferson suggested that John Adams draw up the document. But the latter objected, saying Jefferson could write ten times better than he. The others agreed to let him make the first draft. So Jefferson got to work at a desk he had made himself, in a room at Market and Seventh streets.

On June 28, the group presented the draft; various changes were suggested and made. The discussion of the Declaration continued on July 3 and 4; and late on the afternoon of July 4, 1776, when the daylight was fading, the vote was taken. New York abstained from voting; Pennsylvania and South Carolina voted No; Delaware was divided; but nine other colonies voted in favor of the resolution.

History relates that John Hancock, president of the Continental Congress, was the only signer that day, and he did so just to make it official. All that night, the printer, John Dunlap, and his helpers got out the Declaration on "broadsides" (handbills) which were distributed the following day. The first newspaper to print the document was the *Pennsylvania Evening Post*, on July 6, 1776. After that, the news soon spread through the colonies.

At noon, on July 8, 1776, the Declaration was read for the first time in Independence Square. There was some cheering; however, one contemporary reported that not many "respectable" persons were in the crowd. That evening, for the second time, Philadelphia citizens heard the famous document read at the commons on the edge of the city. There were bonfires and pealing church bells. Also the great bell in Independence Hall rang out. At first its name was the "Province Bell"; later this was changed to "Liberty Bell"; for it had an appropriate inscription:

Proclaim Liberty Throughout All the Land Unto
All the Inhabitants Thereof

By order of General Washington, on July 9, 1776, the Declaration was read "in a clear voice" to his troops, in City Hall Park in New York. Then Boston rejoiced over the adoption, on July 18, with the firing of cannon, while chimes sounded from church steeples. After the news of the adoption had reached remote communities of the colonies, loyal patriots celebrated the event.

On July 19, 1776, the Continental Congress ordered that the Declaration of Independence be "engrossed on parchment" and signed by every member of the Congress. It was on August 2 that the men began to add their signatures; but it was not until several weeks later that this work was completed. By this time things had taken a decided turn for the worse. Washington was outnumbered four to one, so it was really a dangerous proceeding for these fifty-six patriots to sign this paper.

John Hancock—so it is said—signed "with a great flourish," and declared, "There, King George can read that without spectacles!" And as Hancock said, "We must all hang together," Benjamin Franklin replied, "If we don't, we shall all hang separately." When one delegate remarked to Charles Carroll that it should not disturb *him* to sign the document, since there were so many Carrolls, the latter answered by signing, "Charles Carroll of Carrollton," and added, "There is only *one* Carrollton."

It was an inspiring and solemn occasion when those men gave their pledge, by their signatures:

> And for the support of this Declaration, with a firm reliance on the protection of Divine Providence, we mutually pledge to each other our Lives, our Fortunes, and our sacred Honor.

The idea of celebrating the anniversary of the adoption of the Declaration started in Philadelphia the next year, 1777. Bells rang, cannon boomed, and at night there were bonfires and fireworks; also the soldiers at Morristown got an extra gill of rum that day. At a three o'clock dinner for notables the music—strange to say—was furnished by some Hessians who had been taken prisoners at Trenton, New Jersey.

As John Adams walked around Philadelphia that evening, he was delighted to notice that many citizens had placed lighted candles at their windows. He wrote, "I think it was the most splendid illumination I ever saw." However, some homes were dark, and a contemporary reported that overenthusiastic patriots threw rocks through several such windows.

After the Revolutionary soldiers were disbanded on November 5, 1783, some went west to Kentucky, Ohio, and on to the Mississippi and Missouri, where they took up land. They carried with them the love of their country, and in after years in small settlements such men used to meet on July 4 and talk over the events of their struggle for freedom.

(Boston had been celebrating a patriotic day on March 5, the anniversary of the Boston Massacre; however, in 1883 they changed to July 4, and observed their first real Independence Day.)

In 1788, one of the longest and most talked about Fourth of July parades in our history took place in Philadelphia. As there was much rejoicing over the final ratification of the Constitution, this was a very special Fourth. Church bells aroused the people early, and all turned out for the grand procession.

One man rode the horse on which Rochambeau had led the French forces at Yorktown. A carriage shaped like an eagle and drawn by six white horses carried the Chief Justice of the Supreme Court of Pennsylvania. Ten men walked along, with linked arms, as a symbol of the ten states that had ratified the Constitution. A float showing the Federal Building carried a structure whose roof was supported by thirteen columns, three of which were unfinished.

The most spectacular sight was the federal ship, the *Union*, 34 feet long, mounted with 20 guns. Hundreds of citizens from various crafts and organizations, clergymen of different faiths, and other persons took part in this long parade.

The marchers went to Bush Hill where the oration was delivered. Tables were spread with a hearty "cold collation"; at once the hungry crowd thronged around them, ate, and quenched their thirst with American cider or beer. That evening ten ships in the Delaware River were illuminated, and fireworks added to the brilliant scene. Then, "to top it all," nature cooperated "by festooning the sky with an aurora borealis that must have seemed to patriotic hearts a sign of heavenly approbation."

Soon after the beginning of the new century, other places began to celebrate the Fourth of July. By 1810, New York and the national capital were putting on elaborate observances. The idea later spread to the South, but it was discontinued during the Civil War and for some time afterward.

Gradually, there came about a pattern, what we call the "old-fashioned Fourth," consisting of bell ringing, displays of the Stars and Stripes, salutes at sunrise, noon, and evening from forts and men-of-war, parades with militia units, veterans, floats, bands, and marchers from many civic groups. And, after the parade came the "patriotic exercises," including the reading of the Declaration, singing of national songs, and the chief feature—the lengthy oration.

In those times, before radio and television, many persons really enjoyed such oratory. In those Fourth of July speeches the virtues of the Pilgrim fathers, the heroic exertions and sufferings of the soldiers of the Revolution, the growth and power of the Republic, and the great future, which expands before her, were the staple ideas.

It was considered a great honor to be asked to be the orator of the day; and it is said that each year Daniel Webster left his duties in Washington, D.C., to go to his home town in New Hampshire to deliver an eloquent two-hour address.

When the gold rush called thousands of Americans to the West Coast, they clung to the old customs and enjoyed celebrating the Fourth of July. The first observance took place in Los Angeles in 1847, during the Mexican War when Colonel Stevenson and his New York Volunteers dedicated Fort Moore, on the hill, west of the Plaza. This was named to honor gallant Captain Moore, killed in the Battle of San Pasquale by the California Lancers.

Beforehand the colonel had sent some soldiers out to the mountains, where they cut down two tall trees to make a flagpole. At daybreak on July 4 Americans marched up Fort Hill, and the flag was raised on the new pole. The Declaration of Independence was read, both in English and Spanish so the native Californians could understand it. Colonel Stevenson made the speech of dedication; the men had the rest of the day free; and the celebration was climaxed that evening by a gay ball, attended by many of the native senoritas of the "Sleepy Pueblo."

In 1853, there were rousing Independence Day festivities that lasted three days at San Pedro Bay, where a great world harbor now is located. This was put on by a patriotic young Easterner, Phineas Banning, from Wilmington, Delaware, who was starting a forwarding business there. He ran some stages which carried passengers to and from Los Angeles. His lighters also brought travelers and freight in from ships anchored in the roadstead. (Later he founded Wilmington, California, and became the "Father of Los Angeles Harbor.")

On July 3, people began to arrive at the bay by stages, on horseback, afoot, or in ox carts. Banning and his partner had bought quantities of food and drink from the ship, *Laura Bevan*, anchored in the bay. These were spread on a table and everyone helped himself. Since there was no place to sleep (the only building was the old hide house of the San Gabriel Mission), the fun went on all night. Next day, on the Fourth, about a thousand visitors marched around a flagpole and drank a toast of champagne to President Franklin Pierce. On the fifth, a tired but happy crowd of people went back to their ranchos or homes in Los Angeles.

The most important Independence Day, long remembered in Southern California, came in 1876, when the United States observed its centennial. All homes and business buildings in the pueblo were decorated with greenery and bunting. The parade was the longest ever staged and included veterans of the Mexican War and members of varied organizations. Pretty girls, representing the Goddess of Liberty, Peace, Plenty, and Columbia, rode on decorated floats. Later, about sixteen hundred persons gathered to hear the exercises; band music, singing of patriotic songs, reading of the Declaration, a centennial poem, the usual oration, followed by much food, various pastimes, and fireworks.

Sometimes we hear people longing for the "good old-fashioned Fourth," when they lighted firecrackers with "punk"—that Chinese import—and also had the thrill of setting off giant crackers. Since many serious accidents occurred both to adults and children, gradually there came a trend toward a safer and saner Fourth. Now most states have outlawed the use of such dangerous items.

The fact that schools are not in session on Independence Day makes this observance more of a family, or community affair. Varied celebrations are held across the continent. At many playgrounds, trained directors plan entertaining programs that impress young Americans with the significance of the day.

Indians meet for three days over the Fourth, at Flagstaff, Arizona, and hold rodeos and other ceremonies. (This began back in the 1880's.) The colonial capital of Virginia, at Williamsburg, notes the Fourth on July 25; for the good news of the adoption of the Declaration at Philadelphia did not reach there in 1776 until three weeks later.

Since 1843, Lititz, in eastern Pennsylvania, has had a distinctive and beautiful observance. During the winter, thousands of tallow candles are made in old-fashioned tin molds. Then on July 4 the citizens gather at Lititz Spring Park. In the Baby Parade many small youngsters, dressed in patriotic costumes, ride on diminutive floats, decorated in our national colors.

A Queen of the Candles, selected from the senior class of the high school, reigns over the ceremonies. That evening, at the park, boys light the candles, many of which float in the waters. The community joins in this beautiful project, which has no religious significance, but is their unique fashion of noting Independence Day.

Westerners and visitors who yearn to take part in a real old-fashioned Fourth can do so in the small town (only three hundred inhabitants) of Bridgeport, in Mono County, California, on the east side of the snow-covered Sierras.

Before the ten o'clock parade, people gather at the county court-house, where the Declaration of Independence is read. Numerous flags are displayed, and buildings are adorned with red-white-and-blue bunting. Children parade on decorated bicycles, and then comes a great event—a real pie-eating contest. All kinds of persons are in the crowd at Bridgeport, including Indians; and from neighboring ranchos come cattlemen riding good horses with glittering silver-mounted trappings. You can take your own picnic lunch to this affair or buy a real barbecued meal. In the afternoon there are sports events and a baseball game.

In decided contrast to this western Fourth, was one put on by citizens of Scarsdale, New York, in 1959. Instead of spending funds for fireworks, they gave money to the American Korean Foundation,

> . . . which includes help for orphans and Boy and Girl Scouts, the establishment of a special guidance clinic, and vocational training. Scarsdale was awarded the George Washington Medal of Honor by the Freedom Foundation for this effort.

The program for that holiday consisted of a patriotic play, band music, and featured Korean music and dancing. In 1960 they planned to focus attention on Morocco, which had "suffered tragically . . . from drought, earthquake, and the use of adulterated cooking oil." Scarsdale's fine example has been followed by other communities.

During the decade of the 1950's, even though there were many world problems and people were haunted by the A-bomb specter, on Independence Day Americans re-dedicated shrines and battle-fields, where their ancestors had fought for freedom. The governor of Florida spoke at Valley Forge; fireworks attracted thousands to the Washington Monument; and great crowds celebrated at Boston Common, a cradle of American liberty. At the old State House there, now a museum, the Declaration was read by an honor student from the Boston Latin School, one of the earliest in the country. And out in Texas there were rodeos and cowboy reunions; at Belton, one of the oldest ones was given, and four candidates for governor took part.

Philadelphia, always in the forefront in Fourth of July celebrations, noted the 175th anniversay in 1951 by recreating the original dramatic scene of the adoption of the Declaration. A cast of 100 re-enacted history "in all the colorful splendor of Colonial days."

In addition, the City of Brotherly Love put on an unusual "hallowed earth" ceremony. Soil had been brought from Revolutionary battlegrounds of the original colonies and mixed with that of Independence Square. Oak seedlings were planted in it; these were "symbolic of new life springing from earth consecrated by the patriots of 1778." Pots with such seedlings in this special soil were sent to the governors of the forty-eight states.

Washington, D.C. marked the 182nd anniversay in 1958 with a different ceremony. More than 200,000 persons jammed the shores of the Potomac River to see "Theodore Roosevelt Island" dedicated under the glare of the nation's largest display of fireworks. Governor Theodore Roosevelt McKeldin, of Maryland, gave the address of dedication. This island, part of the National Park system, was termed "a place where men may be inspired by Theodore Roosevelt's ideals." It is administered by the Interior Department as a wild life preserve and a site for "peace and quiet."

The 1959 Fourth of July was a "banner day" in more ways than one. For, on it, the new flag, with forty-nine stars, honoring Alaska—the first change in our national ensign, since 1912—became legal.

The first official forty-nine star flag was raised just after midnight at Fort McHenry, in Baltimore, where 145 years before Francis Scott Key had seen the British bombard the city. That evening in the national capital, there was a forty-five minute fireworks display to mark Alaska's entering the Union.

Since so many of the flags flown over the Capitol that day were asked for, one paper reported:

> From midnight, through the dawn's early light, eight arm-weary Capitol guards raised and lowered 1,072 new 49-star flags over the Capitol today.

Several of these ensigns were sent at once by air to be used that same day in celebrating the Fourth.

On July 4, 1960, another new flag with fifty stars (five rows of six stars and four of five each) was flown to denote that Hawaii had become our fiftieth state. This occurred at 12:01 at Fort McHenry. However, it is said that a new banner had been raised ahead of this one at Guam, a United States territory, west of the international date line. When Secretary of the Interior Fred A. Seaton "tugged the halyard to raise the flag at Fort McHenry," he declared that the admission of Hawaii demonstrates "the unparalleled recognition of the rights of man wherever the American flag flies."

At Honolulu, in 1960, there was "a brief and solemn Fourth of July ceremony at Iolandi Palace, before one of the largest crowds ever gathered in the palace ground." People from all over the globe, including crews from Japanese training ships in the harbor, were present.

Four members of the Armed Forces lowered the forty-nine star flag and gave it to representatives of the Hawaiian Society. After the new fifty star flag had flown all day, the two ensigns were placed in the archives of the new state. President Eisenhower had sent the original fifty star flag to Philadelphia to be raised over Independence Hall on that day (July 4, 1960). Then it was presented to Senator Hiram W. Fong for preservation in Hawaii.

Wherever Americans happen to be around the globe on the Fourth of July, they get together for an observance. It is said that this holiday was noted in England for the first time in 1918. Many of our soldiers were on British soil, or fighting with English forces on the Continent. The Stars and Stripes flew alongside the Union Jack. At an important gathering, Lord Bryce and Winston Churchill made memorable speeches. President Wilson's message to the British Isles included the words: "Heartfelt greetings on the 142nd anniversary of American independence."

In 1954, several hundred Americans participated in singing national airs and enjoyed a picnic of hot dogs at the American Embassy in Addis Ababa, Africa, followed by an evening of fireworks.

That same day four of our warships which were in Durban Harbor, in the Union of South Africa, received salutes from other ships in the port, including the British craft.

Denmark seems to be the only land outside the United States where our Independence Day has been regularly observed since 1916. Money was raised to buy land for a site at Rebild—the Danish-American Rebild National Park—a shrine for patriotic American ceremonies. There is a Lincoln log cabin with an interesting collection of Americana, including a covered wagon, cowboy outfits, California redwood, and many Indian relics.

Annually thousands of Danish-Americans go there and celebrate with Danes and other visitors. President Eisenhower sent a message in 1956; and the ambassador, Robert Coe, gave the address. The audience numbered about thirty thousand and included the King and Queen of Denmark. On that occasion tribute was paid to the actor, Jean Hersholt, who had died not long before. Other speakers have been Paul Hoffman, Chief Justice Earl Warren in 1955, and Dr. Lee DuBridge, of California Institute of Technology, in 1958.

In 1960, there were varied observances of this important holiday in Europe. During the rites at Rebild Park, a new fifty-star flag was presented to the Park Committee by the American Legion of New Jersey. At Heidelberg, German, guns saluted the latest banner at the United States Army's European headquarters. The soldiers had a holiday and enjoyed picnics and baseball games.

At the home of the American ambassador—Spaso House—in the city of Moscow, "members of the foreign colony, American tourists and a sprinkling of Soviet guests were invited to a two-hour reception." More than two thousand Americans attended the party given by the Italian envoy, James D. Zellerbach, in the embassy gardens in Rome. Ambassador and Mrs. Amory Houghton held their annual garden party in Paris from 11 A.M. to 12:30; and the affair was largely attended.

However, the biggest observance of the Fourth of July, in Europe took place at Battersea Pleasure Gardens, in London in 1960. The Paris edition of the *New York Herald Tribune* reported:

> Eight thousand American service men, their wives and children virtually took over the Battersea for a picnic, with hot dogs and doughnuts, a band show, and a beauty contest lasting the whole day.

Filipinos also celebrate their national day of independence on July 4. They chose this special date to express their appreciation of an honored American promise to grant them independence. On July 4, 1942, at Manila Bay, the flag of 1898—Admiral Dewey's ensign—was lowered, as the President of the Philippine Islands declared: ". . . not in defeat, not in surrender, not by compulsion, but by the voluntary act of the sovereign American nation."

Atlantic Charter Day—August 14

Early in August 1941—somewhere in the Atlantic Ocean off the coast of Newfoundland—President Franklin D. Roosevelt and Prime Minister Winston Churchill, met on a warship where they conferred for several days. After discussing many points, the two leaders issued a joint statement of the peace aims of the United States and Great Britain.

Their official report, covering the entire meeting, was termed the Atlantic Charter. Its contents were revealed to the public at Washington, D.C., on August 14, 1941. And since that time, this date has been known as Atlantic Charter Day.

These words explain the purpose of the statement:

This charter was intended to set forth certain principles relative to the national policies of the United States and Great Britain and on which the two nations base their vision of a better future for the world.

In their first point, President Roosevelt and Prime Minister Churchill disclaimed any territorial ambitions; two, they wanted no territorial changes that were not in accordance with the freely expressed rights of the lands concerned; three, they expressed their belief in the right of all peoples to govern themselves as they wished and to choose their own form of rule.

The two men also expressed the desire to see sovereign rights and self-government restored to the lands which had been deprived of them by force; four, they promised to try to increase access to raw materials to all nations on equal terms, so they could enjoy economic prosperity.

Five, they desired to help all nations to secure, in the economic field, improved standards of labor and social security; six, after the destruction of the Nazi tyranny, their wish was to see the establishment of a lasting peace by which men could exist safely within their own boundaries, with the assurance of being able to live in freedom from want and fear.

Seven, this peace should permit men to travel on all seas without hindrance. Eight, for both spiritual and realistic reasons, there should be an end of armed force; for this the disarmament of nations was essential. In conclusion, these world leaders declared that their countries would "encourage all other practicable measures, which will lighten for peace-loving peoples the crushing burden of armaments."

V-J Day—September 2

V-J Day (for "Victory over Japan") occurs on the second of September and commemorates the time when World War II officially ended. On that date in 1945, plenipotentiaries on board the *U.S.S. Missouri* signed terms of unconditional surrender.

Before and after the acceptance of the Potsdam declaration by Japan, the expression V-J Day was used to denote the time the Eastern phase of the war would end. At Potsdam President Harry S. Truman and Winston Churchill, with Chiang Kai-shek agreeing, issued an ultimatum to Japan on July 26, 1945, demanding unconditional surrender. Japan would be limited to her islands alone and would be stripped of her ability to carry on war.

At Tokyo Bay, American ships destroyed what was left of the Japanese Navy; flyers strafed the coast for many miles; still Japan did not surrender. Then came the use of atom bombs. The first was dropped on Hiroshima, on August 6, 1945, from an American super-fortress, the *Enola Gay*. Three days later, the second fell on Nagasaki. Thousands were killed, others injured, and countless homes were destroyed. Japan sued for peace immediately.

Her agreement to the peace terms reached Washington on August 14; and on this date our nation celebrated the victory. At 7 P.M., Eastern Standard Time, the news was flashed to the people of New York City by the moving electric sign at the *Times* tower. The jubilation that spread over the country to every town and village has never been equaled. There were victory bonfires, dancing in the streets, and mass singing. The police estimated that at least two million persons were crowded into Times Square.

In accepting the terms, the Japanese insisted that their Emperor remain on the throne; the Allies agreed, but stipulated that he must be under the authority of the Supreme Allied Command; and that later on, there would be a free election by the people in regard to the Emperor's future.

On board the *Missouri,* twelve signatures were placed on the terms of surrender. General MacArthur signed for the Allies, and Admiral Nimitz for the United States; there were eight Allied representatives and two Japanese.

In September 1945 the Stars and Stripes—the same flag that had been flying over the Capitol in Washington on December 7, 1941, the day Pearl Harbor was bombed by the Japanese—flew over Tokyo; and the formal occupation of the city began.

President Harry S. Truman designated the day of the actual signing of the peace terms—September 2, 1945—as V-J Day. Ever since, this anniversary has been observed throughout the United States and at various posts around the world.

Labor Day—First Monday in
September

It's a good old American custom to celebrate the first Monday in September as Labor Day and to honor all workers. This has become one of our most popular holidays, ranking next in importance to Washington's Birthday, Independence Day, and Thanksgiving. Labor Day also marks the end of the summer holidays, the reopening of schools, and the beginning of fall business activities.

In an editorial in the *Los Angeles Times* of September 5, 1954, Theodore Saloutos wrote:

> The willingness to recognize Labor Day in the United States might be attributed to the strength of our representative institutions, the spirit of compromise that prevails, and the dynamic character of our economy, which extends benefits to all who are willing to work. . . .
> . . . Labor Day has become an integral part of the American way of life. It reflects a degree of optimism and mutual confidence on the part of the American way of life. It reflects a degree of optimism and mutual confidence on the part of all segments of society that few countries can equal.

Ever since Bible times, the right of the worker to one day each week for rest has been recognized. The Fourth Commandment says, "Six days shalt thou labor and do all thy work . . ." And the great dramatist, Bernard Shaw, remarked:

> A day's work is a day's work, neither more nor less, and the man who does it needs a day's sustenance, a night's repose, and due leisure, whether he be painter or plowman.

However, for centuries, countless workers were not given their just rights. Through the industrial revolution, various social injustices came about, with the invention of machinery, use of steam and electricity, and adoption of the factory system.

177

During the eighteenth century several persons became justly indignant about the sordid surroundings in which too many workers lived and labored. In the following decades both articles and books appeared championing the cause of the laboring man and crusading for improved conditions. William Morris and John Ruskin praised the beauty and dignity of work well done; in his novels Charles Dickens exposed the sordid surroundings of the workers, their starvation wages, and the tragic poverty of their lives. Thomas Carlyle took up the banner in England as Tolstoy did for the peasants in Russia.

Several poets pleaded the cause of labor; these included Thomas Hood, with his plaintive "Song of the Shirt"; John G. Whittier, in "Songs of Labor"; Henry van Dyke, in his inspiring poem, "Work"; Walt Whitman, "I Hear America Singing"; and Louis Untermeyer's "Caliban in the Coal Mine," while Edwin Markham's "Man with the Hoe" shook many people out of their complacency about the life of a laborer. All these writings helped in the recognition of the dignity of labor.

Artists, too, glorified the worker in their paintings, including Breton's "Song of the Lark"; Adam's "Across the Fields" and "End of Day"; Rosa Bonheur's "Shepherd and His Flock"; Grant Wood's "American Gothic," and many others.

Since so much attention was directed to the importance of labor, it is not surprising that a special day was set aside to honor all who work, and to show the strength and unity of the labor movement. Although Labor Day began as a private annual affair, it was soon converted to a legal and public holiday.

The idea was first suggested in 1882 by Peter J. McGuire, the dynamic president of the United Brotherhood of Carpenters and Joiners of America. He was also an active leader in the Knights of Labor, founded in 1869. McGuire asserted that since we had certain days assigned to represent "the religious, civil, and military spirit," special honor should also be given to the industrial spirit—"the great vital force of the nation."

It was at a meeting on Thirteenth Street, in May 1882, that Peter J. McGuire proposed to the New York Central Labor Union that a "Labor Day" be noted on the first Monday in September. He wanted to observe "a festive day during which a parade through the streets of the city would permit public tribute to American industry." Mr. McGuire chose the September date as it would bring the holiday in pleasant weather, halfway between Independence Day and Thanksgiving.

Peter J. McGuire, the tenth child of a poor Irish-American family, was born in New York City's East Side in 1852. He went to work at the age of eleven when his father joined the Union Army. Peter helped support the family. He worked long hours in piano and furniture factories, and earned the enmity of some employers by pleading for the eight-hour day.

Since McGuire was an eloquent speaker, his fellow workers adopted his idea about a holiday for laborers that day in 1882; and on September 5 of that year the first such parade was staged in New York. Even though men were warned not to leave their jobs, about ten thousand workers paraded around Union Square and up Fifth Avenue to Forty-second Street, headed by a band and mounted police. That afternoon there was a big picnic, with speakers and dancing; in the evening a fine display of fireworks completed the first celebration. Not long afterward, the General Assembly of the Knights of Labor passed a resolution making Labor Day an annual event.

Two years later, on October 9, 1884, in Chicago, the Federation of Organized Trades and Labor Unions of the United States and Canada (which afterward became the American Federation of Labor) voted to make Labor Day a national holiday. In 1887, Oregon celebrated a state holiday honoring labor; and this action was soon followed by Colorado, Massachusetts, New York, and New Jersey.

By 1894 Labor Day was a legal holiday in thirty states; and that year President Grover Cleveland approved an act making it legal in the District of Columbia. In 1928 all forty-eight states and dependencies, except Wyoming and the Philippines, had passed such provisions. Today it is celebrated in all fifty and in the District of Columbia.

Officials of the Presbyterian Church decided that the Sunday before Labor Day should be designated Labor Sunday; and since 1905 special services honoring labor have been conducted on that Sunday in many places. Some time ago, Assistant Secretary of Labor, J. Ernest Wilkins made this statement:

It is fitting that Labor Day, 1955, is being observed in churches all over the nation. The churches and free labor throughout the world have much in common. Both strive to build a world in which fear and poverty will be banished and a secure peace will be established among men.

Even though many Americans are serving in various lands overseas in the Armed Forces, they still have the opportunity to observe our holidays, including Labor Day. For example, in 1958 I had the privilege of attending a Labor Sunday service in the United States Army Chapel near Munich, Germany. It was held in the attractive, modern room, with its bleached walls, pews, and unusual décor; on the right side of the altar was the American flag, with the church ensign on the left.

The chaplain, James H. Terry, used as his text, "And on the seventh day God ended his work." He discussed our attitude toward labor, which is a God-given thing and the fullest expression of man's life. For we can see the results of our labors: great highways, harbors, bridges, buildings, power systems, or fields of golden grain— all the rewards of man's labors.

The chaplain also spoke of the dignity of work, of its great therapeutic value, and of the need for women's finding more happiness in their homes. In conclusion, he urged all "to witness to the divine dignity of work," and to worship God through our vocations.

Once someone remarked that "socially labor has climbed the ladder of recognition." In early times laborers were permitted to watch slaves or captives fight against animals in arenas; during the feudal period, workers could compete with each other, but not with persons of higher social station. Now Labor Day is a time when men from all sorts of vocations can join in a day of recreation.

When this holiday was inaugurated, one writer stated this: "Its celebration takes the form of parades by labor organizations, meetings conducted by labor leaders, speeches, picnics, and athletic events and contests."

By the turn of this century, while various unions still featured their parades, Labor Day was becoming more and more a day for enjoyment, gatherings with friends, picnics at the seashore or in the mountains, for varied athletic contests, attendance at ball games, etc. Nowadays, many use the time for rest, since it is the end of vacation and the beginning of strenuous fall activities.

However, the original purpose of this important holiday has not been lost sight of by labor unions and there are still outstanding celebrations, especially in some larger cities.

In the East on Labor Day 1956, there was an unusual feature. A twelve-year-old girl, Jo Ann McGuire Dougherty (the great-grand-daughter of the founder of Labor Day, Peter J. McGuire), had invited President Eisenhower to attend a celebration in her home town, Camden, New Jersey. There was to be an observance at the grave of Peter J. McGuire to commemorate the issuance of a Labor Day stamp.

As the Chief Executive was unable to accept, he asked Jo Ann to come to the White House. The young girl and eight other descendants of the founder attended ceremonies in the rose garden, and had their picture taken with the President. After his talk, he shook Jo Ann's hand and said, "Thank you very much for the invitation; I hope you will think this a substitute."

In 1959, New York City had the first Labor Day parade in twenty years. It is said to have been the biggest turnout in the history of this holiday, with an estimated 122,000 union members marching through streets thronged with hundreds of thousands of enthusiastic spectators. In the parade were 200 bands, strolling players, show girls, models in bathing suits, and two elephants. In the reviewing stand Governor Rockefeller beamed and wished that Soviet Premier Khrushchev could have seen this outstanding Labor Day observance in democratic America.

It is indeed fitting that the first Monday in September we give deserved recognition to labor and its many achievements. With Walt Whitman we hear each worker "singing what belongs to him or her." On this typically American holiday we are proud to glorify work and to pay our respects to all who engage in it; for truly "the laborer is worthy of his hire."

A well-known California professor and commentator, Dr. Polyzoides has well stated the meaning of Labor Day:

> . . . American labor has set aside the first Monday in September to glorify the dignity of its calling and the strength of its solidarity. In this way it has sharply deviated from the European and South American concept of organized labor that still holds on to May Day for its festival, while clearly lending a political color to the whole event.

Citizenship Day—September 17
(Formerly Constitution Day)

On September 17, 1787, delegates to our Constitutional Convention in Philadelphia proudly signed their names to a remarkable new document, the Constitution of the United States, termed "the finest expression of the determination of a free people to govern themselves and protect their liberty."

This Constitutional Convention had assembled on May 12, 1787 at Independence Hall, with delegates present from all states except Rhode Island. George Washington, a deputy from Virginia, presided over the sessions. The members carefully studied codes of laws, including those of Great Britain, her colonies, the Articles of Confederation, and our own individual state constitutions. One authority, Max Farrand, states: "It is of interest that the New York Constitution of 1777 seems to have been used more extensively than any other."

When the Constitutional Convention had completed its work, after four months of secret deliberation, the members agreed on the final draft and added their signatures. At that time, the instrument consisted of the famous preamble, "We, the people of the United States . . ." and seven Articles.

Strange to say, of the sixty-five delegates from twelve states, ten did not attend; and of those present on that momentous day—September 17, 1787—sixteen "declined or failed to sign."

Among the signers were Alexander Hamilton, James Madison, Gouverneur Morris, James Wilson, John Dickinson, and Benjamin Franklin. (Among our forefathers Franklin had a unique distinction; for he was the only American to sign all four of these important documents—the Declaration of Independence, the alliance with France, the treaty of peace with England, and the Constitution.)

Under the rule of the Constitution, it was to be ratified by nine states before it could go into effect. On December 7, 1787 Delaware had the honor of being the first to approve it. Others followed in this order: Pennsylvania, New Jersey, Georgia, Connecticut, Massachusetts, Maryland, South Carolina, New Hampshire, Virginia, New York, North Carolina, and Rhode Island. Only three states— Delaware, New Jersey, and Georgia—were unanimous in their votes for the adoption of the Constitution.

When New Hampshire ratified the document on June 21, 1788 as the ninth state, her action made it legal. However, the government did not declare the instrument in effect until the first Wednesday in March 1789.

Luckily, the men who framed our Constitution made it difficult to change. The legislatures of three-fourths of the states (or special conventions) must approve each addition. In spite of this restriction, more than four thousand attempts have been made to amend the Constitution. Most of them have dealt with the Presidency, while others were concerned with giving the citizens more voice in national affairs. Few have been directed at the Supreme Court, which acts as a check on "the President, Congress, the states, the counties, the municipalities, and the lower courts, preserving the fundamental tenets of our American system of government."

Here are some measures that have been suggested: The complete abolition of the states, and the division of our country into four sections; changing its name to the "United Nations of the World"; limiting the size of fortunes; prohibiting dueling, divorces, and polygamy; taxing of imports; giving the President a life term; allowing him to veto state laws; and permitting citizens to overrule the Supreme Court.

Other proposed amendments concerned marriage; prohibiting ministers of the gospel from holding political offices; taking away the right to vote from any American who accepted honors from a foreign country or ruler; and the confiscation (without repayment) of private property by the government in time of war. All these suggestions and countless others failed to become part of the highest law of our land. So we are grateful to the creators of the Constitution for their wisdom in making its amendment hard. Result—only 22 additions in over 170 years!

After the ratification of the Constitution, the document was taken to New York, then the seat of government; next, to Philadelphia, when that city served as the national capital; and finally to Washington, D.C. Until 1921 the instrument was kept in a safe in the State Department; then President Warren Harding ordered it deposited in the Library of Congress.

During the years that followed the signing of the Constitution not much notice was taken of the anniversary of its signing until the early part of the present century. Then began a movement for communities to observe the date with fitting ceremonies; the holiday was named Constitution Day and stressed as the proper time for American citizens to take stock of the privileges of living under this democratic body of laws which we enjoy.

This date has been observed more in the city of Philadelphia than anywhere else. An outstanding celebration occurred there on September 17, 1887, the centennial date of this historic event. There was a three-day observance, with long parades. On the last day President Grover Cleveland gave an address, ending with these words:

> . . . as we rejoice in the patriotism and devotion of those who lived a hundred years ago, so may others who follow us rejoice in our fidelity and in our jealous love of constitutional liberty.

The celebration of Constitution Day became popular in the early 1900's; in 1914 the National Security League was organized to promote its observance. Other groups, too, have been active in the movement; for example, the American Bar Association has been sponsoring the project and urging all states to preserve the dignity of the Constitution.

For some time in recent years, a date in May called "I Am an American Day"—was celebrated to honor those foreigners who had just won their American citizenship. On this occasion, and also on Constitution Day in September, many groups worked together to call attention to the importance of our Constitution and of United States citizenship. During the years "I Am an American Day" was observed, it proved effective in attaining its objects.

The idea had originated in Boston, in September 1940, at the national convention of the American Legion; and this movement, to pay tribute to new Americans, spread round the country. In many communities mayors issued proclamations for its observance. The holiday was sponsored by the American Legion Posts and various civic groups. The public was invited to the meetings; outstanding speakers addressed new citizens; and special musical numbers were given. At times the Adult Education Department of the Public Schools staged pageants with scenes from American history.

In 1952, President Truman signed the bill passed by Congress uniting the two holidays as Citizenship Day, to be observed on the day of the signing of our American Constitution, thus ending Constitution Week.

For some time this week was sponsored in Washington, D.C., by the Justice Department and the United States Office of Education. Now the National Conference of Citizens has taken over; it is supported by private subscriptions; and at their last annual meeting, there were eight hundred delegates from about four hundred patriotic and civic organizations. The theme for the week in 1959 was United States Citizenship—Know It—Cherish It—Live It.

That year thousands of Americans assembled to rejoice over their rights and joys as citizens. The climax was welcoming new members on Citizenship Day. In the national capital there was a naturalization ceremony on the grounds of the Washington Monument. District Judge Holtzoff called to order the first outdoor session ever held in that city on Citizenship Day and administered the oath to thirty-five persons born in twenty-three different foreign lands.

Los Angeles has for many years observed this holiday in a distinctive way. In 1959 her civic proclamation urged

> Each and every citizen to remember with honor those who conceived the Constitution on which now rests the greatest country in the world . . . this Constitution will continue to stand only as long as we, individually and collectively, adhere to its principles.
>
> The future of America and the free world depends on an informed, aroused, and inspired citizenry armed with the faith and teaching of this great American document.

A chief feature of this western observance is a playlet, a re-creation of the signing of the Constitution by prominent local lawyers, dressed in colonial garb, and representing famous signers. At the California Museum of Science and Industry in Los Angeles there is a fine display of materials relating to the Constitution—priceless manuscripts, historic flags, and original portraits of our Presidents.

While ceremonies honoring new Americans were staged in this western city, a giant replica of the Constitution, fifteen feet high, hung over the south entrance to the California State Building; and was provided by the Constitution Week Observance Committee.

There has been no period in our national history when it was more important to recall the wise provisions of our Constitution. This document gives us unique rights in a world where today many have lost freedom of the press, of speech, of religion, and of peaceful assembly. Their homes can be searched, and their goods seized. They cannot vote freely or ask for a speedy jury trial. But as Americans we are guaranteed these privileges under our Constitution.

Therefore, it is not surprising that in so many places the celebration of Constitution Week, culminating in Citizenship Day, on September 17, is becoming an important annual celebration, for this holiday stresses the advantages of living under this outstanding, time-tested body of laws. The noted British Prime Minister, William Gladstone, once declared that the American Constitution was "the most wonderful work ever struck off at a given time by the brain and purpose of man."

Rosh Hashanah (Jewish New Year's Day)—Tishri 1

Rosh Hashanah, meaning "head" or beginning of the New Year, occurs on the first day of the Jewish month of Tishri. Its date ranges from September 6 to October 5. (In 1960 the festival fell on September 22–23.) This is also called the Feast of Trumpets. Rosh Hashanah marks the beginning of an observance covering ten days, which is climaxed by Yom Kippur, the solemn Day of Atonement.

The beginning of the Jewish religious year comes early in our fall, and is "a time of stock-taking and heart-searching." A devout Jew does not begin a new year with gaiety; to him it is not the time for idle festivities, but a day "for meditation and self-examination, a solemn occasion, though not a mournful one. . . ."

Some Hebrew authorities have described Rosh Hashanah as "the annual day of judgment when all creatures pass in review before the searching eye of Omnipotence." There is—it is said—a Book of Life in which the deeds of every individual are recorded. Therefore, when Jews greet each other at Rosh Hashanah, they say, "May you be inscribed for a Happy New Year," a reference to this Book of Life.

Before Rosh Hashanah, there is much activity in Jewish families; housewives clean their houses thoroughly, shop for new clothes, prepare for the New Year's feast, and send greetings. The table for the evening meal is spread with the finest linens and set with the best china, and is ornamented with a basket of fruits. Candles are lighted, a special New Year benediction is said over the bread or an apple dipped in honey.

At the synagogue service, the ram's horn trumpet, or Shofar, is blown, symbolic of warning and hope. "Sounded in the temple on solemn occasions [this] reminds the congregation of the gravity of the day and calls them to repent."

There is Bible reading from Genesis, Chapter 22, which begins with the story of Abraham and God's command for him to sacrifice his son, Isaac, to Jehovah. Then comes the climax; Isaac is saved; and the angel expresses his approval of Abraham's willingness to obey God's command.

> And in thy seed shall all the nations of the earth be blessed; because thou hast obeyed my voice.

Then comes the chanting of Psalm 37, which commences with the well-known words:

> Fret not thyself because of evildoers, neither be thou envious against the workers of iniquity . . .

and the promise,

> Commit thy way unto the Lord; trust also in him; and he shall bring it to pass.

Readings from the Torah and also from various prophets are part of the impressive exercises in the synagogue.

> The sanctity of Rosh Hashanah is felt most in the morning service in the synagogues. The prayers make one feel and understand the significance of the day as only great poems can. The Shofar ceremony is an unforgettable experience and to persons of every age. The reading of the Torah, the rabbi's sermon, and the special melodies all lend beauty and meaning to the service.

—Ben. M. Edidin

According to a newspaper item, dated September 23, 1960, temples in the metropolitan area of New York were filled with worshipers at the Rosh Hashanah services the preceding evening. They marked the beginning of the year 5,721, on the Jewish calendar. The observances were to continue throughout the day for Reform Jews, and also on the following one for Orthodox and Conservative congregations.

Yom Kippur (Day of Atonement) —Tishri 10

Yom Kippur, the Day of Atonement—a time of penitence and fasting—falls on Tishri 10 (it was observed on October 2 in 1960), ten days after Rosh Hashanah, the Jewish New Year.

Literally, the word, Kippur, means "to cover"; and this holy day is "the day of the 'covering,' the day when He would blot out the sins of the Jewish nation and remember them no more. . . ." No other Hebrew festival—so it is claimed—is celebrated with such devotion and by so many persons of the Jewish faith.

In Leviticus 23, verses 26 and 27 we read:

And the Lord spake unto Moses saying,

Also on the tenth day of this seventh month there shall be a day of atonement: it shall be a holy convocation unto you; and ye shall afflict your souls, and offer an offering made by fire unto the Lord.

In addition the Hebrews were advised to do no work on the Day of Atonement; the instructions concluded with these words:

It shall be unto you a sabbath of rest, and ye shall afflict your souls; in the ninth day of the month at even, from even unto even, shall ye celebrate the *Sabbath*.

The ten days ("Days of Awe") that intervene between Rosh Hashanah and the Day of Atonement are a time for repentance and prayers for forgiveness of wrongdoing. In ancient times there were early morning sacrifices of animals in the temple, with elaborate rites by priests dressed in special vestments. (Such sacrifices were abandoned after the temple was destroyed in 70 A.D.)

As a climax to this period came the Day of Atonement: . . . "one great annual expiation of all the sins of the whole people." Its ritual culminated in the ceremony of the scapegoat on whom the burden of all sins was loaded.

On this occasion, two goats, contributed by the people, were placed before the high priest, who then cast lots to see which one would become a sin offering, to be sacrificed "unto the Lord." After this ceremony of killing and offering the one goat was completed, the live goat was placed before the priest.

Then he laid "his hands upon its head and confessing over it the sins of the congregation so that it should bear away all the sins of the people 'unto a land not inhabited.' " At once the animal was sent away into the wilderness. This is the origin of our term "scapegoat."

Some modern scholars state that the festival of Yom Kippur is of comparatively late origin, and according to J. F. L. George, it may have begun during the Jewish exile in Babylon.

Today at synagogues, beginning the evening before and continuing until the night of Yom Kippur, there are prayers for forgiveness, and also memorial services for the dead. Children make public mention of their deceased parents and in their behalf give to charity funds. Both in homes and at the temples lights are kept burning, as symbolic of the immortality of departed souls.

On the Eve of the Day of Atonement, the well-known prayer, the Kol Nidre, is recited three times. Then comes the "most solemn moment of the entire year" for devout Hebrews. For as one writer (Levinger) stated, even though the day is decidedly not one of merrymaking, yet it brings a feeling of forgiveness, closeness to God, and "a happiness unequalled by any other Jewish holiday."

Of a recent observance of Yom Kippur, on September 30, 1960, a Chicago reporter said: "Guidance in charting a new life and forgiveness for errors of the last year will be sought by Chicago's Jews in the twenty-four hours beginning at sunset Friday." He also reported that the Hebrews would gather in their synagogues to begin the celebration of the Day of Atonement, the most solemn time in their calendar; that they would engage in fasting and praying for forgiveness for past offenses, and for help in the coming year.

This festival also stresses sincerity in addition to penitence and good resolutions and is considered ". . . the most holy and solemn day of the Jewish year, observed by abstention from all manner of work, from food and drink, and from pleasure."

American Indian Day

American Indian Day (observed on September 23 in 1960), according to one source, was first noted in Rochester, New York, in 1912. Dr. Arthur C. Parker, director of the Museum of Arts and Sciences there, felt the need of a date to honor our native Americans. The Boy Scouts acted upon Dr. Parker's suggestion; and for three years they sponsored the observance of American Indian Day.

When the annual assembly of the American Indian Association met in 1915 at Lawrence, Kansas, there were 1,250 present. The matter of promoting such a day was discussed. During the preceding year, a Blackfoot Indian named Red Fox James had ridden over 4,000 miles, visiting various states and governors in an attempt to win approval for a yearly day honoring his people. On December 14, 1914, Red Fox James had presented endorsements of the plan to White House officials.

Then several months later at their meeting, the American Indian Association approved the idea. Their president, an Arapahoe Indian, the Reverend Sherman Coolidge, asked that such a day be noted; and on September 28, 1915, he issued a proclamation, "which is the first formal appeal for definite recognition of the Indians as citizens." In it he declared:

> Let these things and the means by which they may be accomplished be considered upon American Indian Day. Likewise we do invite every American who loves his country and would uphold its honor and dignity, to celebrate this day and to consider our early philosophy, our love of freedom, our social institutions and our history in the full light of truth and the balances of justice, in honest comparison with the annals of other races, and to draw therefrom these noble things that we believe are worthy of emulation. But we call upon our country not only to consider the past, but to earnestly consider our present and future as part of the American people. To them we declare our needs now as those primarily struggling for enlightenment and competency that is consistent with American citizenship.

We do avow our hopes and our destiny inseparably united to that of the United States of America and that our hearts and minds are now and forever loyal to our country, which we would serve in our fullest capacity as men and Americans.

The first general observance of Indian Day occurred in New York State on the second Saturday of May in 1916. When the governor set this date, he called the attention of his people to the fact that the confederacy of the six nations of the Iroquois had occupied the region before the white settlers had taken over the lands, and he asked "for consideration of the five thousand Indians living on a reservation in the state."

In 1960 Governor Rockefeller of New York proclaimed Friday, September 23, as American Indian Day, in honor of the state's Indians, who "are among our most valued and valuable fellow-citizens." He said also that the Indians of New York have "manifested a fully developed sense of their duties and responsibilities as citizens."

American Indian Day is now set in several states by a governor's proclamation or by legislative enactments. Some observe it on the second Saturday in May; others, on the fourth Friday in September, while some suit the convenience of their citizens as to the date. In 1919 the Illinois legislature, for example, decided on the fourth Friday in September. In 1935 Massachusetts passed an act for the yearly observance of American Indian Day, which was celebrated that year on November 25.

Kids' Day—Fourth Saturday
in September

Kids' Day—on the fourth Saturday in September—is sponsored by Kiwanis International, and observed in thousands of communities in the United States and Canada. Usually the local mayor issues a proclamation in regard to its observance.

The chief purpose of Kids' Day is "to honor youth—our greatest resource." The Kiwanis bulletins describe it as:

. . . a day-long series of community-wide events aimed at recognizing the part played by youngsters in present-day society, and honoring them as the "future hope of the United States and Canada" through public ceremonies, entertainment features, award presentations, etc.

Youth work has been a vital aim of Kiwanis International during its more than four decades of existence. They had been entertaining children for years; but in 1949 they set aside a special day. Originally, Kids' Day was founded to benefit the underprivileged and handicapped boys and girls; now the program takes in all youths. Today this event is well established and traditional in many localities.

In 1958, 2,537 Kiwanis Clubs participated in this annual affair, and entertained 1,752,109 boys and girls. It was estimated that in 1960 the numbers were about 3,000 and 2,000,000.

The major emphasis, in some localities, has been put on fund raising for local youth services; other clubs stress the fact that the day should be devoted to youngsters' recreation and entertainment. Some groups think the educational aspect should be emphasized; that boys and girls should be aided in increasing the breadth of their knowledge and experience, while still others believe that on Kids' Day their contributions and achievements should be recognized.

Therefore, with these varying ideas about the observance of this holiday, the activities differ greatly. To honor the adults of tomorrow there may be field days, picnics, trips to nearby places of historical interest, free admissions to circuses, movies, sports events, amusement parks, rodeos, or ball games.

Often there are amateur talent shows, visits to city halls (sometimes youths are allowed to hold civic administrative positions on Kids' Day), trips to factories, or other business places. Contests are held in the writing of essays, making of posters, or safety plans, bicycle riding, etc., for which prizes are given at an awards dinner. Other ways of celebrating the day include Junior Olympics, hobby shows, model airplane contests, swimming meets, water carnivals, or fishing derbys. Local Kids' Day programs are often stressed in the newspapers, on the radio and over TV.

With these widely differing programs it's not surprising that this holiday has become something of a national one, and quite popular in Canada and the United States.

For several years, both the United States and the Canadian air forces have cooperated on Kids' Day with Kiwanis International in making the occasion a climax to the current Air Force sponsored "Living in the Air Age" Program. Their joint effort is aimed at teaching youth how to prepare for "air age living." And the Air Force "cooperates with Kiwanis in its Kids' Day project by assisting the public and particularly youth to gain a better understanding of the impact of the Air Age through observing the Air Force and its operations."

Most of the bases in both countries hold open house on Kids' Day. The youngsters are taken in buses chartered by the local Kiwanis Clubs. These visits have been very successful and much appreciated by the attendants. And

Both the U.S. and Canadian Air Force regard Kids' Day as one of the finest community activities in which they participate. In most Air Force open houses, displays, demonstrations, and exhibits are designed to be entertaining as well as dramatic, in their picturizations of the exciting vocational opportunities in the Air Force, itself, and in "air age living."

Besides the educational phase of Kids' Day, the raising of money for the benefit of local youngsters is an important project on this holiday. In 1958, for example, Kiwanis International realized more than $1,250,000.

The funds raised are used to help finance such projects as the following: medical clinics, homes for orphans, girls, and crippled children, boys' clubs, schools for the blind, retarded youngsters, Boy and Girl Scout centers, summer camps, athletic fields, playgrounds, and equipment. Some Kids' Day money is lent to students, given for scholarships, or used to buy Christmas gifts and medicines for handicapped children. "Living in the Air Age" projects and scholarships at aviation education workshops also are financed from Kids' Day collections.

Now the fourth Saturday in September—Kids' Day—has become an important American holiday—one with an outstanding purpose. Kiwanis International is to be congratulated on its success in this worthwhile movement.

Sukkoth (Feast of Tabernacles)—
Tishri 15

The Feast of Tabernacles, known also as Sukkoth, Feast of Kings, and Feast of Ingathering, opens on Tishri 15 and is an eight day festival. (In 1960 it was observed from October 6 to 13.) The last day, "a solemn assembly" became known as the "Rejoicing of the Law."

There seem to be differing opinions as to its origin. Tradition says that Abraham observed it; others believe that it began after the Hebrews had finished their wandering in the wilderness and had reached the land of Canaan, and that the Jews adopted it from the Canaanite custom of living in booths at vintage time. By giving the festival a historical aspect—a reminder of the time when the Israelites were leading their nomadic life for forty years—the Hebrews make the feast a double commemoration: for the joys of the ingathered harvest, and of the sufferings of their forefathers.

In Leviticus 23, verses 39–42, the Jews were commanded:

Also in the fifteenth day of the seventh month, when ye have gathered in the fruit of the land, ye shall keep a feast unto the Lord seven days; on the first day shall be a sabbath, and on the eighth day shall be a sabbath.

And ye shall take you on the first day the boughs of goodly trees, branches of palm trees, and the boughs of thick trees, and willows of the brook. . . .

Ye shall dwell in booths seven days; all that are Israelites born shall dwell in booths . . .

And they were told to bring these offerings:

And the feast of harvest, the firstfruits of thy labours, which thou hast sown in the field: and the feast of ingathering, which is in the end of the year, when thou hast gathered in thy labours out of the field.

The Feast of Tabernacles marked the close of "the fruit, oil and wine harvest in Palestine, and was one of the three times when the male Hebrews were required to appear in the holy city of Jerusalem. Naturally there was great rejoicing at the ingathering, for "the nation of Israel knew once more that God had provided for them generously for the coming year."

In early times, maidens danced in the vineyards at this season, and the people lived in booths, typical of the tents in which their fathers had dwelt. The booths were crudely constructed with tree branches laid across the top to protect the inmates from the sun by day, but the stars shone through at night. All except those too ill to stand the exposure were expected to live in this manner during the feast days.

There were daily services, sacrifices, and processions around the great altar in the temple; and four large candles were lighted. The priests marched to Siloam to get water to use at the morning sacrifices. Certain Psalms were sung; and people carried palm branches, "entwined with willow, myrtle, and citron."

After the Jews returned to Jerusalem, following their captivity, according to Nehemiah, the people "made themselves booths, every one upon the roof of his house, and in their courts, and in the courts of the house of God, and in the street of the water gate, and in the street of the gate of Ephraim."

During the reign of Xerxes, there was a Jewish priest named Esdras, who led some of the Hebrews back to Jerusalem. Josephus, in his *Antiquities of the Jews*, Book XI, Chapter V, relates:

> Now when they kept the feast of the tabernacles . . . the people . . . desired of Esdras that the laws of Moses be read to them . . . and this he did from morning to noon . . . they were displeased at themselves and proceeded to shed tears . . . But when Esdras saw them in that disposition, he bade them go home and not weep for there was a festival . . . He exhorted them to proceed immediately to feasting . . . but let their repentance and sorrow for their former sins be as a security and guard to them. . . . So upon Esdras's exhortation, they began to feast, and when they had done so for eight days, in their tabernacles, they departed to their own homes, singing hymns to God. . . .

With the destruction of the temple, many of the ancient rites and customs of this festival had to be given up; but the erection of booths was still observed. And today many Hebrews carry out this custom; some build the tabernacles in their yards and share hospitality with relatives and friends there at this season.

In 1960 one newspaper stated that the Jews were about to start the celebration of this feast saying: "This is the day of rejoicing and reminds Israel of their safety when God was in their midst, and looks forward to a feast of rest forever."

Thus Sukkoth, or the Feast of Tabernacles, is a joyous time among people of the Hebrew faith; and Leopold Cohn has said of it: "No one but a Jew can appreciate the feeling of joy, contentment, and security that comes at the very thought of this most happy and satisfying of all the feasts God gave our people."

Columbus Day—October 12

October 12 is Columbus Day, the anniversary of the landing of Christopher Columbus in the New World. Or as one editor once put it: "Columbus blundered into one of the outlying islands of the Caribbean archipelago, and thought he was somewhere else."

This historic event—the discovery of America—happened before dawn, on October 12, 1492, when the lookout on the *Pinta*, one of Columbus' three little sailing vessels, shouted "Tierra! Tierra!" This happy news came when the dauntless explorer was almost ready to give in to his men's demands that he turn back and give up the expedition.

His son, Ferdinand Columbus, thus described the scene on that memorable day:

> After all had rendered thanks unto our Lord, kneeling on the ground and kissing it with tears of joy for his great favor to them, the Admiral rose and gave this island the name San Salvador. Then, in the presence of the many natives assembled there, he took possession of it in the name of the Catholic Sovereigns with appropriate ceremony and words.

Today, Columbus Day is a holiday in Puerto Rico, and in all states, with the exception of Alaska, District of Columbia, Idaho, Maine, Mississippi, North Dakota, South Dakota, Tennessee, Virginia, and Wyoming. It is termed Discovery Day in Indiana, North Dakota, and Ohio, and Landing Day in Michigan.

Columbus Day is also observed on October 12 in some parts of Canada, in Central and South American countries, and in Italy and Spain, where Columbus, as a sailor, is especially honored. On this date there are church ceremonies, processions, various festivities, and fireworks to end the day's observance.

(In Barcelona, Spain, tribute is paid Columbus in July, when Claudel's dramatic poem, "The Book of Christopher Columbus," is performed. This takes place between the tall monument to Columbus, and the waterfront, at the end of Las Ramblas. Moored here is a replica of his flagship, the *Santa Maria*, in its actual size, 90 feet long, with a beam of 20 feet.

(Seats for two thousand spectators are available for this outdoor production. Most of the action takes place on the shore; but for the mutiny scene, the actors move to the flood-lit deck of the *Santa Maria*. At the end of the drama, the admiral is represented simultaneously by two different actors. One shows him dying in poverty, while the other depicts the great discoverer as "crowned with glory by posterity.")

It is believed that the first celebration of the discovery of America occurred in New York, on October 12, 1792, when the order of Columbia (or St. Tammany) held a dinner in honor of Columbus. At that time the only statue of the great discoverer in existence was situated in New York. However, when we celebrated our centennial in 1876 the Italian citizens of Philadelphia had collected enough money to erect a statue of their compatriot in Fairmount Park.

Congress voted funds to help stage an international exposition as a tribute to the historic event and to Columbus himself. Chicago was chosen as the site. Since it was not possible to complete the grounds and buildings in time for an observance in 1892, the Columbian Exposition took place in the summer of 1893. It was attended by millions of visitors, many from foreign lands.

To make sure that the day would be properly celebrated in October, 1892, as a national holiday, Congress asked the President to issue a proclamation, urging all Americans to observe the four hundredth anniversary of our continent "by suitable exercises in their schools, and other places of assembly."

Therefore, the Chief Executive sent out a proclamation including these statements:

Now, therefore, I, Benjamin Harrison, President of the United States . . . do hereby appoint Friday, October 12, 1892, the 400th anniversary of the discovery of America, as a general holiday for the people of the United States. On that day let the people, so far as possible, cease from toil, and devote themselves to such exercises as may best express honor to the discoverer, and their appreciation of the great achievements of the four completed centuries of American life.

Columbus stood in his age as a pioneer of progress and achievement. The system of universal education is, in our age, the most prominent and salutary feature of the spirit of enlightenment, and it is peculiarly appropriate that the schools be made by the people the center of the day's demonstration. Let the national flag float over every schoolhouse in the country, and the exercises be such as shall impress upon our youth the patriotic duties of American citizenship.

In the churches and in other places of assembly of the people, let there be expressions of gratitude to divine Providence for the devout faith of the discoverer, and for the divine care and guidance with which he directed our history and so abundantly blessed our people.

Following this Presidential Proclamation, citizens all over the United States joined in paying homage to Christopher Columbus.

In 1905 the governor of Colorado asked the people of his state to celebrate the anniversary; in 1906, the mayor of Chicago made a similar request of the citizens. The Knights of Columbus also kept urging the states to make the date a legal holiday. Such a bill became a law in New York in 1909.

On October 12, 1909, two Italian cruisers and several American warships were in New York Harbor. Everyone was thrilled when three small ships, replicas of the *Santa Maria*, the *Nina*, and the *Pinta*, moved slowly up the river, as battleships dipped their colors and cannon boomed out salutes. On the same day, members of Italian societies and other organizations turned out in force to parade up Fifth Avenue to Columbus Circle; and Governor Hughes gave the chief address at a large gathering of the Knights of Columbus in Carnegie Hall.

After this impressive celebration in New York City, public opinion grew in favor of making Columbus Day a legal holiday. Soon several states followed New York's example. In 1909, these states observed the holiday for the first time: Montana, Maryland, Pennsylvania, New Jersey, and Connecticut. Next year, Massachusetts and Rhode Island participated. For the initial celebration in Boston, President Taft traveled to that city and witnessed the parade, the longest since 1904, when the Grand Army of the Republic held its encampment there.

But it was not until September 1934 that President Franklin D. Roosevelt sent out a proclamation, asking all the forty-eight states to observe October 12 as a national holiday. Now, except for religious holidays, it is the only date on which all Pan-American lands join in celebrating.

Throughout the United States communities stage individual celebrations. In 1954, for example, there was a notable one in Columbus, Ohio. A 20-foot, 7,000 pound bronze statue of Columbus—a gift of the city of Genoa, Italy—was dedicated. Thousands of school children and older citizens attended the impressive rites. At a luncheon that day, honoring Italians, Senator John Bricker said:

> This great statue will be a symbol of friendship as long as the city of Columbus lives. . . . In this day there is great need for any good will that can be generated. . . . Today's celebration may be one way to replenish it.
>
> I hope this day is significant of things to come. Columbus will nourish this statue long and protect it well.

In 1957, Boston had a Columbus Day celebration that lasted for three days. Varied activities were provided for the children; religious services were featured; there was an impressive parade; and several Italian societies enjoyed banquets with American-born citizens.

Los Angeles "goes all out" on Columbus Day; religious services sponsored by the Knights of Columbus are held at the Old Plaza Church, or at St. Vibiana's. The procession is headed by the Knights in full regalia. The day is devoted to celebrating; bands play Italian and American numbers; there are banquets, with consular officials as guests. In the evening there is usually an elaborate American consular ball, presided over by a queen and her court.

At the annual Italo-American get-togethers, there are speeches by celebrities; not long before his death, the famous singer, Ezio Pinza, said of Columbus: "Mankind found a new world through the courage of Columbus. Mankind still seeks a new world, and the clash of swords is still heard on the horizon. It will take more courage to find that new world."

On this holiday the Italian flag flies over the City Hall in Los Angeles; usually one of the young Italian movie stars assists in the flag raising. On one such occasion, Mayor Bowron said: "We are proud to see the Italian flag flying over our city on Columbus Day. Our citizens of Italian culture have made rich contributions to all worthy facets of our community life, and we honor them today."

Of course San Francisco does not let Los Angeles get all the publicity; for the northern community stages a three-day Columbus tribute. In 1960 thousands cheered as units marched along famous Market Street, with twelve bands and thirteen drum corps. Among the musical groups were the St. Mary's Chinese drum corps and the Cameron Highland Pipe Band. The Columbus Day queen rode with her pretty attendants on a flower-decked float.

Later, at Aquatic Park, there was a re-enactment of the landing of Columbus; he went ashore from a small craft and was greeted by Indians. Addresses, musical numbers, and athletic contests followed. The climax came that evening with the coronation ball at the Italian consulate.

On Columbus Day in 1960, an unusual event occurred in Florence, Italy. The third of Stanford University's overseas campuses was dedicated there. Dr. Wallace Sterling, Stanford president asserted:

> To locate a study center in Florence seems to us both natural and ideal. The beauty of Florence and of its setting and surroundings, the inspiration of its history and its artistic treasures—all these combined to draw us here. . . . We come to Florence, therefore, to participate in a great intellectual tradition.

Thus Americans at home and abroad observe Columbus Day and honor the man of whom Joaquin Miller wrote:

> He gained a world; he gave that world
> Its grandest lesson: "On! Sail on!"

And another American has stated that Christopher Columbus was

> . . . the greatest educator that ever lived, for he emancipated humanity from the narrowness of its ignorance . . . and taught the lesson that human destiny, like divine mercy, arches over the whole world.

Poetry Day—October 15

In the United States, October 15 has been set as Poetry Day; on this date it is well to note the words of Governor Marvin Griffin of Georgia: "The two-fold purpose of Poetry Day is to remind people that a love of poetry is the heritage of every person, and to encourage the poets who are creating today."

Most sources agree that the movement for a poetry day started in the state of Ohio in 1938, when Teresa Sweazy Webb persuaded the Ohio legislature to proclaim the third Friday in October as Poetry Day. Her idea was "To stimulate interest in poetry through the schools, libraries, press, and radio, in the belief that, through its inspiration, it can lead the way to man's peace of mind and world harmony."

Soon afterward, Iowa, Kentucky, Missouri, Kansas, Colorado, and Arizona had official days; but the observances did not fall on the same day. In Texas in 1947, Lucia Trent promoted the plan of a fixed date and October 15 was chosen. Governor Jester issued a proclamation concerning it.

Later, the poet laureate of Arkansas, Rosa Zagoni Marinoni, brought her state in; in 1947, Lucile Coleman established Poetry Day in New York; and the following year, Mary O'Connor did the same in Pennsylvania, selecting October 15 as the date. So the movement grew; and in 1948 seven western states had proclamations issued by their governors for observing this holiday.

In 1950, Governor Earl Warren of California proclaimed the fifteenth of October as Poetry Day for the first time in his state. He had received many requests for this from heads of poetry clubs and others interested in this important form of literature. By 1951, forty-five states were participating in the movement, and the United States Senate agreed on October 15 as the uniform day.

There is a National Poetry Day Committee, with a chairman, a vice-chairman, a committee of seven regional directors, and a chairman from each member state.

In 1955, Mary O'Connor of Philadelphia became executive director of "World Poetry Day," whose purpose is: "To unite the nations of the world by the indivisible tie of poetry, thereby creating a deeper universal understanding." Now there are representatives of this broader organization in many parts of the globe; and World Poetry Day is "non-sectarian, non-racial, and non-profit."

When October approaches, poetry groups plan special programs for Poetry Day all over the United States. In October 1960, at the banquet of the Ina Coolbrith Circle (named for California's first poet laureate), the chief speaker was Edythe Hope Genee, Poetry Day chairman for the state. She is a poet, editor of *The American Bard*, past president of the California Federation of Chaparral Poets, and acting president of the Poets of the Pacific. She spoke on the subject: "Poetry Publishing and Propaganda." At this meeting the winning poems of the annual contest were read and prizes were awarded.

It is good that each year on Poetry Day we pay just tribute to poets for the inspiration their writings have given the world; for "where there is no vision, the people perish."

United Nations Day—October 24

By Presidential Proclamation United Nations Day, commemorating the establishment of the United Nations in 1945, is observed on October 24.

On April 25, 1945, delegates from fifty countries drove through the rain to meet for the United Nations Conference on International Organization at the flag-bedecked War Memorial Opera House in San Francisco.

Although the delegates came from nations, "small, weak, and strong, and in different stages of political and social development," these earnest individuals were "determined to set up an organization which would preserve peace, advance justice, and constitute a permanent structure for international cooperation."

It is claimed that the idea for such an organization was first stated by President Franklin D. Roosevelt, when the representatives of twenty-six nations, fighting against the Axis, met to study plans for cooperation in winning World War II.

For nine weeks (from April 26 to June 26) the conference worked on the charter. Its preamble is considered by many to be one of the finest expressions of purpose ever set forth in any language.

PREAMBLE TO THE UNITED NATIONS CHARTER
WE THE PEOPLES OF THE UNITED NATIONS DETERMINED

to save succeeding generations from the scourge of war, which twice in our lifetime, has brought untold sorrow to mankind and

to reaffirm faith in fundamental human rights, in the dignity and worth of the human person, in the equal rights of men and women of nations large and small, and to establish conditions under which justice and respect for the obligations arising from treaties and other sources of international law can be maintained, and

to promote social progress and better standards of life in larger freedom,

AND FOR THESE ENDS

to practice tolerance and live together in peace with one another as good neighbors, and to unite our strength to maintain international peace and security, and

to insure, by acceptance of principles and the institution of methods, that armed force shall not be used, save in the common interest, and

to employ international machinery for the promotion of the economic and social advancement of all peoples

HAVE RESOLVED TO COMBINE OUR EFFORTS TO ACCOMPLISH THESE AIMS.

Accordingly, our respective Governments, through representatives assembled in the city of San Francisco, who have exhibited their full powers found to be in good and due form, have agreed to the present Charter of the United Nations, and do hereby establish an international organization to be known as the United Nations.

June 26, 1945

By October 24, 1945, the majority of the signatory nations had ratified the charter, and had sent formal notes to the State Department in Washington, D.C. These signers included China, France, the U.S.S.R., the United Kingdom, the United States, and many others. Therefore, on October 24, 1945, with flags of fifty nations flying together, the United Nations came into being.

In order to stress the charter's importance, in 1947 the General Assembly of the U. N. passed a resolution:

that October 24 shall hereafter be officially called United Nations Day, and shall be devoted to making known to the people of the world the aims and achievements of the United Nations, and to gaining their support for the work of the United Nations.

It was apparent, and also quite important, that the general public should be informed about the content and purposes of the United Nations; therefore an entire week—United Nations Week—was set aside in October, with its chief observance on United Nations Day—October 24.

By 1956 the American committee for the United Nations asserted:

The purpose of United Nations Week is to highlight and to dramatize the continuing efforts of the United Nations in its role of peacemaker for the world. . . . United Nations Week gives opportunity for bringing added strength to the movement in support of the United Nations.

The final decision—peace or war—will eventually rest on the youth of today, who are the citizens of the future.

In order to make the week and United Nations Day of most value, the official American Association for the United Nations sends out information and suggestions for programs with this advice:

> This is United Nations Week. The success of the United Nations in building world peace depends on all of us—on our own understanding and support; know how it works, and what it is doing. Help the United Nations help all of us to a peaceful future.

The committee believes it is very important to plan well ahead, and to choose a local program group that represents varied facets of the community. Good publicity on the radio and television and in newspapers is a vital asset.

In some towns there is a public rally, perhaps at the City Hall, with the Stars and Stripes displayed with the flag of the United Nations. After the mayor has read the proclamation for the holiday, there is usually an address in which the speaker stresses the accomplishments and solid gains—social, political, and economic—which the United Nations has made, often against great odds.

Some shop windows feature products and dress of other lands; a town may put on a colorful "International Festival," with gay songs and dances which depict what is being accomplished. During the week there are forums and panel discussions; in many churches the ministers read the preamble of the United Nations Charter and emphasize our individual moral responsibility in this present-day world. An enjoyable ending for United Nations Day is a banquet with foreign dishes.

An important part of the week's observance is the setting up of information centers, where literature on the work of the United Nations may be obtained. Booths are sometimes placed on main streets, in railway, bus, and air terminals, hotels, stores, libraries, and museums. For instance, it might help some persons to read a bit of information like this: In 1945 the cost per American for World War II was the sum of $633.57, while the cost to each American for maintaining the United Nations per year is about 67 cents, "less than the price of a good breakfast, or a movie ticket in New York," in the words of Henry Cabot Lodge.

The Unitarian Church at Long Beach, California, really carries on a year-round program of United Nations Week. For on their three-acre grounds, they have a flourishing grove of trees from different lands, including

> . . . South African acacias, Norway maple, Australian eucalyptus, English oak, New Zealand casurian, Scandinavian ash and Canary Island pine . . . Egyptian acanthus, cedar of Lebanon, Indian rubber tree, German white birch, Chinese gincko, Monterey pine, and a fiddleleaf fig, which is believed to be the "Bo" tree under which Buddha sat to acquire knowledge.

On United Nations Sunday, Dr. Frenner Nuhn, observer at the United Nations for the American Friends Service Committee, spoke on "Hope for World Order," and the Sunday school children were dressed in costumes of foreign lands.

In 1960, the United Nations had been in existence for fifteen years. One headline read:

STRIFE-TORN UNITED NATIONS MARKS ITS 15TH YEAR;

and in the article were these words ". . . embroiled in bitter East-West scraps over disarmament and the very makeup of the world organization."

As usual, President Eisenhower and the governors of forty-nine states proclaimed the observance of United Nations Day, which this year had as its theme, "U. N. I Believe." More than three thousand American communities joined in celebrating this important day.

One newspaper stated:

> While the great debate at U. N. headquarters in New York makes the headlines, working of the various agencies like UNICEF (International Children's Emergency Fund), UNESCO (U. N. Educational, Scientific and Cultural Organization) and WHO (World Health Organization) continue their efforts to aid backward and underprivileged areas unheralded. Famine, disease, malnutrition, and subsistence living standards have already been markedly improved by teams of workers from the U. N. They render not only direct assistance, but train teams of natives to teach their own people.

This same year—1960—when the General Conference of the Methodist Church met, it passed the following resolution, again giving a positive endorsement of this great movement:

> We believe that the United Nations is a working center of international cooperation which provides our most hopeful avenue leading to peace and world order. The prayers and efforts of churches helped to shape it at birth, and through many of its programs opportunities for the expression of Christian concern arise. We believe that the United Nations with its related agencies should be sustained, unheld, undergirded, and strengthened by all informed and conscientious churchmen.

When our United Nations Permanent Representative, Henry Cabot Lodge resigned in September 1960, he wrote his parting opinion of the United Nations in an article, "The U. N. Begins To Grow Up." In it he told of the many trying problems that faced the organization when he became part of it in 1954. And Mr. Lodge stated that these difficult issues had "either disappeared, or moved toward solution."

He asserted that the entrance of so many new members had injected more life into the organization (and predicted that by 1961 there would be nearly a hundred nations in it).

> Every new member, except a handful of Soviet satellites, is determined to do its share as a sovereign member of the world organization. . . . The U. N. has not only grown greatly in size. It has also been growing up. It has taken on more and more complex jobs, and has acted fast and effectively.

Mr. Lodge spoke of the Congo crisis in which "the U. N. is playing a key part in rescuing a new-born African nation from chaos" as "the most complex and far-flung U. N. operation in history."

In addition, he declared that the U. N. had grown up in its ability to serve the greatest need of new nations: economic development, through the "Special Fund," under Paul Hoffman, and OPEX (Operational and Executive Personnel), started by Secretary Hammarskjöld, both of which have already proved successful. Mr. Lodge ended his inspiring and illuminating article with these words:

> The world is still a dangerous place. The United States, with 6 per cent of the world's population, faces a Communist adversary who rules 40 per cent.
> To hold our own, we need military and economic strength. We

also need friends. We can get and hold those friends, not by command and obedience, which is the Soviet style, but by cooperation among equals and by aid which is free from any suspicion of a desire to dominate. That is pre-eminently the style of the United Nations, and, I truly believe, of the American people.

Navy Day—October 27

Navy Day, on October 27, has as its purpose: "To sell the importance of sea power to our national security and global peace." According to W. Royce Power (editorial director of *Navy—the Magazine of Sea Power*—and other Navy League publications) (1960): "Navy Day, each October 27, sponsored by the Navy League of the United States is still observed as a separate celebration."

In 1902, the Navy League of the United States was founded with the encouragement and cooperation of President Theodore Roosevelt. (As Assistant Secretary of the Navy under President McKinley, he had "instituted target practice and instructed Commodore George Dewey to take Manila in the event of war with Spain.")

When Theodore Roosevelt received the Nobel Peace Prize for his mediation between Russia and Japan in 1906, it is said that he gave part of the money to aid in the development of the Navy League; he also stated:

> It seems to me that all good Americans, interested in the growth of their country and sensitive to its honor, should give hearty support to the policies which the Navy League is founded to further. For the building and maintaining in proper shape of the American Navy, we must rely upon nothing but the broad and far-sighted patriotism of our people as a whole; and it is of great importance that there should be some means by which this patriotism can find an effective utterance. Your society offers just the means needed.

The founders of the Navy League believed that, while the general public is conversant with the wartime work of our Navy, it is not so well informed about its peacetime roles: "of the prestige that its armed strength gives to our statesmen . . . of the protection it gives to our foreign trade; and of its deterrent power. . . ."

Therefore, the Navy League of America declares that "to maintain a sound defense posture" we must control the sea lanes. The organization defined its objectives:

First, we must foster and maintain interest in a strong Navy and Marine Corps as integral parts of a sound national defense.

Second, we must constantly keep before the American people the role of seapower in the nuclear age, and in addition, keep our members informed of the problems which our defense planners face.

Third, we assist the Navy Department in every possible way in the field of public information, recruiting and community relations.

Today the Navy League of America has more than thirty thousand members in over two hundred councils, operating in all fifty states and various foreign countries.

All of our members are American citizens and volunteers who serve without compensation. . . . The Navy League is known as the "Civilian Arm of the Navy," therefore, members of the Armed Forces are *not* eligible for membership while serving on active duty.

The American Navy was founded on October 27, 1775, when the Continental Congress "received a bill providing for the creation and establishment of a Fleet." The date is also the birthday of Theodore Roosevelt. In 1922 the Navy League established Navy Day to honor men and women of the United States Navy and Marine Corps. This observance is "voluntary in nature and under civilian sponsorship."

The Navy is authorized to participate in the Navy Day observance to the extent of having "open house" at its installations and aboard ships, but the major emphasis has been that it is a civilian organization without the expenditure of tax dollars.

Halloween—October 31

Halloween, meaning "holy or hallowed evening," comes on October 31. It was so named because it was the day before All Hallows or All Saints' Day, on November 1.

After the increased spread of Christianity, in the seventh or eighth century, a chapel was consecrated at St. Peter's in Rome, to honor all saints (both known and unknown) on All Saints' Day. However, the rites on the preceding evening, now a Christian observance, really stem from an early pagan festival. It was only natural for some of the heathen customs to become attached to the Halloween celebration.

The Celts, who occupied northern and western Europe (what is now France and the British Isles) had Druidism as their religion. These priests noted two important feasts—Beltane on May 1, and the autumn festival Samhain, on the last day of October. Coming after the harvests had been gathered, this holiday meant the end of summer and the beginning of winter. Their new year began on November 1; and our Halloween was their New Year's Eve.

Druid priests were nature worshipers, and performed mystic ceremonies to the great sun god at such places as a circle near Chartres, France, and at Stonehenge, not far from Salisbury, in England. Today as you visit the latter, you see great stone pillars placed in a circle around which the white-garbed priests are said to have marched.

A supernatural element was part of the autumn festival, for the Druids tried to placate the Lord of Death. It was believed that he allowed the spirits of those who had died during the past twelve months to spend a few hours at their homes at this time. There they could warm themselves at the blazing hearth and enjoy the smell of food cooking on spits in the fireplace.

One of the important rites in connection with the ancient observance of Halloween was the lighting of great bonfires on hilltops to honor the sun god and to frighten away evil spirits who had been released on that special night. For several days beforehand young boys went around begging material for the fires.

Then after the heaps were aflame, people danced and sang around them, often pretending they were being pursued by evil spirits. As many jumped over the flames or dashed through them, their grotesque masks added to the fantastic scene.

This was the time, too, when it was believed that witches rode through the skies on their broomsticks; for the idea that there were women who had sold themselves to the Devil was prevalent among the Druids as it had been among early Egyptians and Romans. On Halloween, these witches were said to dance on the hilltops with goblins and imps, while the Devil himself played the bagpipes, or castanets made from dead men's bones.

This was the night of the full yellow moon, when black cats, bats, elves, and fairies were abroad. Frustrated ghosts were supposed to play tricks on human beings and to cause supernatural happenings. Farmers fastened bells that had been blessed on their cows. They also placed crossed branches of ash and juniper at stable doors to keep witches from harming the animals.

As the people celebrated that night around the massive bonfires, they talked of mysterious sights or weird sounds they had encountered—no doubt, the forerunner of our custom of relating ghost stories on Halloween.

In Ireland, "new fires" were kindled on this occasion. Each householder put out the fire on his hearth, and gathered with others at a certain place. Then the Druid priests rubbed together pieces of sacred oak and started a blaze on the altar. Each head of a family then carried home a new fire, which was to last until the next autumn festival. On Halloween, the farmers often set forkfuls of hay afire and waved them in the air to frighten the witches. This custom is said to have continued in the British Isles until the eighteenth century.

Our modern Halloween has some elements that originated in the ancient Roman feast honoring Pomona, goddess of fruits. After the Romans had conquered Britain, some of their customs were added to those of the Druids. Since the Roman festival also occurred after harvest, today at Holloween parties we feature fruit centerpieces, apples, and nuts. For contests, apples are hung on strings or placed in tubs of water; cider is a popular drink that day; and the nuts used are symbolic of food stored for winter.

With early tribes, Halloween was a time for divination or fortune-telling, for they were eager to learn what might happen to them in the next year. The priests cut an animal open and from the entrails foretold the future, or some used the peculiar shapes of vegetables for this purpose. A young person often peeled an apple, threw the peeling over his shoulder, and from its shape told the initial of a sweetheart. The blowing of candles and opening and closing of doors, too, were means of divination. And there was a belief that if anyone ate a crust of bread before going to sleep, any wish that he made would come true.

Girls tried to discover who their husbands would be in this fashion: a maiden carried a candle along a dark hall, or down a stairway, and hoped to see the face of her future mate in the mirror held in her other hand. At times, a young man was blindfolded and allowed to choose one of three bowls. If he selected the empty one, he would be a bachelor; if the bowl contained muddy water, he would marry a widow, while the one with clear water signified that a young girl would be his bride.

After the spread of Christianity, enemies of the church made fun of the Christians; and on Halloween they worshiped the Devil, set skulls on pretended altars, or painted profane crosses on church walls.

Today when children wear ghost costumes, false faces, or witches' hats, make soap crosses on cars or windows, carry pumpkin lanterns, and use black cats, bats, witches, corn candies, etc., as decorations at their Halloween parties, they are following some very ancient customs. Thus our Halloween, a time of fun and gaiety here in the United States is really a combination of Druid practices and classic and other religious beliefs. Because of its long history as a time of merriment, it is a popular holiday here.

In some foreign lands, Halloween is an austere time; the Miserere is heard; and many persons attend Black Vespers. It is customary to dress in black at this time, pray by the graves of deceased relatives and friends, and set out food for departed souls.

When settlers first arrived in the New World, no notice was taken of Halloween. But after many Gaelic immigrants came, they brought old customs with them, such as building bonfires and meeting at homes for harvest suppers.

American pumpkins were found to be excellent for making Jack-o'-lanterns, and so became a popular Halloween symbol. It is said that this idea originated because a stingy Irishman, named Jack, loved to play pranks on the Devil. Therefore, he was condemned to wander around the world—not going either to heaven or hell—carrying a lantern to light him on his way.

In earlier days in the United States, Americans celebrated Halloween with taffy pulls and corn-popping parties, or by going on hayrides. They also considered it fun to make noises with ticktocks on windowpanes. Other pranks included the changing of house numbers or street signs, lighting bonfires in roads, and taking off gates to permit cows and pigs to wander out into the streets. Sometimes Bossy was found next morning in a belfry; wagons were raised up onto roofs and false fire alarms were sounded.

As years went by, harmless, though often "daring," pranks gave way to behavior that was boisterous and destructive. The spirit of rowdyism increased after World War II. Such pastimes as slitting tires, breaking street lights, and otherwise damaging property led police to issue warnings of punishment for these offenses in an attempt to stop such hoodlumism.

Finally, civic and school groups, especially the P.T.A.'s, decided to try to channel Holloween activities into safer and better ways of celebration. Now, after years of combined efforts, in most communities there are mass observances at schools and parks. These have proved more enjoyable as well as less destructive.

Parents are urged to accompany their youngsters to the festivals; and in some towns radio cars cruise around and ask boys and girls to go to the nearest Halloween party. These carnivals feature costume parades, often with prizes for "the scariest, funniest, and most original" dress or mask. There are booths decorated in black and orange Halloween colors, with various emblems of the holiday. The children can buy hot dogs, candied apples, popcorn, candy corn, peanuts, or other refreshments.

Usually skits and interesting contests are arranged, fun-provoking games—bobbing for apples, or climbing a greased pole, or perhaps a tug of war. There may be a board with a large pumpkin on it, with lighted candles showing through the holes. The object of the game is to put out the lights with a water squirt gun. Or there may be a game of Cats on the Fence, a row of plywood animals to be knocked over by throwing beanbags.

At some city parks, the youngsters gather boxes, crates, and so forth for a big bonfire. In the parade around the flaming pile are witches with their broomsticks, devils carrying pitchforks, sheeted ghosts, and skeletons "with glowing bones." And for teen-agers and adults there is dancing at park club houses or on tennis courts after the costume parade.

Of course Halloween is the ideal time for home parties too; and the small fry still go out to ring doorbells and shout "Trick or Treat!" This is said to have stemmed from the old custom of poor persons going to homes of well-to-do neighbors and begging for "a soul cake" on All Souls' Eve.

Anoka, Minnesota, is said to have been one of the first places to stage a community affair back in 1921. Each year this town is gaily decorated; the younger children parade in the afternoon, and older marchers at night. There are floats, bands, and a queen with her attendants. The annual Pumpkin Bowl football game takes place that evening in the high school stadium. At roped off Bridge Square there are games, contests, and dancing; the Anoka Jesters, members of the Junior Chamber of Commerce, add to the fun; and this gay party ends at 9:30 P.M.

Someone in Memphis, Tennessee, had a bright idea which sends the children home early. A radio station telephones a hundred or more youngsters who registered at the community carnivals. The telephone call will come in at a certain specified time and every boy and girl rushes home hoping he will be among the lucky ones. Prizes are donated by local merchants.

In 1960, Anaheim, California, put on its thirty-seventh Halloween festival, which lasts several days. Everyone gets a bad case of "Halloween fever." "The citizens turn their thoughts to nothing but ghosts and goblins, spook decorations, and civic celebrations—all devoted to the memory of All Hallows' Eve!"

After an opening community breakfast, the children "get into the act with a window decoration contest in business establishments," and winners receive awards. At the stadium show, there is a Whiskerino contest; also the Exchange and Optimist clubs run a kangaroo court.

Among the special features of the day is a downtown Kiddies Parade, a sidewalk bazaar, and a parade of floats which takes place at a local park. As many as two hundred thousand spectators have watched this procession. There is a calliope; and the floats are especially attractive, some designed by Walt Disney. One year Donald Duck with his Voice was the grand marshal. When the parade motif was an Indian one, a chief in full regalia led the procession.

Another enjoyable feature of the annual event is the costume breakfast (sometimes attended by two thousand persons in varied dress); here participants enjoy eggs, pancakes, and coffee at the outdoor affair. Later there is a real western barbecue. Altogether this is an outstanding event, and the town of Anaheim has solved the problem of Halloween fun.

An interesting sidelight on our Halloween celebration is the fact that costuming of the youngsters for parties, "Trick or Treat" excursions, and carnivals has become big business. Formerly children draped themselves in sheets as ghosts, or mothers managed to contrive home-made garb. But today as a reporter for the Los Angeles *Times* declared:

It takes more than a whacked up bedsheet and a jack-o'-lantern to outfit a respectable spook for Monday's trick-or-treat circuit.

The canny little ghoulies and ghosties have learned that clothes make the mischief maker and no spectre of any substance wants to be shaded sartorially.

During the past decade the Halloween costume business has become nationally a multimillion-dollar project. These people have problems, for it is a seasonal affair and an uncertain one. Many children want costumes like those of characters they have seen on television. Therefore, "A suitmaker can see a lot of money go down the drain if he guesses wrong and a TV star topples before next Halloween."

While this holiday is an exciting and happy time for children, it can also be a dangerous one. Fire Chief Frank S. Sandeman of Long Beach, California, released good advice to parents. Children, if dressed in dark costume, should have a spot of bright color on them

—preferably a strip of reflecting tape. It is also wise to carry a small flashlight—but *no* candles. Here are other safety rules issued by the chief:

1. Be sure all costumes, no matter what the color, are made of fireproof material. Of course, no paper costumes.

2. Try to temper some of the youthful exuberance that goes with the night by re-emphasizing the usual safety rules so that your little witches won't use up all their little lives crossing one street.

3. Have an adult accompany the kiddies on their trick or treat rounds, particularly if the kids are small and have to cross any streets.

4. Don't let that funny, funny mask obstruct the tot's vision. Better yet, use make-up for his disguise.

5. Give them white or luminous bags to collect their booty in. Not the usual dull brown sacks. If you will follow these simple instructions, your children will not only have a good Halloween this year, but will also have a good chance for a happy one next year.

According to Barbara Brundage, in an article, "Trick or Treat," in *Presbyterian Life,* in 1953, an excellent Halloween project was started by members of the Presbyterian church in the late 1940's. This was the collecting by children of shoes, soap, money, and so forth for underprivileged boys and girls of the world. This was a substitution for the usual "Trick or Treat" gifts for themselves. Then the results of the project were sent to the United Nations for distribution.

As a result, UNICEF (United Nations International Emergency Children's Fund) was organized in 1946 to obtain money for powdered milk. It is not financed through the regular United Nations budget but by voluntary contributions from individuals and governments. To local group leaders, the national organization sends suggestions for publicity, kits with posters, stickers, UNICEF arm bands for the children. Now its funds are used not only for milk but to fight disease in underprivileged lands.

The boys and girls who collect this fund at Halloween carry milk cartons with the UNICEF label. It is amazing how the small amounts collected add up. In 1959 American children raised $1,500,000. As a result: "Daily milk rations reached 5,500,000 youngsters in 63 countries; over 2,200 maternal and health centers were equipped."

Here is what the sponsors of UNICEF hoped for in the year 1960:

UNICEF's aid this year will reach about 55 million children and mothers in 72 countries. It is providing milk and other proteins to combat malnutrition; distributing insecticides to combat malaria; sending penicillin for treatment of yaws; Aureomycin for the treatment of trachoma, BCG for the control of tuberculosis, and sulfone for the arresting of leprosy. The UNICEF Halloween will contribute substantially to the program.

And best of all, this idea of the youngsters' taking part in this UNICEF movement is an excellent way to turn youthful energy into a really worthwhile Halloween pastime, one that is truly characteristic of America.

General Election Day—November

In 1845 Congress set the First Tuesday after the First Monday in November as the time for the Presidential elections. General Election Day is a legal holiday in

All the states plus Guam, Puerto Rico, with the following exceptions: Alabama, Connecticut, District of Columbia, Georgia, Kansas, Kentucky, Massachusetts, Mississippi, Nebraska, New Mexico, Utah, Vermont. In Ohio, a half holiday, after 12 noon. (Observed usually only when Presidential or General Elections are held.)

The United States Constitution provides for the election of various officers, including the President, Vice-President, members of the Senate and the House of Representatives. Also, each state, county, and city must elect its officials. Therefore, today, in most of our states, the date of general election is also used for state and local elections as well as national. (Since Maine holds hers in September, the rest of the country views her returns with interest.) Naturally, our most exciting elections come in the Presidential campaign years.

Our Constitution contains these two Amendments, dealing with the voting rights of our citizens:

ARTICLE XV

The right of the citizens of the United States to vote shall not be denied or abridged by the United States, or by any state, on account of race, color, or previous condition of servitude.

ARTICLE XIX

The right of citizens of the United States to vote shall not be denied or abridged by the United States or by any state on account of sex.

According to the World Almanac, 1959, page 614, "A voter must be at least 21 years of age (18 in Georgia and Kentucky), a citizen; not a convict; must be registered. Literacy tests and payment of a poll tax are required in some states."

Mary J. Brundage (in *Together*, March 1960) asserts that too many American voters simply don't know their "ABC's" about voting; that some lose their votes because they fail to register after changing their addresses; also women often do not register under their new married names. It is said that at least three million persons lose this privilege after moving.

However, some states now allow new residents to vote in Presidential elections if they are registered elsewhere. It is strange that many voters seem to be unaware of the fact that they may obtain absentee ballots if they are away or unable physically to go to the polls. In 1960 there were three million potential voters living outside of the United States, with about one-third of them in Europe. There was much interest shown in the Presidential campaign by many Americans abroad. The reason given was "the stress on foreign affairs which means more to them because of the nature of their existence than to most Americans at home."

For many years numerous Americans have taken their voting rights for granted; countless others have not exercised this priceless privilege, denied in some other countries. Fortunately, nowadays, our newly naturalized citizens and young people as they come of age are being trained and instructed about voting by civic-minded groups such as the League of Women Voters and the American Heritage Foundation.

The World Almanac gives these recent figures in regard to the voting in our Presidential elections:

CIVILIAN POPULATION OF VOTING AGE[1]

Date	Estimated Population	Votes Cast	Percentage
Nov. 1936	80,055,000	45,647,117	57
Nov. 1944	90,599,000	47,976,263	53
Nov. 1948	94,877,000	48,833,680	51.5
Nov. 1952	98,133,000	61,551,978	62.7
Nov. 1956	102,743,000	62,027,040	60

[1] In 1956 88 per cent of the citizens in West Germany voted; 83 per cent in France; 79 per cent in England; and 77 per cent in Japan.

The World Almanac (1961) states that the 1960 Presidential election was the closest one since 1916. The popular vote (as reported on December 16, 1960) was 34,226,925 for the Democrats and 34,-

108,662 for the Republicans. More than 69,000,000 ballots were cast, setting a new record in our voting history. The 1960 election was the fourteenth in United States history in which a Presidential candidate was elected by a minority, or less than half of the popular vote.

Early estimates after the 1960 election were that about 80 per cent of the registered voters turned out, leaving about seventeen million who could have helped elect the Chief Executive of the United States.

Richard M. Scammon, director of elections research for the Governmental Institute, a private organization, tells who these millions are:

They are the very young and the very old among the voting-age citizenry. They include more women than men. They're people without any roots, living in trailer courts, big-city boarding houses, working on construction jobs, stationed in military camps.

They come from the less well-educated, less well-paid segment of the population. A lot of them are Negroes in Southern states who aren't able to define a clause of the Constitution to the satisfaction of election officials.

And some of them . . . are sitting this one out because they don't like the candidates.

The columnist, Hal Boyle, declared that the No. 1 United States public enemy is "the man or woman who took the trouble to register—but won't take the trouble to vote," and adds:

A million men have shed their blood on a thousand battlefields around the world in the last 185 years to keep this procedure—the right to a free and secret ballot—intact. It is still the first and last frontier of our liberty, a liberty that has never faced a greater or wider challenge than now.

Both Presidential candidates in 1960 gave excellent advice to American voters: (*Parade*, November 6, 1960)

Every one of us who is eligible to vote should help choose our national leaders this Tuesday.

For all of us voting is a responsibility. Unless it is exercised by every qualified voter, the election returns cannot truly reflect the will of our people. . . .

Let me assure you that a single vote is not only important but at times crucial. In 1884, less than one vote in each of New York State's precincts would have elected Republican James G. Blaine President over Grover Cleveland. . . .

Then vote according to your considered judgment of what is best for your community, your state, and your nation. That is the way to affirm our faith in the freedom we enjoy.

—Richard M. Nixon

This is the most important election of the century, and perhaps of our whole history. . . . In this election the question is the preservation of civilization.

YOU will make the decision. You alone will win this election—or lose it—for the professional politicians know that elections are lost more often than won. You win by going to the polls, no matter what. You lose by staying at home.

In 1948 President Truman carried Ohio and California by less than one vote per precinct, and these two states provided his margin of victory. . . .

So if you are told that in 60 or 70 million votes your vote is of no importance, don't believe it!

Don't sell your vote for baubles of the moment—a movie, or a holiday drive, or a day hunting. Whatever else you do on Election Day, vote!

—John F. Kennedy

Veterans' Day (Formerly Armistice Day)—November 11

Veterans' Day (formerly Armistice Day), November 11, is the anniversary of the signing of the Armistice in the Forest of Compiègne by the Allies and Germans in 1918, thus ending World War I, after four years of conflict.

Veterans' Day has been observed generally in the United States by Presidential Proclamation; in Canada, as Remembrance Day, in the British Commonwealth countries, and in France. Here it is a legal holiday in all states (except Oklahoma, where it is optional) the District of Columbia, Canal Zone, Guam, and Puerto Rico.

When at 5 A.M. on Monday, November 11, the Germans signed the Armistice, an order was issued for all firing to cease; so the hostilities of the First World War ended. This day began with "the laying down of arms, blowing of whistles, impromptu parades, closing of places of business." All over the globe there were many demonstrations; no doubt the world had never before witnessed such rejoicing.

Next year, in November 1919, President Woodrow Wilson said in his Armistice Day proclamation:

> To my fellow-countrymen: A year ago our enemies laid down their arms in accordance with an armistice. . . . The soldiers and people of the European Allies had fought and endured for more than four years to uphold the barrier of civilization against the aggressions of armed force. We ourselves had been in the conflict more than a year and a half. . . .
>
> We were able to bring the vast resources, material and moral, of a great and free people, to the assistance of our associates in Europe. . . . The war showed us the strength of great nations acting together for high purposes, and the victory of arms foretells the enduring conquests which can be made in peace when nations act justly and in furtherance of the common interests of men.

To us in America the reflections of Armistice Day will be filled with solemn pride in the heroism of those who died in the country's service and with gratitude for the victory, both because of the thing from which it has freed us and because of the opportunity it has given America to show her sympathy with peace and justice in the councils of the nation.

Armistice Day was observed all over the United States by veterans' parades, public services both religious and secular, with two minutes of silence to honor the dead. In 1920 an Unknown Soldier was buried in Westminster Abbey, the burial place of kings and queens; that same year a French Unknown Soldier was interred at the Arc de Triomphe in Paris, where a perpetual flame burns.

In 1921, the American Unknown Soldier, symbolizing all the unknown dead, was chosen in an unusual way. Six soldiers of the American Army of Occupation in Germany were selected from different sectors to act as pallbearers. They met at Châlons-sur-Marne, and were interviewed by General Rogers. Next day, Sergeant Edward F. Younger of the 59th Infantry was asked to make a choice among four caskets, with unidentified bodies disinterred from American cemeteries at Bony, Belleau Wood, Romagne, and Thiaucourt.

When the sergeant was ready to perform his solemn duty, he received a bouquet of white roses, with instructions to proceed into the City Hall at Châlons, where the four caskets stood. Sergeant Younger realized fully the grave importance of his action; and after bowing his head, he walked around the coffins three times. On the fourth round, he seemed involuntarily drawn to the second one. Reverently, he laid the roses on it, saluted, and reported to his commanding officer that he had accomplished his mission.

The body of the Unknown Soldier was brought home on the cruiser, *Olympia*, reaching Washington, D.C., on November 9, 1921. For three days thousands of people passed by as the body lay in state in the rotunda of the Capitol.

For this important Armistice Day in 1921, President Harding requested that flags be flown from sunrise to sunset at half mast, and that all Americans pay silent tribute as the casket was lowered into the tomb at 11 A.M. on November 11, 1921.

There were elaborate ceremonies, and the President's address was heard by high army, navy, and other service personnel, along with diplomats, who had followed the caisson to Arlington. Many wreaths came from all over our country, and from abroad; these were placed on the plain white marble tomb, on which are these words:

> *Here rests in honored glory*
> *An American Soldier*
> *Known but to God.*

Six years later—1927—Congress resolved:

That the President of the United States [Calvin Coolidge] is requested to issue a proclamation calling upon the officials to display the Flag of the United States on all government buildings on November 11, and inviting the people of the United States to observe the day in schools and churches or other suitable places with appropriate ceremonies expressive of our gratitude for peace and our own desire for the continuation of friendly relations with all other peoples.

But it was not until 1938 that Congress passed a bill that *each* November 11 "shall be dedicated to the cause of world peace and . . . hereafter celebrated and known as Armistice Day." That same year President Franklin D. Roosevelt signed a bill making the day a legal holiday in the District of Columbia.

For sixteen years the United States formally observed Armistice Day, with impressive ceremonies at the Tomb of the Unknown Soldier, where the Chief Executive or his representative placed a wreath. In many other of our communities, the American Legion was in charge of the observance, which included parades and religious services. At 11 A.M. all traffic stopped, in tribute to the dead; then volleys were fired and taps sounded.

The celebration of Armistice Day reached its climax in the years just before the beginning of the Second World War. However, public interest seemed to wane. There were many new veterans who had little or no association with World War I. The word, "armistice," means simply a truce; therefore as years passed, the significance of the name of this holiday changed. Leaders of Veterans' groups decided to try to correct this and make November 11 the time to honor *all* who had fought in various American wars, not just in World War I.

In Emporia, Kansas, on November 11, 1953, instead of an Armistice Day program, there was a Veterans' Day observance. Ed Rees, of Emporia, was so impressed that he introduced a bill into the House to change the name to Veterans' Day. After this passed, Mr. Rees wrote to all state governors and asked for their approval and cooperation in observing the changed holiday.

> Veterans' Day certainly has wider connotation than Armistice Day. Its name is self-explanatory; it embraces all veterans. . . . We should see that it gets the observance it deserves . . . and recall the earlier purpose of November 11 as stated by Congress: "expressive of our gratitude for peace and our desire for the continuance of friendly relations with all other peoples."

The name was changed to Veterans' Day by Act of Congress on May 24, 1954. In October of that year, President Eisenhower called on all citizens to observe the day by remembering "the sacrifices of all those who fought so gallantly," and through rededication "to the task of promoting an enduring peace." In his proclamation, the President referred to the change of name to Veterans' Day "in honor of the servicemen of all America's wars." Now the purpose is to pay tribute to more than thirty-one million men who were engaged in our different conflicts. Therefore, Spanish War veterans take part in the ceremonies with men from the two world wars and the Korean engagements.

Veterans' Day in 1954 had an outstanding feature—that of welcoming to American citizenship over 50,000 new members. At these "dramatic mass-naturalization ceremonies" intellectuals and artists mingled with refugees from distant lands. At New York several thousands were sworn in, many others in Mobile, Alabama, while Bremerton, Washington, admitted 80; San Francisco, 3,500, and Philadelphia, 1,300.

At a thrilling scene in Hollywood Bowl, at Los Angeles, where Jean Hersholt, a naturalized citizen, acted as master of ceremonies, exactly 7,568 were welcomed in an inspiring speech by United States Judge Pierson Hall.

On the sunken battleship, *Arizona*, at Honolulu, an unusual observance of Veterans' Day took place in 1957. Men stood at attention and women wept, as flowers were placed at the base of the *Arizona*'s flagpole. Lovely flower leis were dropped into the sea to honor the 1,102 men entombed in the ship.

In 1958, on this holiday, authorities designated five American cities to hold official Veterans' Day celebrations. At one of them, Long Beach, California, for instance, the largest veterans' parade ever staged in the West was viewed by more than 100,000 spectators. There were 130 different units, numerous bands, displays of military might from our various defense branches, floats, drill teams, over 4,000 veterans, public officials, and servicemen from nearby posts, bases, and ships.

As usual, on this day in 1959 there were ceremonies in Arlington at the Tomb of the Unknowns; and here General Albert Wedemeyer warned the audience: "We lose our freedoms by default, simply because we take them for granted."

And not long ago a newspaper editor asserted:

> So Veterans' Day is our annual renewal of our pledge of unending indebtedness to the great host of Americans who have been called to stand between the homeland and its enemies.
>
> If we have been disillusioned by the failure of the original Armistice Day to fulfill its place in history as the end of all war, we still live in hope that the objective of permanent peace will some day be achieved, with faith that the ultimate destiny of mankind will thus be served.

Veterans' Day in 1960 was noted all over the United States with impressive rites. As usual one of the outstanding observances occurred beside the Tomb of the Unknowns at Arlington National Cemetery.

Veterans' Administrator Sumner Whittier placed at the base of the national shrine a wreath sent by President Eisenhower. At exactly 11 A.M., forty-two years after the guns became silent on the Western Front ending the First World War, many representatives of veterans' and other patriotic groups bowed for a moment of silence until this was broken by the sounding of taps by an Army trumpeter.

An unusual feature of the 1960 exercises in the amphitheater at Arlington, and a highlight of the inspiring ceremonies was the gift of a flaming torch. This had been lighted in Antwerp, Belgium, flown to the United States, and was presented by a Belgian flying officer to Sumner Whittier. In accepting it, the latter called it "a symbol of the timeless effort for peace." This torch will continue to burn in Arlington in memory of our war dead.

The former commandant of the Marine Corps, General Lemuel C. Shepherd, led the audience in paying "symbolic tribute in this bivouac of the dead to the immortal memory of the veterans of all wars." In his address, the general warned that there seems to be "no end in sight" for the struggle between the free world and the Communists and declared that our country and our allies "will continue to be assaulted on our ideological, political, and economic fronts."

As one editor remarked, we must admit that though "worthwhile peace carries a risk, there is a kind of peace not acceptable—the peace of slavery."

Therefore, it was especially fitting that our observance of Veterans' Day in 1960 had as its theme: "Peace with Honor."

Thanksgiving—Fourth Thursday
in November

Thanksgiving Day, "a peculiarly American feast," occurs on the fourth Thursday in November, and is proclaimed by our President and governors. Thanksgiving is a legal holiday in all states, the District of Columbia, the Canal Zone, Guam, Puerto Rico, and the Virgin Islands.

With its roast turkey, cranberry sauce, and pumpkin pies, "of all the holidays observed in this country, there is none so distinctively American as Thanksgiving, a legacy of the Pilgrims, cherished because of the traditions attached to it." This holiday is enjoyed not only by the descendants of the Pilgrims but by all Americans; and Thanksgiving is primarily a time for giving thanks for the harvests, and for other blessings the year has brought.

The idea of such a day was not a new one with the Pilgrims; in fact it is claimed that the Chinese observed such rites thousands of years ago. Thanksgiving can be traced back to the ancient Jewish Feast of Tabernacles, which lasted eight days; also to a nine-day celebration, the Greek feast for Demeter, goddess of agriculture; and to the Roman Cerealia, honoring Ceres. Both the Greek and Roman festivals featured sacrifices to the deities; and these ceremonies were combined with music and feasting.

Following a traditional autumn feast of the Druids, the Anglo-Saxons held their "harvest home" celebration, the high point of the year in rural districts. As the last cartload of grain was being brought in from the fields, reapers and other workers followed the wagon, singing

> Harvest Home, harvest home,
> We have plowed and we have sowed,
> We have reaped, we have mowed,

> We have brought home every load,
> Hip, Hip, Hip, Harvest Home!

After the ingathering there was a hearty supper—sometimes served in the barn—for all farm workers. There were "substantial viands," abundance of ale, with the master and mistress presiding over the festivities. Toasts were drunk to the pair: one began

> Here's a health to our master,
> The lord of the feast,
> God bless his endeavours
> And send him increase.

In Scotland, such a gathering was called a "kern"; often after a special service at the church, which was decorated with autumn flowers, fruits, and vegetables, a harvest feast was served to all attendants.

From time to time England celebrated special days of thanksgiving; for example, in 1386, after the Black Prince had defeated the French; in 1588, following the victory over the Spanish Armada; also for more than two hundred years the British observed a day of gratitude for the failure of the famous Gunpowder Plot in 1605. Other countries besides England had thanksgiving celebrations in the fall, notably Russia, Norway, Poland, and Lithuania.

After the small Pilgrim band had landed at the bleak shore of Plymouth, they passed a winter filled with sickness and hardships. Forty-seven of the 103 *Mayflower* passengers died and were buried on a nearby slope.

However, with spring came new hope. Each family had a home; and a friendly Indian, Squanto (who had been taken to England, where he learned English) brought the Pilgrims some corn. He taught them how to cultivate it, also how to net fish. So that spring the settlers planted twenty acres of corn, six of barley, and some peas. Naturally they watched the fields with great anxiety; for they knew their lives depended upon their crops. Fortunately, the corn and barley did well, but the peas, while in blossom, were parched by the hot sun.

During their stay in Holland, the Pilgrims had seen the Dutch celebrate a day of thanksgiving for their victory over the Spanish in October 1575. Therefore, after their own long strain of anxious waiting was over and the harvest proved plenteous, it seemed appropriate to have a day set aside for feasting and celebration. Governor Bradford chose a date late in 1621. One settler reported: "Our harvest being gotten in, our governor sent 4 men fowling so that we might after a special manner rejoice together, after we had gathered the fruit of our labors."

The hunters returned with many wild turkeys, wood pigeons, partridges, geese, and ducks. Others brought in clams, eels, and various kinds of fish. The women were busy preparing the foods, making Indian pudding, hoecake, and so forth. It is said that Priscilla Mullins (who married John Alden) was one of the best cooks; and that she worked in the largest kitchen and produced some special dishes.

Since the Pilgrims had made a treaty of peace with the Indians and their chief, Massasoit, they decided to share hospitality with the natives. But they were indeed surprised when ninety redmen answered the invitation. However, these Indian visitors killed five deer for the feast, and are said to have introduced the settlers to eating oysters.

At the three-day get-together, the women served the men at long tables. At that time two people usually ate from one trencher, a wooden plate with a hollowed-out center, about twelve inches square. After dinner, the Pilgrims and their guests engaged in races and other athletic contests.

Although we would naturally expect that some religious service would be included in the observance of thanksgiving for the bounty of nature in 1621, historians state that official records of the time contain no reference to anything of the sort.

In 1622, some rather undesirable settlers arrived and started a community at Weymouth, Massachusetts. They came in two ships, but did not bring enough food supplies with them, so the colonists at Plymouth had to share their crops. In addition, the newcomers made trouble with the Indians.

During the summer of 1623, the Pilgrims faced starvation. After a long gloomy winter, they had planted seeds, but in May came a severe drought, "without any rain and with great heat," and this almost destroyed the plants. Therefore, Governor Bradford ordered a day of fasting and prayer. For nine hours the praying continued. Finally "He was pleased to give them a gracious, speedy reply.

"Small clouds appeared in the sky; then came "a long refreshing rain," which saved the crops. To show their gratitude to God, the Pilgrims set a day of Thanksgiving on November 23, 1623. Some authorities say that this second observance, rather than the one in 1621, was the real start of our present holiday, for it was religious as well as social. Here is the proclamation issued on that occasion:

TO ALL YE PILGRIMS

Inasmuch as the great Father has given us this year an abundant harvest of Indian corn, wheat, beans, squashes, and garden vegetables, and has made the forests to abound with game and the sea with fish and clams, and inasmuch as He has protected us from the ravages of the savages, has spared us from pestilence and disease, has granted us freedom to worship God according to the dictates of our own conscience; now, I, your magistrate, do proclaim that all ye Pilgrims, with your wives and little ones, do gather at ye meeting house, on ye hill, between the hours of 9 and 12 in the day time, on Thursday, November ye 29th of the year of our Lord one thousand six hundred and twenty-three, and the third year since ye Pilgrims landed on ye Pilgrim Rock, there to listen to ye pastor, and render thanksgiving to ye Almighty God for all His blessings.

William Bradford
Ye Governor of ye Colony

After the first two Thanksgivings, there is no evidence that such a day was regularly observed. When settlers of other faiths reached New England, it was decided to let the governors set the dates. The Dutch people of New Amsterdam—later New York—began to observe "Thank Days" in 1644, and continued them after coming under British rule.

The custom of combining the religious elements at these Thanksgiving Days gradually spread from New England to other settlements.

During the American Revolution, the Continental Congress set several Thanksgiving Days for the people to rejoice in their homes and churches for victories won. In 1778, George Washington proclaimed a day on which to give thanks for the treaties just concluded with France. Some years later, in 1789, he designated Thursday, November 26, to honor the adoption of the Constitution, . . . a form of government that would make for safety and happiness."

In his 1789 proclamation, President Washington declared: "It is the duty of nations to acknowledge the providence of Almighty God, to obey His will, to be grateful for His benefits, and humbly to implore His protection and favor. . . ."

Three years after the War of 1812, President Madison proclaimed a special Thanksgiving for peace. Later, there were scattered observances at varying dates in some states, mostly in the North. It is said that when the governor of Virginia considered proclaiming such a day in 1853, he was dissuaded, and years passed before it was the custom in that section.

But gradually the feeling grew all over the land that we should have a uniform national Thanksgiving Day. Sarah Josepha Hale, the dynamic editor of the popular magazine, *Godey's Lady's Book*, was for forty years the chief sponsor of this idea.

For more than two decades Mrs. Hale wrote editorials in her magazine, sent letters to Presidents, state governors, and many others, and gave countless speeches urging the adoption of a uniform national Thanksgiving Day. In one editorial Sarah J. Hale wrote:

> The unifying effect of such a festival can hardly be overrated. The pulpits, during the day, one in every year, will be occupied with the stirring incidents of national history, and with a retrospect of the moral and religious progress of the nation. . . . The people of our country will learn to value the bond of national union when they know with what mighty labors and sacrifices it was wrought.

Mrs. Hale advocated the celebration of Thanksgiving on the same day as Independence Day, July 4. Since she and many others realized the approaching break between the North and South, in her 1859 editorial ("Our Thanksgiving Union") she declared:

> If every state would join in Union Thanksgiving on the 24th of this month, would it not be a renewed pledge of love and loyalty to the Constitution of the United States, which guarantees peace, prosperity, and perpetuity to our great Republic?

In September 1863, Sarah Josepha Hale's last editorial urging a national Thanksgiving Day appeared in *Godey's Lady's Book* and no doubt it helped bring action.

After the victory at Gettysburg, there was great rejoicing in the North. Then President Lincoln issued a proclamation (the second ever made by a Chief Executive) and named the last Thursday in November as the date. He gave reasons for this act, and concluded with these words:

> And I recommend to them, that while offering up the ascriptions due to Him for such singular deliverance and blessings, they do so with humble penitence . . . commend to His tender care those who have become widows, orphans, or mourners, or sufferers in the lamentable civil strife in which we are unavoidably engaged, and fervently implore the interposition of the Almighty hand to heal the wounds of the nation, to the full enjoyment of peace, harmony, and Union.

When families and friends met for Thanksgiving dinner that year, they ate practically the same foods served today on this holiday. Here is a menu used on Thanksgiving Day 1863:

Cranberry Juice

Roast Turkey with Dressing   Cranberry Sauce

Sweet Potatoes   Creamed Onions   Squash

Pumpkin Pie   Plum Pudding   Mince Pie

Milk   Coffee

It's interesting to get the viewpoint of an Englishman, George Augustus Sala, who reached New York late in 1879, in time to watch Americans celebrating Thanksgiving. In his book, *America Revisited* (published in London in 1885) he gives an excellent account of the occasion.

Mr. Sala declares that while in the old Puritan days here Thanksgiving no doubt was a strictly religious observance, he could not help "fancying that the Pilgrim Fathers were by no means averse to good living, when they could enjoy their cheer in a sober and serious manner."

He commented that the Americans of that period—the 1870's—did "a gigantic amount of eating and drinking" on the holiday; that everyone who had "joined a church" went to his own church in the morning, where "sermons galore" about "abundant harvests and reviving prosperity" were preached.

Charity, too, so the Englishman said, played a big role on Thanksgiving; he decided that the day was really "rough" on turkeys. "The poorest of the poor, the meanest of the mean, the lowest of the fallen were regaled with the succulent white meat. The destitute and the infirm, the prisoners and captives were abundantly fed." Mr. Sala even gave the number of pounds of turkey prepared for the feasts at the Almshouse and the Tombs. At the latter a volunteer choir went through the corridors trying to cheer the prisoners.

The writer seemed especially glad that the children in reformatories and poor districts were well fed on Thanksgiving. Even though Mr. Sala had been told that there was much poverty and suffering in New York, he found that on this day ". . . the Good Samaritan was out and about in every street of the great city on Thursday, laden with the good things of the earth, and sedulously seeking for the poor folks to relieve their bodily needs, and comfort them with kind words."

We are indebted to Mr. Sala for including a poem that had appeared in a New York paper on Thanksgiving. It was entitled "A Thanksgiving Anthem" and began with this stanza:

> In Sixteen Hundred and Twenty-one,
> When the Pilgrims' first year's work was done,
> When the golden grain and the Indian corn,
> And the wild fruits plucked from the forest thorn,
> Were gather'd and stor'd 'gainst the winter's wrath
> Till the drift should lift in springtime's path,
> Far into the woods, on fowling bent,
> Four good men Governor Bradford sent. . . .

And the Thanksgiving song concluded with these words:
> 'Tis now of years full thirteen score
> Since thus our fathers blessed their store,
> But each recurring year has brought
> The blessings which our fathers sought—
>
> Rich harvests ripe with golden grain,
> And rarest fruits and turkeys slain,
> But still that pious "Let us pray"
> Is heard on each Thanksgiving Day.

Since several famous early travelers from England to the United States wrote some caustic criticisms about our way of life, it's refreshing to find that this Britisher even praised our climate—on this holiday which he spent in New York:

Thanksgiving — lived back thru the ages of the Canaanites, from whom the children of Israel were delivered

"And they went out into the fields, + gathered their vineyards + trod the grapes, + went into the house of their god, + did eat + drink."

. . . to crown the blessings of Thanksgiving Day, the Indian summer shone with all its mellow brilliance on the 27th of November—the sun glittering in an atmosphere as elastic and as exhilarating as that of Athens, the sky a lapis-lazuli blue. . . .

But most of all we are indebted to Mr. Sala for the vivid detailed description he has given of the way the New Yorkers celebrated after their church attendance on Thanksgiving:

> The rest of the day was devoted to pleasure; and Broadway and Fifth Avenue became moving panoramas of holiday-makers. From Fifty-ninth Street to Washington Square the sidewalks were densely thronged; and in the afternoon the roadway was crowded with carriages, bound to the exterior boulevards of the Empire City. In the leading thoroughfares all the great stores were closed; but eatables, drinkables, and cigars could be bought at will in the side streets. All the theatres and other places of amusement were open at night, and at many of them afternoon performances were given.

After 1863 Abraham Lincoln issued other Thanksgiving proclamations, and later Presidents followed his example. It is interesting to study such documents for they reveal the state of the nation and tell why the country was grateful. In a message in 1938 Franklin D. Roosevelt said:

> Thus from the earliest recorded history, Americans have thanked God for their blessings. In our deepest natures, in our very souls, we, like all mankind, since the earliest origin of mankind, turn to God in time of happiness. "In God we trust."

It was President Harry S. Truman, who in his message in 1952 asserted:

> We are grateful for the privileges and rights inherent in our way of life, and in particular for the basic freedoms, which our citizens can enjoy without fear.

And President Eisenhower, in his proclamation of 1958 called upon all Americans to give thanks for the many blessings which have "signalized our lot as a nation."

> We are grateful for the plentiful yield of our soil. . . . We rejoice in the beauty of our land. . . . We deeply appreciate the preservation

of those ideals of liberty and justice which form the basis of our national life, and the hope of international peace. . . .

Let us be especially grateful for the religious heritage bequeathed us by our forefathers, as exemplified by the Pilgrims, who, after the gathering of their first harvest set apart a special day for rendering thanks to God for the bounties vouchsafed to them. . . .

While the New Englanders were giving thanks for their blessings, days of thanksgiving were also observed on the Pacific coast. Historians say the first one celebrated in California occurred in July 1769.

Officials in Mexico City feared the British and Russians would get a foothold on the Pacific coast; so they decided to forestall this by sending up expeditions to establish colonies. Three ships left the western coast of Mexico, while two parties set out by land. One vessel was never heard of again, and many persons in the land groups met disaster.

Only 126 of the more than 300 who started reached San Diego. Almost without food and surrounded by hostile natives, the members of the group were desperate. Fortunately, Father Junipero Serra and Portola's soldiers arrived with supplies. On a day of thanksgiving—July 1, 1769—Father Serra sang the Mass; the men joined in the Te Deum; and there was much rejoicing that the survivors had escaped with their lives.

In 1847, at Portsmouth House, in San Francisco, there was a Thanksgiving dinner, said to have been the first served in that city. And during gold rush days, miners from the East tried to celebrate the day, even though food was scarce and quite expensive. Late in 1849, just a year before California entered the Union, Brigadier-General Riley set October 24 as Thanksgiving Day.

By the 1860's grapes were plentiful in Southern California, and after these had been gathered in one year during this decade, a vineyardist named Frohling invited two hundred guests to his home for an Old World Thanksgiving, or "Harvest Home."

Another long-remembered autumn celebration took place in Los Angeles on November 29, 1875, when Mat Keller (owner of the famous Rancho Malibu) invited 125 people, including members of the City Council and other officials, to his Harvest Home. Here is the menu served on that occasion:

DINNER

Soups
Mock Turtle   Oyster
Fish
Oyster Patties
Boiled
Rump Beef (Corned) with Cabbage, Leg of
Mutton, Caper Sauce
Roast
Beef   Mutton   Lamb
Pork with sage and onions
Entrees
Blanquette of Chicken
Veal Cutlets, breaded
Steak and Kidney Pudding
Curried Pigs' Feet, with Rice
Macaroni and Cheese
Dessert
English Plum Pudding   Mince Pie
Blackberry Pie
Apricot Pie   Green Gage Pie
Fruit & Etc.
Apples   Pears   Grapes
Nuts   Raisins
Mixed Candies
Coffee   Tea
Claret   Eldorado   Madeira   Angelica
White wine   Sherry   Port

Many toasts were offered, songs sung, and dancing continued for several hours. Then the guests sat down to the customary midnight "cold collation." This featured cold chicken, various meats, cakes, pies, ice cream, nuts, raisins, candies, and different drinks. Mat

Keller's Harvest Home party broke up at 5 A.M. and the sleepy Angelenos made their way home.

On Thanksgiving afternoon, all over America, many have followed the Pilgrims' idea of staging athletic contests. By the end of the nineteenth century Kansans, for instance, were enjoying bicycle or horse races on this day; also the new game of football was becoming popular. And "Turkey Day" contests are still held on many football fields.

At St. Paul's Roman Catholic Church in Washington, D.C., there is a Pan-American celebration which began in 1909. Here representatives of the Western world join in giving thanks. At the initial service of this kind, President Taft and his Cabinet were present. This marked "the first time in the history of the Western World that all the Republics were assembled for a religious function."

In 1942, during World War II, Great Britain was introduced to our American Thanksgiving Day. Our soldiers attended special services in several English churches. In London, the affair was held in Westminster Abbey. There the meeting was conducted for the first time in its nine hundred year history under other auspices, this time by American army chaplains. Enlisted men served as choristers; and the American flag was carried through the ancient building to the high altar. Men of different ranks and from various branches of the Services, army nurses, Red Cross workers, and many others attended this unique, nonsectarian Thanksgiving service.

On Thanksgiving Day in 1952, while the two American destroyers, the *Roberts* and the *Royal*, were in Plymouth Harbor (from which the Pilgrims sailed in the *Mayflower*), children from a local orphanage were invited aboard the two ships. The men entertained them with a typical Turkey Day dinner ending with American ice cream and followed by a program of entertainment and movies.

Nowadays, all over our country, especially in schools and churches the re-enactment of the first American Thanksgiving is often staged. Such a performance is given each year at Plymouth, Massachusetts. The players represent all the characters who took part in the original celebration in 1621. In Puritan attire, they gather on Leyden Street (the first thoroughfare of the colony) and then at the base of the famous rock, they bow their heads in gratitude. The procession, with the men carrying old-fashioned muskets, marches to

Burial Hill—where the Pilgrims who died that first winter are buried —and there a memorial and thanksgiving service is held.

At this same season, three thousand miles away, across the continent, at Pilgrim Place, in Claremont, California, another group of modern Pilgrims stages a special Thanksgiving celebration. This unique community is a home for retired ministers, missionaries, doctors, and various Christian workers—275 in all. Several are descendants of *Mayflower* passengers. "These pioneers in low cost retirement living" are really showing that "the spirit of pioneering is not a monopoly of youth."

Pilgrim Place, founded in 1915, on arid land, now has over a hundred houses, and includes one of the best botanical gardens in Southern California. The residents engage in interesting hobbies, run a monthly newspaper, and carry on club work.

To earn funds for their community projects, such as the infirmary, they put on a two-day Thanksgiving festival, which has been a tradition here since 1949. In their proclamation of this event, the residents say: "We, the retired Christian missionaries, living at Pilgrim Place in Claremont, call on all friends to join us in thanksgiving and good cheer."

Pilgrim Place takes on the atmosphere of a seventeenth century New England settlement; all the men don Puritan attire, including tall hats and buckled shoes, while the women wear typical colonial costumes.

Visitors to this unique affair can tour the grounds in a replica of the good ship, *Mayflower* (this one on wheels), have their pictures taken sitting in the stocks, visit the bazaar, and buy articles made by the sponsors of this interesting Thanksgiving project. Also turkey dinners are served by the costumed ladies.

Each year a pageant, "Pilgrims Triumphant," is staged, and in 1959 it was seen by more than five thousand visitors on the two days. This dramatic presentation shows the life of the original Pilgrims from the time of the persecutions in Scrooby, their stay in Holland, the journey to America, and the first Thanksgiving in Plymouth. And all who see this production have a better idea of what these courageous settlers did in helping to found our country.

One of the fine ways in which the United States, generally, celebrates Thanksgiving is the sharing with the less fortunate. Churches, rescue missions, school classes, and many philanthropic organizations see to it that no one goes hungry on this truly American holiday.

Church services are held in many localities; and often persons of different faiths worship together on Thanksgiving. There are appropriate Scripture readings, hymns such as "We Gather Together," and reading of the national and state Thanksgiving proclamations. The ministers usually stress our religious heritage and traditions in their sermons.

Afterwards comes the typical and long-observed Thanksgiving dinner, with the "gathering of the clan," Arthur Guiterman once wrote of this holiday:

> So once a year we throng
> Upon a day apart,
> To praise the Lord with feast and song,
> In thankfulness of heart.

Hanukkah (Chanukah) Jewish "Feast of Lights" (Begins on Kislev 25)

Hanukkah (Chanukah), the Jewish Feast of Lights (observed from December 14 on, in 1960), is also known as the Feast of Re-dedication. It is an eight-day festival, beginning at sundown on the twenty-fifth of Kislev, the ninth sacred month of the Jewish calendar. It is celebrated in synagogues all around the world, by all three degrees of Judaism—Reform, Conservative, and Orthodox. This observance is "a feast of liberation, symbolic of the victory of the few over many, and of the weak over the strong."

The Syrian-Greek king, Antiochus IV, ruler of part of the old Greek Empire, sent his armies against the little state of Judea, and tried to suppress the Jewish religion. He set up pagan idols in the country, and his men desecrated the temple at Jerusalem by making offerings to Zeus on the main altar.

An old prophet, Matthias, killed a Syrian official who was trying to make the Jews worship an idol. Then, Matthias and his five sons, the Maccabees, fled to the hills and gathered forces of "all those zealous for the Law." After fighting the Syrian legions for three years, the Jews were able to re-establish their independence and their freedom to worship as they wished.

One of the sons, Judas Maccabaeus, purged the temple and brought in new sacred vessels and a large candlestick with several branches. He took down the altar defiled by the Syrians and built a new one of stones. Tradition tells that the Jews found only enough oil to light the temple lamps for one day. But miraculously the oil burned during the eight days they were completing their task in the building. This is the reason that Hanukkah is observed for eight days. It commemorates not only the rededication of the temple but also "the miraculous re-lighting of the perpetual light."

After the building had been completely purged, on the twenty-fifth day of Kislev, the priests lighted the candles, offered incense, laid loaves of shewbread on the table, and made sacrifices on the new altar. Thus the temple was rededicated to the worship of Jehovah; and this feast is symbolic of Jewish "steadfastness of faith against the oppressor" and of the fight for religious freedom.

In Book XII, Chapter VII, of his *Antiquities of the Jews*, Josephus describes this celebration:

> Now Judas celebrated the festival of the restoration of the sacrifices of the temple for eight days; and omitted no sort of pleasures thereon; but he feasted them upon very rich and splendid sacrifices; and he honored God, and delighted them by hymns and psalms. Nay, they were so very glad at the revival of their customs, when, after a long time of intermission, they unexpectedly had regained the freedom of their worship, that they made it a law for their posterity, that they should keep a festival on account of the restoration of their temple worship, for eight days. And from that time to this, we celebrate this festival, and call it "Lights." I suppose the reason was, because this liberty beyond our hopes appeared to us; and that thence was the name given to that festival. . . .

During the modern Jewish observance of Hanukkah, there are special services at the synagogues; sometimes several join together on these occasions. Choirs sing traditional Hanukkah music, including Jewish folk songs and selections from Handel's Judas Maccabeus. Often the children of the religious school put on special programs for their parents. Since the events of this observance are quite dramatic, plays, such as *A Gift of Light* are sometimes staged. Fellowship hours for young and old and various social events add to the week's enjoyment.

In the synagogue there are impressive candlelighting services; the account of the historic Jewish victory and rededication of the temple is read from the Book of Maccabees; and prayers of thanksgiving for the miraculous survival of the Hebrew people are offered. However they have subordinated the theme of their national victory to a spiritual theme—the relighting of the temple and its rededication.

In Hebrew homes, Hanukkah rites continue for eight days, with a cherished tradition the lighting of the candles in the candelabrum (the Menorah) as the chief feature. Each evening one is lighted until all eight are used. The tapers are emblematic of "the eternal light shining through the spirit of the Jewish people." During this celebration the members of the family eat traditional dishes, play games, entertain guests, and exchange gifts.

Giving presents is an important part of this festival not only among families and friends, but the spirit of the season is revealed in the generosity shown to others not so fortunate. For example, many Jewish women collect gifts and send them to children in Israel and other lands. Often parties where Hanukkah rites are carried out are given at institutions for children, the aged, and at veterans' hospitals.

This is one of the happiest and most popular of Hebrew festivities —"one of thanksgiving and gift-giving for a spiritual heritage that has stood for peace and freedom." And Rabbi Solomon F. Kleinman, western regional director for the Union of American Hebrew Congregations, recently stated:

> The holiday is as meaningful today as it was when Judas Maccabaeus and his band of Jewish warriors recaptured the temple in Jerusalem from the Syrians in 165 B.C.E., cleansed it, re-dedicated it, and proclaimed an eight-day dedication of the altar.

Bill of Rights Day—December 15

Today, in communities all across our continent, December 15 is observed as Bill of Rights Day. In fact, in many places an entire week, including the date December 15, is celebrated as Bill of Rights Week.

This commemorates the ratification of the first ten amendments to the Constitution by three-quarters of the states, which took place on December 15, 1791. These were subsequently incorporated into the Constitution and became known as the Bill of Rights.

In 1941, President Franklin D. Roosevelt noted the 150th anniversary of this ratification by proclaiming December 15 as Bill of Rights Day. He urged all Americans to display the flag on this date, and to plan appropriate ceremonies honoring the occasion.

After the Constitution had been written and ratified, numerous citizens objected to it. They feared that they would not have sufficient protection under its provisions. Even that great Revolutionary patriot, Richard Henry Lee asked: "Where is the contract between the nation and the government? The Constitution makes no mention of those who govern and never speaks of the rights of the people who are governed."

Therefore, to correct this lack, at the very First Congress in New York on September 25, 1789, James Madison introduced twelve amendments. There was much debate over them; but they were approved and sent to the states for ratification. Two proposals (one in regard to the apportionment of Representatives, and the other concerning Congressmen's salaries) were discarded. The other ten were enthusiastically received, and were ratified by the required number of states.

At the present time, even though many decades have passed since the Bill of Rights was accepted, Americans join annually in celebrating the addition of these first ten Amendments to our Constitution.

For they are a guarantee, as was the Magna Charta, of the "rights of free men against tyrants." They are concerned with these topics:

1. FREEDOM OF RELIGION, SPEECH, PRESS, ASSEMBLY, PETITION
2. RIGHT TO KEEP AND BEAR ARMS
3. RIGHTS REGARDING THE QUARTERING OF SOLDIERS
4. REGULATION OF SEARCH AND SEIZURE
5. PROTECTION OF PERSONS AND THEIR PROPERTY
6. RIGHTS OF PERSONS ACCUSED OF CRIME
7. RIGHT OF TRIAL BY JURY
8. PROTECTION AGAINST EXCESSIVE FINES, BAIL, PUNISHMENT
9. GUARANTEE OF UNSPECIFIED RIGHTS
10. POWERS RESERVED TO STATES AND THE PEOPLE

In many communities, the observance of this holiday stresses the importance of the Bill of Rights; and in doing so, community leaders, churches, schools, women's clubs, P.T.A.'s, patriotic and fraternal organizations—all unite in putting on programs.

In some places, thousands of school children take part in varied exercises. Student speakers from junior and senior high schools and city colleges give talks or present skits and short patriotic pageants in costume before city and county officials, service groups, and other organizations, to emphasize the significance of the day and week.

Adult speakers also note this vital anniversary, and newspapers, radio, and TV stations give it publicity. Often essay contests on the Bill of Rights stimulate interest in the occasion. Some newspapers have been sponsoring yearly contests for students. Prizes of United States savings bonds for the senior and junior high school winners are the rewards for the best essays. In some cities facsimiles of the Bill of Rights are distributed to students to remind them of their rights and privileges under our Constitution.

The actor, Dennis Morgan, a speaker at one Bill of Rights observance, declared:

> Down through the glorious summers and winters of American history, while our nation has grown and flourished in a manner unequalled in the history of the world, our Bill of Rights has stood as a signpost of freedom, and a guardian of the rights of man.

Joe Crail, an enthusiastic advocate of Bill of Rights Day stated some years ago:

This election year of 1952 saw more people take advantage of their right as citizens to cast ballots in the American tradition. We expect Americans enthusiastically and reverently to participate in the Bill of Rights Week with the same patriotism they displayed at the polls.

And some time later, Mr. Crail expressed his satisfaction at the progress made in celebrating this important American holiday:

> One of the most encouraging facets of the local observance has been participation by students, who through study, are finding the original meaning of the Bill of Rights as our fathers meant them to be. They are putting this learning to energetic, aggressive work for the benefit of all.

Today, when our world is filled with conflicting ideologies, each striving for supremacy, it is more necessary than ever before that Americans *know* what our government stands for. Therefore, the observance of Bill of Rights Day (or Week) is vitally important to all citizens, and should be noted and stressed in *all* American communities.

Forefathers' Day—December 21

Forefathers' Day—sometimes called Pilgrims' Day—though not a legal holiday is celebrated to honor the landing of the Pilgrims on December 21, 1620. It is observed mainly in New England to pay tribute to the first settlers there and to show reverence for them. This follows a British tradition, revealed in the battle cry, "Think of your forefathers and your posterity," used when the Britons were fighting against the Roman invaders.

The observance of Forefathers' Day started, it is claimed, in Congregational churches in New England in the eighteenth century. And today descendants of the Plymouth and other colonies, and members of New England societies all over the United States celebrate the occasion.

The first Forefather's Day was noted on December 22, 1769, by the Old Colony Club. (There has been some variation in the date; some believe it should be observed on December 22, while most keep to December 21.)

At such meetings—usually banquets—there are speeches, toasts, and poems. Often the famous poem by Felicia Hemans, beginning, "The breaking waves dashed high . . ." is heard. On one occasion, at Plymouth, William Cullen Bryant read one of his poems. On Forefathers' Day in New England, famous orators like Daniel Webster, Edward Everett, Rufus Choate, and Charles Sumner delivered important addresses.

In his impassioned speech in 1850, Daniel Webster challenged the descendants of the Pilgrims to cherish civil and religious liberty; to be willing to shed their blood to transmit these to posterity. "Then," he concluded, "you will be worthy descendants of Bradford, Standish, or Winslow, and the rest of those who landed from stormy seas on the Rock of Plymouth."

In noting the true significance of Forefathers' Day, Edward M. Deems once declared:

It calls for the American people to honor these men truly [the Pilgrims] but with them *all* those first settlers of our land who were actuated by the same noble motives, and in whose hearts thrilled the same love of freedom and hatred of oppression.

Our Forefathers' Day speakers stress the facts that the Pilgrims fled from the Old World because of religious intolerance and persecution; and that they wished to found a new colony as "a place of freedom and equality." Even though many of the men died that first winter in Plymouth, the rest worked on in their struggle for survival in the New World.

Fortunately they had such fine leaders as Carver, Brewster, and Bradford. The latter, in his *History of Plymouth Plantation*, (which Page Smith terms "one of the greatest achievements of American letters"), has given an excellent account of the development of the new settlement.

During the voyage on the *Mayflower* the Pilgrim Fathers, realizing the need for some "mode of civil government," drew up the famous Mayflower Compact. While the ship was lying off what is now Provincetown on November 21, 1620, forty-one men signed this agreement. They pledged themselves to submit to officials chosen by common consent, and to obey laws for the good of all. This created the first free government in our history and was typically American.

The Mayflower Compact contained the ideas of freedom of worship, popular suffrage, and freedom of speech. The historian, George Bancroft, declares that November 21, 1620 was "the birthday of constitutional liberty."

Therefore, on Forefathers' Day it is fitting to read this document again, and to study these significant passages:

. . . having undertaken, for the glory of God and the advancement of the Christian faith and honor of our King and country, a voyage to plant the first colony in the northern parts of Virginia, do by these presents solemnly and mutually in the presence of God, and one another, covenant and combine ourselves together into a civil body politic, for our better ordering and preservation and furtherance of the ends aforesaid; and by virtue thereof to enact, constitute, and frame such just and equal laws, ordinances, acts, constitutions, and offices, from time to time, as shall be thought most meet and convenient for the general good of the Colony; unto which we promise all due submission and obedience. . . .

By 1920 on the 300th anniversary of Forefathers' Day, much attention was paid to this historic event; and impressive celebrations occurred all over the United States. Many well-deserved tributes were paid to the founders. The following words, spoken by President Calvin Coolidge, are worthy of repetition on each Forefathers' Day: "On their abiding faith has been reared a nation, magnificent beyond the dreams of Paradise. No like body has ever cast so great an influence on human history."

Christmas—December 25

The year's "most joyous feast"—Christmas—is celebrated on December 25, both in homes and churches, to observe the anniversary of Christ's birth. In the second chapter of Luke is the story of this memorable event, with its never-to-be-forgotten passages:

> And she brought forth her firstborn son, and wrapped him in swaddling clothes, and laid him in a manger; because there was no room for them in the inn.

Luke tells of the shepherds keeping watch over their flocks, and of the light that shone down on them from heaven, as they heard "the tidings of great joy." For a Saviour had been born in the little town of Bethlehem. Then came the triumphant song of the angel chorus:

> Glory to God in the highest, and on earth
> peace, goodwill toward men.

The exact date of Christ's birth is not known; and during the first two or three centuries little note, apparently, was taken of the anniversary. For church officials opposed such celebrations as savoring of paganism. Clement, of Alexandria, Egypt, mentions the observance of the birth of Jesus by Christians about 200 A.D. Other sources state that this day was noted in scattered places on varying dates.

During the fourth century—about 350 A.D—the Bishop of Rome set December 25 as Christ's birth date. Western churches observed this day but for some time the Eastern ones celebrated on January 6.

Some authorities claim that the choice of December 25 was made because it coincided with that of the Mithraic feast of the sun god; also that of the Roman Saturnalia. In addition, the Jews celebrated their Feast of Chanukah (or Hanukkah) about this time; and the people of northern Europe observed their important winter solstice feast. So it appears that old pagan customs were given new meanings as the church fathers turned such occasions to "the adoration of Christ the Lord."

At first Christians noted Christmas just as a religious holiday; but gradually it took on a secular aspect, with feasting, exchange of gifts, and general rejoicing. During the Middle Ages, Christmas was the most popular holiday of the year, observed both in churches and homes.

CHRISTMAS IN THE BRITISH ISLES

Christmas, at first, was called jule, or yule, in England; but later its name became "Christes Mass." When we think of holiday celebrations, the British festivities come first to mind; for nowhere was this season observed longer or more joyously. Sir Walter Scott described this in *Marmion:*

> England was merry England, when
> Old Christmas brought his sports again . . .
> A Christmas gambol oft would cheer
> The poor man's heart through half the year.

From early times we get accounts of elaborate holiday gaieties which reached their height in the sixteenth and seventeenth centuries. From the poorest cottage to the king's palace Christmas was planned for and then enjoyed with much revelry. The people did not stop just with Christmas Day itself, but kept up the festivities until Twelfth-night, the evening before Epiphany—January 6.

HOLIDAY GREENERY

Evergreens, symbolic of eternal life, have long been used for decorating at yuletide. Teutonic peoples believed that certain greens would frighten evil spirits away. The Saxons hung holly, ivy, rosemary, or laurel in their homes and churches. In the great manor houses, walls, pillars, and windows were adorned with branches of greens. A bunch of mistletoe hung from the door or the ceiling. Each time a man stole a kiss under it he had to pluck a berry from the bough.

It is said that early Roman enemies made up their quarrels when they met under the mistletoe; this is believed to be the origin of kissing under the green. This plant was not used in churches (because of its association with the pagan Druid ceremonials). There was one exception to this—at York Minster—where a bunch was laid on the high altar "with a benediction for peace and goodwill."

As early as 1444, greenery was used on the streets of London as Christmas decorations, and the custom grew through the years. Holly has long been a favorite holiday green. There are several legends connected with it. One is that Christ's crown of thorns was made of holly. Some say the idea of making Christmas holly wreaths came from His crown, as the berries resembled drops of blood. Today holly wreaths, with their glistening green leaves and contrasting berries, are among our most distinctive holiday decorations.

THE YULE LOG

There was a gay ceremony when several men and boys dragged in the yule log. (Some say this custom originated in the bonfires at the time of the winter solstice feast.) Often the log was selected months beforehand and stored for drying. After the men had carefully placed it in the great fireplace, it was set afire by the brand saved from the log of the previous year. The ashes, also, were preserved, to protect the home from storms, thunder, and lightning. These remains—many thought—could heal wounds, and make animals and fields fertile.

On Christmas Eve children were allowed to stay up until midnight. All members of the family and the servants sat around as the flames from the yule log rose higher and higher. They believed that this fire "would burn out old wrongs and heart burnings, and cause the liquor in the wassail bowl that was quaffed to down ancient feuds and animosities." And in many English homes there was a huge Christmas candle, which was lighted each of the twelve holiday evenings.

THE LORD OF MISRULE

At the king's court, as well as at universities and manor houses a Lord of Misrule had charge of the sports, games, and ceremonials during the yule season. In London, for instance, this personage paraded along the streets with his followers and organized festivities for the populace. In homes games were played, one of the favorites being Snap Dragon, the attempt to pull a raisin from a bowl of flaming spirits.

THE MUMMERS

From early times in the British Isles there were bands of mummers, masqueraders, guisers (going about in disguise, reminiscent of an old Roman custom at the Saturnalia) who went from hall to hall, singing, dancing, or staging rude plays. The latter usually contained such characters as St. George, the Dragon, Hector, and Alexander the Great.

In 1377, a "mummerie" was given before Richard, son of the Black Prince. When Henry IV observed Christmas at Eltham, he was visited by twelve aldermen and their sons as mummers. Much later, Henry VIII sent out a proclamation against mumming or guising (a person could be jailed for three months for this offense) because many crimes, even murders, were committed during the mumming season.

THE WAITS

An important part of early English Christmases was the group known as "waits." At first they were minstrels who sang and played at the court; afterward, watchmen, used to guard the streets. Finally the word was applied to the people who went from home to home singing Christmas carols; for their efforts, they received small gifts or their suppers.

CAROLS AND CAROLING

Caroling was a popular pastime in England, where it is said to have come into common use after the Norman Conquest. Various religious carols composed in other lands were sung, and Englishmen produced some of our most beloved carols, including "Hark, the Herald Angels Sing," "Joy to the World," "Angels from the Realms of Glory," and the secular ones, such as "God Rest Ye Merry, Gentlemen," "Deck the Halls," and several wassailing songs.

The custom in England of going around the neighborhood caroling is well described by W. E. Duncan in his book, *Carols:*

> On Christmas Eve, country carol singers spent half the night tramping the ice-bound ways and frosty woodlands, now and anon striking up their old melodies, which sang of the heavenly birth and earth's substantial comforts and joys with impartial mixture. A fine hearty welcome greeted them at the houses and farmsteads, whose occupants sat up in impatient anticipation. . . .

CHURCH SERVICES

At midnight on Christmas Eve, church bells pealed and many people went to services in honor of the Babe of Bethlehem. Also there were well-attended church meetings on Christmas Day. In his *Diary*, Samuel Pepys tells that in 1662 he walked to church where he heard an exceptionally long sermon. Also, three years later, after the Christmas address, he saw a wedding at the church. On this holiday in 1666, Pepys wrote that his wife stayed in bed, as she had sat up until four o'clock that morning, watching her "mayde" make the mince pies. In contrast, "I, to church, where our parson Mills made a good sermon . . . thanks to God Almighty, for the goodness of my condition at this day."

THE ENGLISH CHRISTMAS FEAST

On Christmas Day the great feast was served; this often lasted for several hours at the king's court, and in the castles of the nobility. After the lord had seated himself at a table, on a dais, trumpeters and minstrels announced the coming of the Lord of Misrule. This dignitary was followed by the chief servingman bearing a massive silver platter. On this rested the boar's head with garlands of rosemary, and an apple or lemon in its mouth. Then a procession of knights and ladies entered and took their places.

The boar's head was set down before the lord, who served portions to his guests. Another unusual feature was the baked peacock, in all the glory of its colorful plumage and spreading tail. A beautiful highborn lady always carried in this distinctive dish.

On the long tables were immense haunches of beef, meat pies, roast ducks, geese, and young pigs. For dessert, there was "plumb porridge"—the forerunner of plum pudding. Mince pies, symbolizing the richness of the gifts of the Wise Men, and fancy cakes called "yule babies" also graced the board. There were steaming bowls of wassail, and numerous toasts were quaffed on this festive day.

After several centuries, the holiday gaiety reached its climax in England; finally such celebrations were banned by the Puritans from 1642 to 1652. Even though Charles II restored the yuletide observance when he came to the throne, the holidays never regained their former popularity and were shorter than the earlier "Twelve Days of Christmas."

Today British shops are filled with gifts for weeks beforehand, and elaborate preparations are made for church services, musical entertainments, and family gatherings.

ST. NICHOLAS OR SANTA CLAUS

Naturally the mystery as to who brings their gifts has long added to the joy experienced by children at Christmas. Since ancient times the presents have been accounted for in various ways. As the Three Kings carried rich gifts to the Christ Child at Bethlehem, Spanish boys and girls were told to set out their shoes for Balthasar to fill as the Magi rode toward Jerusalem. Italy has a female Santa Claus, Befana; Denmark, a gnome, Jule-Nissen; in some places the children believe the Christ Child brought their gifts, while in England Father Christmas greets the youngsters in the big department stores.

However, the idea developed rather early in northern European lands that St. Nicholas, the patron of children and young people, was the source of holiday giving. He was an actual person, a bishop who lived in Asia Minor during the fourth century. He was famous for his generosity, and the story of his furnishing money for the dowries of three Italian sisters became well known. Each time he had thrown a bag of money in the window. Later, the bankers of Lombardy used the three bags (or balls) as signs over their places of business. As they lent money, this insignia became associated with pawnbrokers.

December 6—the day of his death—is the feast day of St. Nicholas. Children were told that the saint had come to their homes the preceding evening, dressed in his red bishop's robe and riding a white horse to inquire about their behavior during the past year. If he received satisfactory reports, he returned the next day in full regalia (donned for the occasion by father, uncle, or other suitable substitute) to distribute presents to the delighted children.

The Dutch who settled in New Amsterdam brought with them the idea that St. Nicholas was the gift giver. On his feast day they had a parade in which the saint's image was carried; and their boys and girls received presents at that time.

However, with the change to English rule, and the arrival of many people from England in the colony of New York, the two holidays, December 6 and 25 gradually merged. Through the Dutch influence St. Nicholas, or Santa Claus, lost his lean look; and became a chubby character with a beard, dressed in a red suit, especially after the famous poem, "A Visit from St. Nicholas," by Dr. Clement C. Moore appeared. A noted cartoonist, Thomas Nast, a German immigrant, first depicted Santa Claus with a sleigh and reindeer on a visit to give presents to the soldiers during the Civil War.

CHRISTMAS IN THE UNITED STATES

When the Puritans reached New England, they brought with them their dislike for any observance of Christmas and levied fines on those who dared to celebrate the holiday. It was not until the nineteenth century (after many German and Irish immigrants had arrived) that holiday celebrations really became popular in that part of the country.

In the southern colonies, in Virginia, for example, there were gay gatherings of families and friends, with bountiful feasts and gala balls by candlelight. The aristocratic plantation owners carried on many of the holiday traditions that had prevailed for centuries in the home country. Often the slaves were not required to work as long as the yule log burned.

The Moravians who made homes in eastern colonies, because of religious persecution in the Old World, continued their usual customs. On Christmas Eve, carrying lighted candles and singing a Christmas hymn, they marched into a stable, thus recalling Christ's humble birthplace. And in our Southwest, people of Spanish and Mexican ancestry staged old holiday plays such as *Los Pastores* and *Las Posadas,* brought here from Spain via Old Mexico. Scandinavian settlers in the Middle West, cherished their native traditions, as have their descendants. Therefore, our American Christmas observance is a most interesting and unusual one; for it includes varied customs from faraway lands.

CHRISTMAS GIFTS

Gift giving at yuletide dates back to the Roman Saturnalia, when those people presented their friends "strenae" (fruits, pastries, and even jewelry). Also we remember the rich gifts that the Magi, or the Wise Men, brought to the Christ Child in the manger at Bethlehem.

In recent years the custom has caused much discussion here in the United States; for it must be admitted that the exchange of presents can, at times, be a burden instead of a pleasure. Many deplore the fact that our Christmas, like other holidays has become tinged with commercialism. Often too much pressure is put on by advertisers to encourage lavish holiday buying. On the other hand, the production, transportation, and distribution of this merchandise *does* give employment to thousands of workers.

To offset this undesirable phase of our modern Christmas, we should remember the fine spirit of friendliness that is shown by the millions (perhaps billions) of Christmas messages that go through our mails. Also the feeling of generosity that prevails in schools, churches, clubs, and in individuals, which brings Christmas joy to countless needy persons, shut-ins, and underprivileged children. Another evidence of the true yuletide spirit is revealed in the movement, started in 1904, by a Dane, Einar Holboell, who promoted the first Christmas seals, today an important factor in fighting disease.

CHRISTMAS DECORATIONS

Centuries ago, Romans decorated their homes, public buildings, and temples on festive occasions, and we have followed this ancient custom. In most communities, at Christmas there are beautifully decorated store windows, often depicting holiday scenes.

The merchants along New York's famous Fifth Avenue vie with each other in originality and spare no expense in the creation of luxury and beauty. The final displays attract such vast crowds that special roped-off areas are necessary and the public is kept moving by uniformed guards. In many cases the air is perfumed with some special fragrance and music accompanies the changing scenes of animated figures inside the windows.

Weeks before Christmas a giant Christmas tree is set up with much ceremony in the center of Rockefeller Plaza, decorated with huge colored baubles, and the lighting of the tree is the official opening of the Christmas season. The entire length of Park Avenue is lined with its own lighted Christmas trees, and it is a beautiful sight in snow. Many New York skyscrapers—always dramatic against the night sky—are also aglow with red and green lights in honor of the occasion.

While New York goes all out for a brilliant, sophisticated Christmas emphasizing luxury with a touch of frivolity, other cities celebrate in their way. In some where traffic hazards do not prevent, the downtown streets are festooned with colored lights, bells, stars, candles, and other yuletide emblems.

Many American cities are famed for their distinctive street decorations, which visitors often drive many miles to see. For instance, since 1920, the city of Fresno, California, has featured its Christmas Tree Lane. This is slightly less than two miles in length and is said to be the longest in our country. The project began on a small scale, but by 1930 the great cedars lining Van Ness Avenue had been lighted with colored bulbs for a quarter of a mile. Then, in 1959, more than 300 stately trees had been festooned with lights, and over 121,000 people visited the unusual scene.

In addition to the beauty of the tree illuminations, the home owners along this handsome street set up holiday displays on their lawns, picturing varied Christmas stories or traditions. These bring visitors from every state and many foreign countries. This holiday spectacle is the result of the altruistic devotion of many Fresno citizens, who unselfishly give their time, energy, and funds to promote this incomparable yuletide display.

CHRISTMAS TREES

Some sources trace the origin of the Christmas tree to the Romans and Egyptians; others give Germany the credit. One story relates that in Germany during the eighteenth century the missionary St. Boniface urged the Germans to discontinue their bloody, pagan rites in dark forests, and instead to carry fir trees into their homes at yuletide. Martin Luther is said to have set up a tree lighted with candles for his children; and this idea spread through northern Europe, and then to the New World.

Opinions differ as to who set up the first Christmas tree in the United States. Several sources give credit to Charles Follen, who had a lighted tree at his home in Cambridge, Massachusetts in 1832. And, according to Frank J. Dutcher, the community of Hopedale, in the same state, used some of the earliest trees in New England. Adin Ballou, founder of Hopedale, stated in his autobiography:

I presume that the reputed anniversary of the Saviour's birth was never celebrated . . . in the vicinity, until the year 1838. Traditionary prejudice, an inheritance from our Pilgrim and Puritan ancestors, was strongly against it. But I suggested and encouraged a change from the long-prevailing custom, to which my people readily consented. Our sanctuary was accordingly appropriately and gracefully trimmed and well lighted for the evening of December 24, when I delivered a specially prepared discourse to a large and deeply interested congregation. . . . Since that time, celebrations of the event have prevailed more and more in churches of this general region. . . .

The Reverend Ballou also gave an account of Christmas exercises in 1853 in the Hopedale church. Songs, pieces, dialogues, and dramatic sketches by children were featured.

> About an hour before the speaking closed, the curtains, which had through the afternoon concealed the Christmas tree, were drawn aside, and we were permitted to behold the pliant branches of the hemlock, drooping under a load of presents, whose rich colors were pleasing to the eyes. At seven o'clock in the evening, the distribution of presents commenced. . . .

Now, all over the United States many communities make a large Christmas tree the center of their holiday activities, where young and old join in caroling and in sharing the holiday spirit. Several such trees have become traditional; the outstanding one at Rockefeller Center in New York City; the "Nation's Christmas Tree" (the General Grant) in King's Canyon National Park, near Sanger, California; and the tree in Washington, D.C., whose lights are turned on each Christmas Eve by our Chief Executive.

MANGER SCENES

Another popular custom—the setting up of manger scenes of the Nativity—has become almost universal here. This idea started in 1223, at Greccio, Italy. St. Francis of Assisi assembled such a scene with real people and live animals; for he wanted to make the story of Christ's birth real to his followers.

This movement spread through Italy and to other lands, especially in southern Europe, where manger scenes rather than the Christmas tree form the center of the holiday observance. In the United States each year more churches, clubs, and homes use such displays, both indoors and out. The Moravian family sets up an elaborate Christmas scene—the "Putz"—which pictures not only the Holy Family, but also village scenes showing the life of the people.

While the celebration of Christmas was becoming more general in the East and Middle West, those living on the Pacific Coast also had their festivities. In California, these became a mixture of eastern, southern, and Spanish customs, and included bell ringing, fireworks, church services, bullfights, fandangos, and gay fiestas.

Now, for many decades, our American celebration of Christmas has been a combination of world-wide holiday customs, making it one of the most interesting anywhere. To many people this is the most sacred day of the year, a time that has inspired some of the world's greatest artists, poets, and other writers. The incomparable Shakespeare paid tribute to Christmas in this passage from Hamlet:

> . . . the crowing of the cock.
> Some say that ever 'gainst that season comes
> Wherein our Saviour's birth is celebrated,
> The bird of dawning singeth all night long;
> And then, they say, no spirit dare stir abroad;
> The nights are wholesome; then no planets strike
> No fairy takes, no witch hath power to charm,
> So hallow'd and so gracious is the time.

Bibliography

BOOKS

BOYT, CLARA, *American Patriotic Holidays*. New York: Pageant Book Company, 1955.

CHAMBERS, ROBERT, editor, *The Book of Days*, vols. 1 and 2. London and Edinburgh: W. R. Chambers, 1863, 1864.

DEEMS, EDWARD M., *Holy-Days and Holidays*. New York and London: Funk & Wagnalls Co., 1906.

DILLON, P. R., *American Anniversaries*. Philadelphia: Philip R. Dillon Publishing Company, 1918.

DOUGLAS, G. E. (Revised by HELEN DOUGLAS COMPTON), *American Book of Days*. New York: H. W. Wilson Co., 1948.

DUNCAN, W. E., *Carols*. New York: Charles Scribner's Sons, 1911.

EDDY, LLOYD C., *Holidays*. Boston: Christopher Publishing House, 1928.

EDIDIN, BEN M., *Jewish Holidays and Festivals*. New York: Hebrew Publishing Co., 1940.

GAISTER, THEODOR, *New Year*. New York: Abelard-Schuman Limited, 1905.

HANSEN, HARRY, editor, The World Almanac and Book of Facts. New York: *New York World-Telegram*, 1959, 1960, 1961.

HAZELTINE, MARY E., *Anniversaries and Holidays*. Chicago: American Library Association, 1944.

HONE, WILLIAM, *Everyday Book*. London: William Tegg, 1864.

——, *Table Book*. London: William Tegg, 1864.

HOOKE, SAMUEL H., *New Year's Day*. New York: William Morrow & Co., Inc., 1928.

HUMPHREY, GRACE, *Stories of the World's Holidays*. Springfield, Massachusetts: Milton Bradley Company, 1923.

JOHN, RAYMOND, *Concise Dictionary of Holidays*. New York: Philosophical Library, Inc., 1958.

JOSEPHUS, FLAVIUS (translated by William Whiston), *The Works of Flavius Josephus*. Cincinnati, Ohio: Morgan and Sanxay, 1836.

MEYER, ROBERT, JR., *Festivals U. S. A.* New York: Ives Washburn, Inc., 1950.

PAULMIER, HILAH and R. H. SCHAUFFLER, *Pan-American Day*. New York: Dodd, Mead & Co., 1943.

RICE, SUSAN T., compiler, *Mother's Day*. Edited by R. H. SCHAUFFLER. New York: Moffat Yard & Company, 1915.

SALA, GEORGE AUGUSTUS, *America Revisited*. London: Vizetelly & Company, 1885.

SCHAUFFLER, R. H., *Arbor Day*. New York: Moffat Yard & Company, 1909.

——, *Mother's Day*. New York: Moffat Yard & Company, 1915.

——, *Thanksgiving*. New York: Moffat Yard & Company, 1907.

——, *Washington's Birthday*. New York: Moffat Yard & Company, 1916.

SECHRIST, ELIZABETH H., *Poems for Red Letter Days*. Philadelphia: Macrae Smith Co., 1951.

——, *Red Letter Days*. Philadelphia: Macrae Smith Co., 1940.

UNTERMANN, ISAAC, *The Jewish Holidays*, vols. 1 and 2. Philadelphia: Federal Press, 1939.

WEBSTER, HUTTON, *Rest Days*. New York: The Macmillan Co., 1916.

YOUNG, GORDON, editor, *The Army Almanac*. Harrisburg, Pa.: The Stackpole Co., 1959.

MAGAZINE ARTICLES

ASCH, JOHN, "May Facts and Fancies," *American Home*, May 1949.

ATKINSON, T. M., "Halloween of Long Ago," *Classmate*, October 31, 1948.

BARTLETT, LANIER, "The Fourth Has Grown Up," *Western Family*.

BASKETTE, FLOYD K., "Why Celebrate It as Good Friday?", *Classmate*, March 5, 1950.

BATTISTA, O. A., "Last Evening in October," *The Christian Family*, October 1952.

BENGSTON, BENNIE, "New Year's Day," *Classmate*, December 31, 1950.

——, "The Palm: Symbol of Peace," *Classmate*, April 2, 1950.

BRUNDAGE, BARBARA, "Trick or Treat," *Presbyterian Life*, October 31, 1953.

CARRICK, MARGARET, "Wel-come be thou, Fair Freshe May," *Los Angeles Times Home Magazine*, May 1950.

CRUMP, SPENCER, "California's First Thanksgiving," *Southland*, November 1954.

CURTIS, OLGA, "Leap Year," *Parade*, December 27, 1959.

CYMBALA, WILMA T., "The Fabulous Easter Egg," *Together*, March 1959.

DOERFFLER, ALFRED, "Journey to Bethlehem," *This Day*, December 1959.

DUGAN, JAY, "Halloween," *Ford Times*, October 1952.

FLEMING, T. J., "Ireland, Land of Smiles and Surprises," *Reader's Digest*, June 1960.

GARDNER, MARY M., "A Universal Festival," *Classmate*.

GILMER, CAROL L., "Trees for Tomorrow's Children," *Coronet*, April 1947.

HARDESTY, BETTY, "Procession of Pilgrims," *Southland*, November 23, 1958.

HARPER, CANON H. V., "Days and Customs of All Faiths," *Los Angeles Examiner*.

HOWARD, MARJORIE, "Celebrating Easter Around the World," *Think*, April 1954.

IKERMAN, RUTH C., "Easter's Cross at Sunrise," *Christian Advocate*, April 10, 1952.

JOHNSON, HELEN, "It's an Old Easter Custom," *Southland*, April 18, 1954.

KENNEDY, J. F. and R. M. NIXON, "Your One Vote Counts," *Parade*, November 6, 1960.

KERIGAN, FLORENCE, "Pageant of Easter," *Classmate*, August 4, 1949.

LeBUFFE (S.J.), FRANCIS P., "Story of Easter," *American Weekly*, March 28, 1948.

LILE, LETHA O., "Hail the New Year!" *Classmate*, December 26, 1954.

LODGE, HENRY CABOT, "The U. N. Begins to Grow Up," *New York Herald Tribune* (Paris Edition), September 5, 1960.

LORANT, STEFAN, "Inaugurations Generally Rough on Generals," *Long Beach Press-Telegram*, January 18, 1953.

MILLER, MARGARETTE S., "How the Pledge of Allegiance Was Written," *Parade*, June 13, 1954.

MILLER, R. C., "Pilgrim Place," *Los Angeles Times*, November 21, 1954.

MOHLER, IRA M., "Father Has a Day, Too," *Together*, May 1959.

OFFEN, CHARLOTTE, "Old Favorite," *This Day*.

PEATTIE, D. C., "Declaration of Independence—America's Gospel," *Coronet*, July 1948.

POLYZOIDES, "Labor Day Differs from Europe Fetes," *Los Angeles Times*, September 7, 1955.

POWELL, J. H., "The Day of American Independence," *Woman's Day*, December 1950.

REECE, RUTH, "California Thanksgiving, 100 Years Ago," *Southland*, November 19, 1950.

SALOUTOUS, THEODORE, "Labor Day History," *Los Angeles Times*, September 5, 1954.

SANDERS, BOB, "Chief Cautions Goblins," *Long Beach Press-Telegram*, October 25, 1960.

SMITH, PAGE, "It Is Good to Admire the Pilgrim Fathers," *Los Angeles Times*, November 26, 1953.

———, "There Never Was a Parade Like This One of 1788," *Los Angeles Times*, July 7, 1953.

SNEED, J. RICHARD (Dr.), "Palm Sunday: Jesus' Day of Triumph in Jerusalem," *Los Angeles Times*, March 22, 1959.

TRUE, BARBARA, "She Started Mother's Day," *Together*, April 1958.

UNGER, HENRY F., "All Eyes on Washington," *Highway Traveler*.

WILLIAMS, VERA, "International Grove Planted by Church," *Long Beach Press-Telegram*, October 26, 1960.

WILLIS, MARY JAYNE, "Most Voters Don't Know Their A.B.C.'s," *Together*, March 19, 1960.

——, "What Does He Do When He Plants a Tree?" *American Home*, April 1948.

ENCYCLOPEDIAS

American People's Encyclopedia. Chicago: Spencer Press, Inc., 1948–1961.

Collier's Encyclopedia. New York, Toronto: P. F. Collier and Son Corporation, 1959.

Compton's Pictured Encyclopedia. Chicago: F. E. Compton Co., 1910.

Encyclopedia Americana. New York: Americana Corporation, 1959.

Jewish Junior Encyclopedia (Naomi Ben Asher and Hayim Leaf, editors). New York: Shengold Publications, Inc., 1957.

New International Encyclopedia. New York: Dodd, Mead & Co., 1915.

Picture World Encyclopedia. New York: Picture World Encyclopedia, Inc., 1959.

World Book Encyclopedia. Chicago: Field Enterprises, Inc., 1958.

Index